Fanning
the Flame

Fanning the Flame

Bible, Cross & Mission

Meeting the Challenge in a Changing World

General Editors
Paul Gardner • Chris Wright • Chris Green

ZONDERVAN™

GRAND RAPIDS, MICHIGAN 49530 USA

We want to hear from you. Please send your comments about this book to us in care of zreview@zondervan.com. Thank you.

GRAND RAPIDS, MICHIGAN 49530 USA

WWW.ZONDERVAN.COM

ZONDERVAN™

03 04 05 06 07 08 09 /❖ CLY/ 10 9 8 7 6 5 4 3 2 1

Contents

Introduction

This book is written primarily for English Anglican evangelicals preparing for their meeting in Blackpool, England, in September 2003, but we hope it will have a wider readership and more long-term value. Many evangelicals around the world are wrestling with the challenges and opportunities of seeking to be faithful to God and his revelation in Scripture at the start of this third millennium, and it is increasingly the case that Anglican evangelicals are concerned with issues beyond their own congregations or dioceses. These are critical times as we begin to prepare for the next international Lambeth Conference in 2008, and we recognize that our ties with our international communion are closer and more necessary than ever before, because the pressures we face are increasingly global. The open expression of the debt that English Anglican evangelicals owe to others for the courageous stands they made at Lambeth 1998 is a new, and refreshingly humble, characteristic. The currents in our local denominational waters find deep similarities with those that others face. Militant secularism, militant Islam, militant materialism and militant liberalism are alike in recognizing no geographical borders, and just as our Blackpool meeting will have a deliberately international dimension, so the contributors to this volume come from evangelical Anglicanism around the world.

The Background to This Book

The National Evangelical Anglican Congress of Blackpool 2003 stands in a famous line of such Congresses that began at Keele University in 1967. For many, Keele marked a signal moment as they committed themselves to be faithful and traditional both as evangelicals and as Anglicans, and to interpret those commitments in a radical and imaginative way as they spoke to a lost world. Of course, many people were already committed to the structures and debates in the denomination, and many had held senior positions within it. Keele, though, marked a fresh and new moment of common commitment to the structures and Councils of the Church of England. Both the preparatory book and the subsequent statement reflected that.[1]

The second Congress, at Nottingham University in 1977, was much more ambitious in scope, and produced three significant books beforehand, and a much more global statement from its debates.[2] It became clear at Nottingham, though, that Anglican evangelicals (or, as some would prefer, evangelical Anglicans) no longer spoke with a single voice, even on Scripture or on our experience of God. There was a need for informed and intelligent debate not only with our world and with our denomination, but with each other.

This book stands in the tradition of the Keele and Nottingham studies. The papers here are designed to introduce the Congress's main themes, but they are not narrow, interest group themes. These are issues that should interest and captivate all Christians, and particularly evangelicals. Yet all three themes are subjects of intense debate. We have chosen to look at the Bible (because that is what defines us), the Cross (because that is what unites us) and Mission (because that is what inspires us). All three presume the living, active, loving and speaking Trinitarian God of traditional Christian orthodoxy. Clustered around these themes, there is variety, if not disagreement, among us. But as the Scripture section will make clear, we need to reinforce that there is a God-given method for solving such disagreements. We should not shrug our shoulders as if God has not made himself clear to us. He has spoken.

The style and complexity of the essays in this volume varies considerably and deliberately. We hope there will be chapters here to stimulate thinking and discussion among us all whether we have been 'theologically trained' or not. For those who find reading a volume like this 'hard going', then we suggest you might start with some of the challenging essays borne of practical pastoral experience of the authors. On the Bible, you might wish to begin with Dave

Fenton's and Wallace Benn's articles; on the Cross, with Rico Tice and Gerald Bray; on Mission, with Phil Baskerville and Simea Meldrum de Souza.

The Background to the Congress

It is now sixteen years since the last Congress at Caister-on Sea in 1987. Strictly speaking, that was not a 'congress' but a 'celebration', planned as a festival and held at a family holiday camp and, in line with that motif, it produced neither a book nor a statement. In the background, senior leaders were expressing concern at this change of direction, and the failure to produce anything permanent.[3] For many delegates Caister-on-Sea was a much-needed exploration of the confidence they felt, not merely in the gospel, but in the increased influence of evangelicalism within the denomination. As senior Anglican after senior Anglican took the stage, they were celebrating the success of the Keele strategy in gaining positions of influence. For a sizeable minority, though, while they agreed that this was the fruit of Keele, it was not something to celebrate. On their reading of history the very clarity, focus, intensity and biblical emphasis of evangelicalism had been lost in the Keele process. This division, which first broke surface in the wake of Caister-on-Sea (although it had been present at the two previous Congresses, with hindsight) has been one of the main dominant divisions in Anglican evangelicalism in the last fifteen years. Another division has been over charismatic theology.

There is no doubt that the growth of evangelicalism among English Anglicans between Caister and Blackpool has resulted in a greater self-confidence and less feeling that we 'need' to get together to keep in touch. Nowadays most evangelical Anglicans are in frequent contact with other churches. The various networks of contact, often centred around particular meetings or conferences, have diminished further the 'felt need' for a large and inclusive gathering. Many more Anglican evangelical scholars are now widely published, so we do not need a Congress specifically for us to hear their views. Many more resources are available online to help local churches conduct their disciple-making task, so there is less need to travel to dedicated resource conferences. And, of course, many evangelical Anglicans meet up at annual conferences such as Spring Harvest, Word Alive, New Wine, etc., and do so in an ecumenical setting in which the 'evangelical' content of their faith is probably more important than their identification as Anglicans.

This change between 1988 (Caister-on-Sea) and 2003 (Blackpool) is, on the whole, hugely encouraging. We need only think of the way different groups have mushroomed and become a force to be reckoned with within the church. Although some of the following were already in existence prior to 1988, it is worth pausing to remember the significance and impact among many evangelical Anglicans and on the denomination as a whole, of groups such as the Alpha network, the Evangelical Anglican Leaders' Conference, the Reform network, the New Wine network, the Fellowship of Word and Spirit, the Evangelical Group on General Synod and so on. An exhaustive list would include some big groupings and some much smaller, yet all significant and helpful to many. We also still have the important work of the long established evangelical societies such as the Church Pastoral Aid Society and the Church Society. All of this means that the inclusive gathering such as this National Evangelical Anglican Congress takes a lower priority in many minds these days, than when we were small, defensive and lacking leaders.

This wide-ranging list of groupings has some features that are quite predictable, but others that are surprising and inexplicable to many non-evangelical observers. Given that evangelical Anglicanism has grown markedly in the last forty years, and given the developments within our denomination, it should surprise no-one that some read that as a success story and some as a decline, that some see engagement with and learning from other theological traditions as a strength while to others it is a capitulation. The predictability of such fault lines does not preclude any debate over which view is correct, but any competent observer in the 1960s would have predicted both the emergence of a more theologically *avant garde* grouping and a network for the more traditionally minded. It was only a matter of time that, as evangelicalism ceased to be a ghetto and became a fashionable suburb, some would embrace considerable bulldozing and renovation, while others would moan about the neighbourhood not being what it was and forming a residents' committee to oppose new development.

The other side of this coin is that the very 'tribalism' often reflected in the healthy multiplication of different groupings has also taken its toll on the gatherings of evangelical Anglicans. It is probably precisely a sign of the numerical gains among us that now, apparently, we can afford to divide into our various tribes. Some of these divisions are no doubt simply pragmatic. In God's church where all have Spirit-given gifts and interests with which to bring glory to God, it is inevitable that groups of like-minded people will gather, some to focus, for example, on evangelism, some on the gifts of the Spirit, some on worship, some on preaching and so on. The church needs all these and, provided such foci are always relating back to the living, rounded and Christ-centred church, only then can they be of real help to the church's mission.

However, even though such groupings usually begin from the best of motives, our surrounding secular culture and thought processes can begin to distort valuable 'groupings' into 'tribes' at conflict with other 'tribes' in the same church. It is *de rigour* in our society that people meet in small communities of like-minded people. In an age when people seek to deny meta-narratives and universal ideas, in an age when each person is entitled to hold an equally valid view on a matter, even when these are diametrically opposed, community is formed by like-minded people coming together and often avoiding serious debate.

On the other hand, many Anglican evangelicals experience a profound unease when they encounter their denominational structures. It can seem as though that same denial of a universal truth has placed the ground of our Anglican unity not in the Lord Jesus where it rightly belongs, but in our structures, orders, services, procedures and especially in personal loyalty to the bishops. Thus some evangelicals have become increasingly concerned that, to be thought 'authentically Anglican', a person must be so tolerant of other divergent forms of Anglican belief and practice, that theological and unbiblical compromise is almost inevitable. The recent and essentially bureaucratic definition of Anglicanism mentioned here has led to a phenomenon in which those who dissent are sometimes treated as 'not truly Anglican'.

There are many easy but false ways out of these mazes within and without evangelical Anglicanism. One is the way of irrationality, which is to deny that differences matter, or to claim that if intelligent scholars disagree there can be no hope of clarity, or that the Bible is a human-made code of outdated views, or that if something cannot be easily understood then it cannot be important, or that serious thought should be avoided because 'doctrine divides'. Another view, fatally tempting to evangelicals, is to try to find some middle ground between two opposing views, as if it were enough to affirm both without engaging in their substantive disagreements where they are mutually contradictory. We have, historically, always tried to find balance, but we should remember that, biblically speaking, truth is found by searching the Scriptures, and then adhering to God's mind, whether that be central, extreme or difficult to grasp. Being English, we love balance, but balance is not always biblical.

So our discussions cannot be an exercise in *naiveté*! There are genuine theological differences between some who call themselves 'charismatic' and some who call themselves 'classical evangelical', between some who call themselves 'open evangelical' and some who call themselves 'mainstream', between some who are – to put it crudely – 'pro-Keele' and those who are 'anti-Keele'. We need to find a way to engage in debate as fellow evangelicals without losing ourselves in tribalism

Tribes

The three-fold trouble with tribalism is that, first, it diminishes the church's witness to Christ, not just in the sense of 'doing mission together' but in the sense of witnessing to Christ in our corporate life as church. Second, tribalism fails to enable the Bible-centred, Spirit-led discussion between us that should be taking place on matters where serious theological differences and concerns arise. Third, it hinders our ability to function properly within our own denomination. We so often find ourselves unable to pursue together the biblical agenda that we espouse. We have not even talked together about our priorities, about ways in which, despite some important theological differences, we can work together on many matters. So entrenched have some become in their groupings that they will not venture forth.

It is sometimes suggested that evangelicals currently have 'the ball at their feet' in this denomination. There have been those making similar claims since 1967 (perhaps in the light of England's World Cup victory in 1966!). Some will claim that the reason for not taking advantage of that position has been a refusal to follow the lead of those evangelicals who gained senior positions. Others will claim that those same people used the 'ball is at our feet' slogan to mask a shift from pure evangelicalism to a more compromised position. History will have to decide.

Truly we thank God for his grace in the numerical advance of churches that remain faithful to his Word and to the preaching of 'Christ crucified'. But it would be our contention that, whatever the position in the past, today we simply do not have the 'ball at our feet'. We *could* have, but do not, and at least a significant reason for this is our own inability to work together in our denomination.

The organizers hope that one of the outcomes of this Congress in Blackpool will be a renewed ability among us to appreciate and understand what is going on in the ever-expanding evangelical Anglican constituency. Unlike previous Congresses, there has been a deliberate attempt this time to expose a large number of evangelical Anglicans to the wider community, and to engage in an ongoing global evangelical Anglican debate.

—Paul Gardner, Chris Green and Chris Wright
General Editors, on behalf of the executive
committee of NEAC4

A study guide to this book can be found
on the Congress website: *www.NEAC.info*

Notes

1. J.I. Packer, ed. *Guidelines: Anglican Evangelicals Face the Future,* London, Falcon, 1967; Philip Crowe, ed. *Keele '67: The National Evangelical Anglican Congress Statement,* London, Falcon, 1967.

2. Under the general editorship of John Stott, and under the common title of *Obeying Christ in a Changing World,* the books were subtitled *Volume 1: The Lord Christ,* ed. John Stott, *Volume 2: The People of God,* ed. Ian Cundy and *Volume 3: The Changing World,* ed. Bruce Kaye (Fountain, 1977). *The Nottingham Statement* issued by the Executive Committee of the Second National Evangelical Anglican Congress, London, Falcon, 1977.

3. See Timothy Dudley-Smith, *John Stott: A Global Ministry,* Leicester, Inter-Varsity Press 2001, p. 275–78.

Part One

Chapter One

The Bible, Its Truth and How It Works

Timothy Ward

In this chapter Timothy Ward deals with the issue of truth. He points out that, for the Christian, all truth pivots on the person of Jesus Christ. But it is in the Bible that we discover who Jesus is, which leads on to the issue of biblical 'infallibility', 'inerrancy' and 'inspiration'. The author investigates the meaning of these terms in the light of their traditional evangelical understanding. More recently 'speech-act' theory has appeared. Ward argues that this new way of viewing scriptural truth, although it has pitfalls, is a valuable part of the Christian's arsenal. He also examines the 'sacramental' view of the Bible, but rejects this as being a helpful hermeneutical tool.

Introduction

The true focus of Christian faith is Jesus Christ. Christianity has at its heart the Bible, but the purpose of the Bible is to point us to the person of Jesus Christ. The words of the Bible exist only to serve the Word made flesh. One of the greatest theologians of the early church, Augustine, expressed the point well. We ought to use Scripture, he said, 'not with such love and delight as if it were a good to rest in, but with a transient feeling rather, such as we have towards the road, or carriages, or other things that are merely means'. The aim of Scripture is to bring us to God, he points out, and Scripture is just the means to that end.[1] Paraphrasing Augustine, we might say that he warns against the danger of becoming a Christian 'trainspotter' – loving the means of transport (Scripture) so much that we neglect the destination (a relationship of love with God).

It is important to begin a discussion of the truth of the Bible this way because it is often alleged that the classical evangelical under-standing of the Bible as itself the Word of God attracts attention away from Jesus Christ as the Word of God. It is feared that, in some evan-gelical churches and in the lives of some evangelical believers, trust in the Bible somehow displaces trust in Christ, and that high claims made for the words of Scripture focus attention on them, and away from the living spiritual reality to which they point. Of course, if and when that happens a grave mistake has been made, for Christ calls us first of all to be disciples, not bookworms. All faithful Christian living, and all faithful Christian theology, have at their heart the per-son of Jesus Christ. In fact, all the best writing throughout Christian history on the topic of the Bible and its truth focuses on Christ.[2]

The first sections of this chapter present some of the main argu-ments that have been advanced in favour of the classical evangelical view of the Bible as itself the Word of God. Some readers may not have encountered these arguments together in one place before, even in brief form, and will find their presentation here helpful. Other readers, especially those who find the classical evangelical view of the Bible problematic in various ways, may feel some impatience at the rehearsal of these arguments in the first part of this chapter. Such readers are encouraged to note the extent to which these arguments are, in their best form, remarkably Christocentric. (These readers may also find it helpful to engage with the notes; in a short chapter aimed at a wide readership it has been necessary to relegate some important material, both traditional and contemporary, to the notes.) It is regularly alleged that the classical evangelical view of the Bible, under the influence of various Enlightenment philosophies, replaces

Christ's spiritual authority with the primary authority of the Bible, established independently of him.[3] What follows here is intended to suggest that, though frequently made, this criticism is seriously open to question.

Evangelical theology must have a healthy respect for its own traditions; that they are old and widely criticized does not necessarily mean that they are erroneous. Yet it is also true that faithful theology never stands still in its formulation of the truth, and is never uncritical of inherited traditions. Theology always needs to learn from the best of new thinking across a variety of fields, in its ongoing reformation. Later sections of this chapter, discussing the question of how the truth of the Bible works, will therefore engage with some contemporary issues of concern, especially questions of hermeneutics, language and personhood. I shall suggest that recent work in these fields can and should inform evangelical thinking about the Bible in creative and stimulating ways. Indeed, in the work of such writers as Anthony Thiselton, Kevin Vanhoozer and Nicholas Wolterstorff this kind of reformation of the evangelical understanding of Scripture is already taking place.[4]

The Truth of Jesus' Own Words

Jesus makes staggering claims for the origin of his own words. He claims not only that he has been sent by God the Father, but also that the words that he speaks come directly from the Father: 'I declare to the world what I have heard from him' (John 8:26 NRSV); 'the words that you gave to me I have given to them' (John 17:8 NRSV; see also John 12:49). That means that the words spoken by the Word incarnate are the very words God the Father has spoken to God the Son within the life of the Trinity itself. It is possible to get tied up here in questions to which we cannot know the answer – such as, in what language do the persons of the Trinity speak to each other? What is important, though, is to take seriously what Jesus presents to us in simple but striking terms: when we hear him speaking words in ordinary human language (in the Aramaic language he spoke, or translated into our own language) we are hearing divine language. God the Son is telling us what he has heard God the Father say. God, by definition, speaks only what is perfectly true, so in the words of Jesus we encounter perfect truth.

This has a significant implication for everyone who has not met Jesus in the flesh, and Jesus draws this out shortly before his death. He prays to his Father, regarding his disciples, 'the words that you gave to me I have given to them . . . I ask not only on behalf of these, but also on behalf of those who will believe in me through their word, that they may all be one. As you, Father, are in me and I am in you, may they also be in us' (John 17:8, 20–1 NRSV). Jesus passed on the Father's own words to the disciples, who, after his ascension, passed those words on to others. In doing so, they did not just bear witness to what they had heard and seen of the Word incarnate, although they certainly did that. As they faithfully passed on what Jesus had said, they also spoke words God himself had spoken. To hear the Twelve pass on the words of Jesus was therefore to be addressed by God. This is exactly the point the apostle Paul makes when he calls himself an ambassador for Christ, 'since God is making his appeal through us' (2 Corinthians 5:20 NRSV). It also explains why Jesus, in the verses from John 17 just quoted, links the hearing of God's words through the first disciples with coming to be 'in' the Father and the Son. To respond in faith to the apostles' proclamation of the words spoken by the Word incarnate is both to be addressed by God himself and to come into relationship with God himself.

Jesus and the Truth of the Old Testament

Of course, only a small part of the Bible is spoken directly by Christ during his earthly ministry. In thinking about the claim that can be made for the truth of the rest of the Bible, we turn first to the Old Testament. As before, we begin with Jesus. Many writers have documented in great detail that, for Jesus, what the Old Testament says is both historically accurate and of divine origin.[5] First, Jesus constantly refers to characters and events in the Old Testament with the assumption that he is referring to real history. It is sometimes argued that Jesus was here accommodating himself to the literal interpretation of Scripture of his Jewish contemporaries, but Jesus seems to go further than that. For example, his references to Abraham at the violent climax of the long discussion with the Jews in John 8 (vv. 52–8) make little sense if significant details given about Abraham's life are not historical. As John Wenham has pointed out, Jesus had no qualms about overturning dearly held religious beliefs, if they were in fact wrong. Had parts of the Old Testament in fact been historically inaccurate, he would not have baulked at correcting his hearers' view of their Scriptures.[6]

Second, for Jesus the Old Testament is not just historically true. It is also, and much more importantly, of divine origin, in the strong sense of that claim: whatever it says is what God says. For Jesus, God is the ultimate author of the Old Testament. It is therefore true in what it says about matters that go beyond ordinary history, such as the theological interpretation it gives to history, as well as prophecy, the creation, the nature of humanity and the character and actions of God himself. Jesus often uses the phrase 'it is written' to introduce a quotation from the Old Testament. This phrase seems to be tantamount to saying, 'God says'. This is particularly clear in his temptations in the wilderness (Matthew 4:1–11). Three times Jesus responds to Satan with 'It is written' and a quotation from the Old Testament. This response to the Tempter can only be thought of as effective if in these verses Jesus is quoting a spiritual authority higher than Satan. That Jesus does not need to bolster his responses to Satan with 'God says', but is quite happy with 'it is written', strongly suggests that for him the two phrases are interchangeable and identical in meaning.

A further very illuminating example is found in Matthew 19:4–5. Here Jesus quotes Genesis 2:24 ('For this reason a man will leave his father and mother and be united to his wife, and they will become one flesh'). In the context of Genesis, these words are not put explicitly into God's mouth, but are simply part of the narrative. However, Jesus introduces them as being spoken directly by God: 'the one who made them at the beginning ... said'. That would be an extraordinary mistake to make for a Jew who knew his Scriptures well, if a clear distinction had to be drawn between God saying something and merely Scripture saying something. Jesus, though, draws no such distinction. For him, 'Scripture says' and 'God says' are interchangeable phrases of identical meaning.

It is worth noting that other parts of the New Testament equate the voice of God and the voice of Scripture in the same way. The apostle Paul introduces a quotation from the Old Testament thus: 'the scripture says to Pharaoh' (Romans 9:17 NRSV). In fact, though, what he quotes are words that, in the Old Testament context, God spoke directly to Pharaoh. Words can have no greater mark of authority and truth than when God speaks them, so why would Paul be happy to ascribe the words simply to 'scripture'? It can only be that, for Paul, as for Jesus, to say that 'Scripture says' is no less a claim to truth and authority than to say, 'God says'. Paul does exactly the same in Galatians 3:8. He introduces some words that, in the Old Testament, God spoke directly to Abraham; thus, 'the scripture, foreseeing that God would justify the Gentiles by faith' NRSV. Paul does something remarkable here. He personifies Scripture, saying that it 'foresees' something that only God can foresee, and ascribes to it some words in fact uttered by God. When Scripture is put on this level, it can only be that for Paul, as for Jesus, 'Scripture says' and 'God says' are interchangeable terms, with identical meaning and force.

Jesus and the Truth of the New Testament

I have discussed Jesus' views of the truth of his own words and of the words of the Old Testament. What, then, about the rest of the New Testament? As before, we begin with Jesus himself. Jesus promised his disciples that he would send them the Holy Spirit, his Spirit, who 'will teach you everything, and remind you of all that I have said to you' (John 14:26 NRSV). This Spirit is also the Spirit of truth, who will declare to the disciples whatever he hears from Jesus: 'When the Spirit of truth comes, he will guide you into all the truth; for he will not speak on his own, but will speak whatever he hears ... he will take what is mine and declare it to you. All that the Father has is mine. For this reason I said that he will take what is mine and declare it to you' (John 16:13–15 NRSV). These are crucial words, for in them Jesus promises his disciples that the process of the communication to them of divine words from the Father through the Son will not end with the Son's ascension. Instead, the ascension will enable the sending of the Spirit, who will speak only what the ascended Son gives him to say, who in turn is given everything he has by the Father.

Jesus is giving us here a trinitarian explanation of revelation. The Father gives everything he has to the Son, who sends the Spirit to speak only what the Son gives him to say. We are on the verge of deep theological waters here, but in the context of the upper room, shortly before his death, Jesus is making one clear practical point. He is explaining that, after his ascension, certain human beings will be given by the Holy Spirit words to speak that are of equal divine origin and character to words uttered directly by the Father or by the Son. The fact that all the disciples remain sinners till the day they die does not alter the fact that, if they faithfully pass on what the Spirit gives them to say, their words are God's own words, just as much as the Ten Commandments or the Beatitudes.

However, the full implications of this promise do not apply to every believer. Not everything that you and I say is also at the same time God speaking. You may write me a letter of Christian teaching and exhortation, but that letter, however 'inspired' it may be, should not be added to Scripture. We may feel that the Spirit is telling us certain things, but we should not claim unqualified scriptural authority ('God says to you') for those words. Exactly the same point was recognized in the early church, during the process of discerning what was really Scripture, and so belonged in the Bible, and what was not. Not everything that every Christian wrote about Jesus in the early centuries, and not every letter that was written, was added to the Bible. Over time, the early church weighed the writings of the earliest Christians, to determine in which of them God was speaking by his Spirit and in which of them he was not. And one of the chief marks of *canonicity* (that a text really does belong in the canon of Scripture because it really is a medium of God's speech) came to be *apostolicity* (that it was written by one of the apostles, or by someone closely associated with them). Whether or not the apostles in the upper room realized it, it becomes clear that the promise Jesus made to them (John 16:12–15) was directed specifically to them, and was laying the groundwork for more Scripture to be written – that is, for more of God's words to be written down – after his ascension. Jesus therefore intended and foresaw that more Scripture *should* be written after he had returned to his Father, and made provision, by the sending of the Spirit, that such Scripture *could* be written.

Later New Testament writings begin to show awareness of the implications of this promise. Peter refers in an almost off-the-cuff way to Paul's letters as 'Scripture'. Some people twist the meaning of Paul's letters, he says, 'as they do the other scriptures' (2 Peter 3:15–16 NRSV). This statement assumes without argument that Paul's letters are Scripture – and this, as we have seen above, is the same as claiming that Paul's words are not his alone but really God's words. A second example is found in 1 Timothy 5:18. Here Paul introduces two quotations under the heading 'the scripture says'. The first is from Deuteronomy, and the second is identical to some words uttered by Jesus in Luke 10:7. Whether one thinks that, in the second saying, Paul is quoting directly from Luke's Gospel, or from a collection of Jesus' sayings, which later found its way into the Gospel, depends on the respective dates one gives to 1 Timothy and Luke. Whichever is the case, it seems that Paul places sayings of Jesus on exactly the same level as Old Testament law: they are both Scripture, and so are both God speaking.[7] A third example may be given. Paul tells the Thessalonians he thanks God that 'when you received the word of God that you heard from us, you accepted it not as a human word but as what it really is, God's word' (1 Thessalonians 2:13 NRSV). When the Thessalonians heard Paul speaking, what they really heard was God speaking to them. When that happened, the Father was answering Jesus' prayer for the apostles that, through the words the Father had given to him and he had given to them, people would come to faith and so come to be united with the Father and the Son (John 17:8, 20–1). The Father answers Jesus' prayer the same way every time someone hears and responds in faith to the gospel communicated to them in the words of an ordinary sinful human preacher or evangelist.

The Bible as God's Inspired Word

So far I have been describing, first, Jesus' view of the Bible, and second the Bible's general view of itself. This kind of description of the Bible is often summarized by saying that the Bible is God's inspired Word.[8] We need now to consider both what is and is not meant when we say that the Bible is 'inspired' by God.

Discussions of biblical inspiration, especially scholarly discussions, are often confused and confusing. The main reason for this is the failure to distinguish 'inspiration' in its biblical and theological sense from the way we often use the words 'inspire' and 'inspiration' in everyday English. This is vital, for the two are very different. A teacher who inspires her pupils gives them the ability to achieve things that they would never have achieved without her. An artist may find the inspiration to paint a picture more beautiful than he's ever painted before. The idea is of some gift or motivation being given to someone – something, as it were, breathed into them (in-spired).

The idea of Scripture being 'inspired', though, is quite different. It comes from the well-known verse 2 Timothy 3:16, and specifically from the Greek word used there, *theopneustos*. This verse, in the traditional English translation, says that 'all Scripture is inspired by God'. This translation can give the impression that the writers of Scripture were helped, nudged and motivated by God to produce better and truer writing than they could ever have produced on their own. That may be true, but it misses what the word *theopneustos* was intended to convey. This word almost certainly does not have the sense of God breathing some influence or inspiration *into* the minds of the Bible-writers; rather, it asserts that God has *breathed out* Scripture. The NIV has captured this well, in its translation of the verse: 'All Scripture is God-breathed'. *Theopneustos* therefore says nothing about *how* God worked in and through the Bible-writers to produce Scripture; it is rather about Scripture's divine *origin*. This is important because much contemporary writing on the doctrine of biblical inspiration, including some evangelical writing, simply assumes that *theopneustos* just means 'inspired' in the normal English sense of that word.[9] This ignores the lengthy research that previous generations of evangelical scholars have carried out to establish the particular theological meaning of the word.[10]

Thus the doctrine of inspiration asserts that Scripture's ultimate author is God. It does not have very much to say about the exact process by which God worked in and through the Bible-writers to produce Scripture. The doctrine of inspiration is often derided by its critics, and has occasionally been described by its proponents, as a 'theory of divine dictation'. When the critics of biblical inspiration describe it in this way, they are pointing out that the Bible very clearly looks like a set of human texts written by real people in real situations, whose lives and characters marked what they wrote. A secretary taking a letter from a boss by dictation has no personal input into what she writes; that does not seem to be the case with the Bible. When the more thoughtful proponents of the doctrine talk about 'dictation', however, as they occasionally do, what they mean is that the Bible is so completely God's book that he could not have been its ultimate author to any greater degree *if* he had actually dictated it word by word to the writers, like a boss dictating a letter to a secretary. They are not claiming that this is what God actually did.[11]

Lurking behind this debate is the doctrine of providence, which is the biblical idea that God sovereignly brings about the good he intends for the world, while working through the actions of free and responsible agents. The crucifixion is a classic example. Those who called for Jesus' crucifixion and who put him to death were acting out of their own free choice. Yet God was at work in and through them to bring about his own purposes. The idea that the Bible is inspired by God is the application of this doctrine of providence to the production of Scripture by God by means of human agents. It is not that God waited for believers to write of their own accord exactly what he wanted to say, and then authorized what they had written as Scripture.[12] It is not that God found a few deeply spiritual human writers, and gave them extra special promptings to help them to write exactly what he wanted to say. Neither of these views fits with the biblical picture of how God works in the world. Instead, God worked *concursively* with, in and through the thoughts and character of the human writer. To recognize that the Scriptures are thoroughly human texts, written in ordinary human languages, with histories of editing and copying, does not exclude them from also being thoroughly divine texts: divine providential activity and free human activity are not in competition with each other. One of the clearest and most thoughtful writers on this topic is the early twentieth-century American theologian B. B. Warfield. He defines what is meant by God working 'concursively' with the human writers: 'By "concursive operation" may be meant that form of revelation illustrated in an inspired psalm or epistle or history, in which no human activity – not even the control of the will – is superseded, but the Holy Spirit works in, with and through them all in such a manner as to communicate to the product qualities distinctly superhuman.'[13] Many denials of this understanding of the production of Scripture effectively reject or ignore the underlying doctrine of divine providence on which it rests.[14]

This understanding of inspiration is sometimes rejected by people who fear that it has unfortunate practical consequences for the way we interpret the Bible. They fear that it leads us to treat every single verse of the Bible as a direct message from God to the individual believer, ignoring the literary, historical and theological contexts in which that verse stands.[15] Certainly, evangelicals have often been guilty of (mis)reading the Bible in this way. However, it is not their doctrine of inspiration that is to blame. In fact, the classical doctrine of inspiration, if properly understood, will aid specifically in not treating the Bible this way. If the idea is taken seriously that God has worked concursively with the full personality of the Bible-writer, then the reader will look very carefully at the literary and contextual character of every biblical verse. The reader will ask such literary questions as 'Is this poetry or history?', such historical questions as 'Is it written to people before or during the exile?', and such theological questions as 'Where does this fit in the course of God's progressive revelation?' All this will be with the aim of faithfully hearing what God was saying in authoring that part of the Bible at that time in that way, and what he is now saying through the canonical function of that part of the Bible. It will produce readings of Scripture that find meaning in every verse, but not meanings of equal significance. The classical understanding of inspiration does not therefore necessarily lead to a flat reading of Scripture. To assert, as the evangelical doctrine of inspiration does, that 'Whatever the Bible says, God says,' does not ignore the fact that the Bible 'says' what it says in complex literary forms, and in literary, historical and theological contexts; in fact, it should warn readers to be sensitive to these forms and contexts.

What Should We Make of Infallibility and Inerrancy?

'Infallible' is a traditional description of the Bible, asserting that it is *wholly trustworthy*. 'Inerrant' is a more recent term, (although the concept is not new), which has been used most regularly since the nineteenth century; it asserts that the Bible is *wholly true*.[16] Since the terms themselves are not directly biblical ones we should not attach too much weight to them, although the concepts to which they refer are important.

The claim that the Bible is both infallible and inerrant is usually argued to follow on from the claim that it is 'breathed out' by God. If the Bible is ultimately authored by God, who cannot lie, then it must be trustworthy and true in every respect. In fact, both infallibility and, especially, inerrancy have recently been hotly debated topics among evangelicals, and many people have understandably tired of these debates. The prominence of these topics has occasionally given the impression either that the *first* thing some evangelicals want to say about the Bible is that it is without error, or the most important implication of biblical inspiration is that God gave us a book without error. This has in turn led many Christians to be wary of holding to inerrancy, because they fear it will lead them to read Scripture primarily as a book of facts (especially facts about ancient history) and not as a life-changing word from God to which they must submit; they also fear it will attract them away from devotion to Christ into an unhealthy interest in the details of biblical history. These are understandable fears: simple errorlessness and factuality do not seem to be an overriding concern of Christ and Scripture.

Infallibility and inerrancy are indeed poor concepts with which to begin thinking about the Bible's truth, because they actually claim too little. I presume that my local telephone directory is without error (it has proved itself perfectly trustworthy and true to me so far), but to say so does not claim very much. That is why the *first* things we should want to say about the Bible should be biblical and theological: what Christ says about it, and the purposes for which God spoke it. This is indeed where I began in this chapter. Nor is it the case that infallibility and inerrancy are the most significant corollaries of biblical inspiration. Instead, I want to think about infallibility and inerrancy on a different basis from the usual.

A good place to start in thinking biblically about these two concepts is Isaiah 55:11 (NRSV):

> so shall my word be that goes out from my mouth;
>> it shall not return to me empty,
> but it shall accomplish that which I purpose,
>> and succeed in the thing for which I sent it.

God promises that his word will infallibly perform the purpose for which he sent it. This verse reveals something to which the whole Bible bears witness: God's words fundamentally perform actions. God does also make statements and state propositions, but at the root his words perform actions.

We need to step back a moment and think about language and words in general, because God's words are not unique in having as their primary purpose the performing of actions. All language does two things, and the ordinary human language of the Bible is no exception: it states (or implies) certain *propositions* about the world, and it performs *actions*. There are some particular kinds of 'speech-acts' – for example when the foreman of a jury pronounces the word 'guilty', his simple act of speaking that word performs the further act of turning the defendant from innocent to guilty in the eyes of the law. That example, though, is not a special case; all language has this characteristic. For example, the words 'I'll see you at the party tomorrow' state the proposition that I will be at the party tomorrow. More than that, they perform the act of promising you that I will indeed be there. Proposition and action cannot, though, be separated: every time we speak, the two are inextricably linked together in our words. The truth of my words therefore has a double aspect. There is a factual aspect to their truth: they are true if I do indeed turn up at the party. But there is an additional aspect to their truth, which is to do with the personal trustworthiness of the person who speaks them: they are true if I prove trustworthy and keep the promise to which they give expression.

This analysis of language and how it works can seem too obvious to be worth describing like this. However, philosophers of language have tended to concentrate on the stating of propositions as the primary task of language. The contrasting view of language given above, which concentrates on language as performing actions, has come to be termed 'speech-act theory'. It was outlined by the Oxford philosopher J. L. Austin,[17] and has been developed by several writers, notably the American philosopher John Searle.[18] It has been applied to the Bible in some fruitful ways by theologians and philosophers, notably Anthony Thiselton, Kevin Vanhoozer and Nicholas Wolterstorff,[19] and I will draw on this application of speech-act theory later in this chapter. It will be immediately clear that God's words, and the Bible as a whole, are well described as a 'speech-act'.[20] God creates simply by speaking. His words, spoken by his prophet, build up and tear down (Jeremiah 1:9–10). God's written word has the purpose of bringing us to repentance and faith (e.g. John 20:31). In performing these actions, God makes or implies countless propositional statements about the world (e.g. that Abram left Haran at the Lord's command, that a rich tax-collector called Zacchaeus climbed a tree to see Jesus, etc.). Purpose and action, therefore, are two distinct aspects of language, but are closely interlinked whenever language is used; there cannot be one and not the other.

This point will help us get to grips with some recent discussions of inerrancy and infallibility. Some evangelicals hold to infallibility but not inerrancy – that is, they believe that Scripture infallibly performs the purpose for which God sent it, even though some of the propositional statements it makes about the world are likely to be incorrect (e.g. that Jericho was razed to the ground, or, more controversially, that the infant Jesus was visited by magi). John Goldingay, in a rich book on Scripture, states this general view. Thinking of the Bible as a whole as a witness to Christ, and drawing on the parallel of a witness in a law court, he argues, 'we are not dependent on witnesses making no mistakes, nor are we troubled when they contradict each other over certain matters. The concept of witness carries within it the notion of general reliability, but not that of inerrancy.'[21]

Two things may be said about this view. First, the analogy with the law court reveals a potential weakness. A witness at a trial may in fact be correct in her testimony about the defendant, but if her testimony about a number of incidental but related matters is shown to be incorrect, then her overall trustworthiness is rightly thrown into question, as any interrogating lawyer will attempt to demonstrate. Of course, if a few details of Old Testament history are plain wrong, it is true that the whole edifice of faith in the crucified and risen Christ does not immediately crumble. However, establishing which historical details of Scripture may safely be shown to be wrong without damage to the faith, and which may not, is a difficult and probably arbitrary task. In other words, it is not at all easy to disentangle Scripture's overall purpose from the propositional statements about history that it makes along the way in carrying out that purpose. Purpose and proposition are inextricably bound together in all language – they are each abstractions, describing different aspects of a single speech-act. This is especially true of Scripture's fundamentally historical revelation.

Second, Goldingay, following an argument put forward by Richard Bauckham, says that biblical historical narrative, like all historical narrative, carries the implicit qualification 'This is as accurate as my sources allow', and so probably contains some errors.[22] His point is that the model of inspiration outlined above works well for prophecy, in which God speaks directly to the prophet, but cannot easily be stretched to cover narrative, for which the Bible-writer has to do his research like any other historian (as Luke 1:1–3 makes clear). However, if the NIV's translation of 2 Timothy 3:16 is correct then Scripture itself describes historical narrative, as well as prophecy, as directly 'breathed out' by God. This, perhaps surprisingly, ascribes to biblical history qualities that might be thought to adhere only to prophecy – specifically the heading, whether stated or implied, 'Thus says the Lord'. The Bible itself does not know the distinction between the divine inspiration of prophecy and the divine inspiration of narrative, which it might seem natural to us to draw. Both infallibility and inerrancy do seem to be necessary doctrinal consequences of biblical inspiration. However, they are not the practical and devotional heart of inspiration. To explore that heart, we need, in a final and necessarily all too brief section, to open up the question of how the Bible's truth works.

How the Bible's Truth Works

Detailed studies of how the Bible uses the words 'true' and 'truth' tend to reveal two main areas of meaning. The first, unsurprisingly, is simply 'conformity to fact' – stating something accurately. (This corresponds to *inerrancy*.) This is how we usually think of 'truth' in everyday speech. However, there is a second area of meaning, which perhaps doesn't occur to our Western minds so readily: truth as the faithfulness, trustworthiness or reliability of a person. (This corresponds to *infallibility*.) As one writer has put it, 'Truth, in the biblical sense, is ultimately associated with the triune God Himself as a perfection of His being . . . He is always true to His word, so that faithfulness appears as a wonderful feature of His being, grounding full confidence on the part of believers.'[23]

Thus any description of the nature and function of the Bible's truth must lead us to, and be directly related to, God as the true God – that is, the truth-speaking and trustworthy God. Many writers fear that the belief that the Bible is inspired, infallible and inerrant, in the forms in which I have outlined these beliefs, is misleading and even dangerous, because it leads us away from God himself. It is alleged that it leads to a form of Bible-reading which so focuses on the words of Scripture that the reader forgets that those words exist only to lead us to a spiritual encounter with God. Such Bible-reading would indeed be a serious abuse of the Bible.

I have already suggested that the conception of the Bible as a speech-act leads us to view infallibility and inerrancy as inextricably linked. In a moment I shall argue, in addition, that a speech-act view of the Bible is the most appropriate overall description of the Bible's nature and function – especially so, if we want to encourage Bible-reading which seeks above all to encounter God through that reading. This is not to do away with the idea of the Bible as the 'Word of God'; it is to point out that by Word we really mean 'speech-act'. First, though, we shall consider an alternative suggestion for the Bible's overall nature and function. Namely, that we should understand the Bible to be 'the Word of God' in a sacramental sense, and should even think of the Bible as itself a sacrament.

Stephen Wright has recently proposed this view of the Bible,[24] and makes high claims for it: 'I suggest . . . that to view Scripture as sacramental is perhaps the only way to save the Church from either fundamentalist misreading or effective marginalization of Scripture.'[25] He starts by making a very helpful distinction between 'receiving' and 'using' Scripture:

> 'Receiving' any literary text – including . . . the Bible itself – entails a readiness to be immersed both in 'the words on the page' and the realities to which they point. It implies that the reader (or hearer) is drawn out of themselves in a transcendental moment of encounter. It is contrasted with the mere use of a text in order to confirm our prejudices, echo our experiences, or satisfy our lower desires.[26]

He argues that to think of the Bible as 'the Word of the Lord' in the traditional evangelical sense in fact hinders 'reception', and tends towards 'use', since we are led away from encounter with the spiritual reality to which the text points, and towards an unfortunate focus on the words themselves. He proposes instead that we relate the words of Scripture and the truth towards which they point *sacramentally*. Wright sets out the basis for his sacramental account of Scripture with this analogy:

> In the paradigmatic sacraments of baptism and eucharist, ordinary, created things – water, bread and wine – become, through

God's promises received in faith, the vehicles of extraordinary, transcendental meeting. To speak of the elements themselves as extraordinary removes the sacramental mystery and paradox, and leads to error and superstition. So surely it is with Scripture.

One advantage, for Wright, of this sacramental view of Scripture is that it helps us avoid hearing the words of Scripture, as he says, 'in the flat, as if they did not point beyond themselves to the mystery of the gospel'.[27]

I am very much in sympathy with Wright's aims to promote Bible-reading which leads to spiritual encounter, and to warn against 'flat' Bible-reading. But I find his proposal unconvincing, and this for two reasons. The first is broadly philosophical. The analogy between the Bible on the one hand, and the water of baptism and the bread and wine of the Lord's Supper on the other, fails to acknowledge that words are not things in the way that water, bread and wine are. We can be deceived into thinking that words are 'things' when we observe them laid out in a dictionary, or when we are thinking about language as a system (what Saussure called *langue*). But of course a dictionary is only a selective archive of language-in-use, and *langue* is an abstraction derived from (what Saussure called) *parole*: language-in-use. The basic unit of language-in-use is not the individual word but the speech-act. Moreover, whenever we perform a speech-act (i.e. whenever we speak), we identify ourselves with our words: if I make you a promise, I take to myself the responsibility to keep that promise. In addition, if you either trust or distrust my promise, in so doing you either trust or distrust me.[28] To put the point philosophically, the ontology of language-in-use, unlike the ontology of objects (including sacramental elements), is closely related to the ontology of action and of personhood. Speech-acts are a kind of extension of the self; in no sense is this true of objects, even when used sacramentally by God to point to himself.

My second objection to the description of the Bible as sacramental is theological. Sacramental elements point effectively beyond themselves to divine spiritual reality only because they were given in the past by Christ with explanatory words, and because their contemporary ritual use is accompanied with words. This is Augustine: 'Let the word be added to the element and it will become a sacrament.'[29] Calvin describes the relation of Word and sacrament thus: 'a sacrament is never without a preceding promise but is joined to it as a sort of appendix, with the purpose of confirming and sealing the promise itself'.[30] That promise itself of course comes to us only in and through the words of the Bible. The Bible cannot be a sacrament, because it is that which, among other things, makes sacraments possible – making them meaningful and capable of pointing beyond themselves. To say either that the Bible is a sacrament, or that it functions sacramentally, introduces a theological confusion. It is certainly true that the Protestant Reformers regularly compared the effectiveness of the sacraments to the effectiveness of the ministry of the Word: 'the sacraments have the same office as the Word of God: to offer and set forth Christ to us, and in him the treasures of heavenly grace'.[31] But this point cannot be argued in reverse. The Reformers were offering not a sacramental account of the Word, but a Word-related and non-sacerdotal account of the efficacy of sacraments.

I am not suggesting that sacramental elements and Scripture have no common functions; they clearly both exist to point us beyond themselves to spiritual encounter. However, any overarching description of the *nature* of Scripture, directing us towards appropriate *reading* of Scripture – which is what Wright intends his description of the Bible as sacrament to be – must be able to show that it is fundamentally sound philosophically and theologically. The above arguments suggest that it is neither. I have already argued that to view all language as a speech-act is philosophically the most coherent and fitting approach; I want now to suggest that it also provides a more coherent and fitting biblical-theological description of the Bible than the 'sacramental' account, while leading just as naturally to the kind of Bible-reading Wright rightly wishes to recommend.[32]

In the Bible, God himself, his actions and his words are intimately related. We have noted that words do not just point to actions, but are the means for the performance of actions – simply in uttering the words of a promise, for example, God makes that promise to us. Moreover, God himself is intimately related to his speech-acts.

Two examples may be given. First, throughout Scripture God establishes his relationship with people primarily by uttering words of a covenant-promise to them. He presents himself to them as the God who makes that promise. When people respond in faith, obedience and love to the words of that promise, they are responding to God; there is not an initial response to the promise and a subsequent response to God himself. Responding in faith to the covenant is not the gateway to an encounter with the God who stands some distance behind the promise; the promise does not exhaust who God is, but yet he is truly and faithfully present to us in his promise. Thus there is no faithful response to God apart from a faithful submission to the speech-acts he performs in relation to us – and to respond in faith to God's speech-acts simply is to respond to him.

Second, in the discourse on the vine and the branches, Jesus refers both to his *words* abiding in us and to *him* abiding in us (John 15:1–12). He seems to use the two interchangeably; they are practical synonyms. The words of both the Father and Jesus, then, are a kind of extension of themselves. We encounter the words of the covenant and the words of Christ only in Scripture. In the words of the Bible, therefore, God *presents* himself to us as the true God in that he will faithfully keep the promises he makes to us.

To read a text is therefore to encounter the actions of another person, and so to encounter a kind of extension of that person. In interpreting texts, readers thus acquire all the same moral responsibilities entailed by an encounter with another person in the flesh, and by speaking to them face to face. Kevin Vanhoozer, in his recent work of theological hermeneutics, identifies what he calls 'two deadly interpretive sins': *pride* and *sloth*. Interpretive pride assumes that we know what the speaker or writer is saying or doing in his words before we have properly listened to them; interpretive sloth shirks the reader's responsibility to attend carefully to the text for himself.[33] Both ignore the voice and the action of the author on the reader, exercised through the text. Speech-act theory provides a rich account of why such readerly attitudes really are sins, for to read or to listen is to encounter the action and also therefore, in some sense, the person of another.

Conclusion

It is impossible to attend overmuch to the words of a text – as long as the reader is attending to the words with the right interpretive goal in mind. A model of Scripture that focuses us profoundly on the words of Scripture (as the classical model of an inspired, infallible and inerrant Scripture does) does not necessarily hinder encounter with God, but in fact leads us into deeper encounter with the God who presents himself to us in those words.

A flat reading of Scripture is not one that attends to the words too much; it is one that attends to them wrongly. We can attend to the words wrongly by attempting, for example, to treat every biblical sentence as a direct communication from God to us, taking no account of its literary, canonical, historical and theological context. Or we can attend to them wrongly by focusing on grammar and semantics, refusing to come to understand and submit ourselves to the speech-act being performed by means of the words. The corrective to these abuses of the Bible is not, though, to attend less to its words and more to the spiritual reality to which they point. To present the solution in these terms is to present a false dilemma, because that spiritual reality is none other than the God who presents himself to us in the speech-acts performed in and through the words. The corrective, rather, is to attend to the words more carefully, in order to encounter God more truly.

Notes

[1] Augustine, *On Christian Doctrine*, Nicene and Post-Nicene Fathers 2, ed. Philip Schaff, Grand Rapids, Eerdmans, 1956, 1.35, 39.

[2] It is regularly asserted that in the post-Reformation period orthodox Protestant doctrines of Scripture lost the dynamic Christocentric focus of first-generation Reformation theology (e.g. Carl Heinz Ratschow, *Lutherische Dogmatik zwischen Reformation und Aufklärung*, vol. 1, Gütersloh, Gütersloher Verlagshaus Gerd Mohn, 1964, p. 72). It is certainly true that seventeenth-century Protestant theology became significantly

more scholastic in its written form. Whether this form took the content of the doctrine of Scripture itself in a formalistic direction away from its grounding in Christ is by no means as certain as is often assumed (see e.g. Robert D. Preus, *The Theology of Post-Reformation Lutheranism: A Study of Theological Prolegomena*, Saint Louis, Concordia, 1970, p. 411; Timothy Ross Phillips, 'Francis Turretin's Idea of Theology and Its Bearing Upon His Doctrine of Scripture', PhD thesis, Vanderbilt University, 1986, pp. 13ff.).

[3] This criticism is often made with regard to the orthodox Protestant doctrine of the inspiration of Scripture: see William J. Abraham, *The Divine Inspiration of Holy Scripture*, Oxford, Oxford University Press, 1981, pp. 72–74; Kern Robert Trembath, *Evangelical Theories of Biblical Inspiration: A Review and Proposal*, New York, Oxford University Press, 1987, pp. 99, 115. For a longer critique of Abraham, Trembath and others see Timothy Ward, *Word and Supplement: Speech Acts, Biblical Texts, and the Sufficiency of Scripture*, Oxford, Oxford University Press, 2002, pp. 270–80.

[4] E.g. Anthony C. Thiselton, *New Horizons in Hermeneutics*, London, HarperCollins, 1992; Kevin J. Vanhoozer, 'God's Mighty Speech-Acts: The Doctrine of Scripture Today', in *A Pathway into the Holy Scripture*, eds. Philip E. Satterthwaite and David F. Wright, Grand Rapids, Eerdmans, 1994, pp. 143–81; *Is There a Meaning in This Text? The Bible, The Reader and the Morality of Literary Knowledge*, Leicester, Apollos, 1998; Nicholas Wolterstorff, *Divine Discourse: Philosophical Reflections on the Claim that God Speaks*, Cambridge, Cambridge University Press, 1995.

[5] See e.g. John Wenham, *Christ and the Bible*, 3rd ed., Grand Rapids, Baker, 1994, ch. 1.

[6] Wenham, *Christ and the Bible*, p. 27.

[7] It has been argued either that 1 Timothy 5:18 only refers to the first quotation (from Deuteronomy) as Scripture, or that the second saying was a common proverb, to which Jesus

also happened to refer (see J. N. D. Kelly, *A Commentary on the Pastoral Epistles*, Black's New Testament Commentaries, London, Adam & Charles Black, 1963, p. 126). It is not likely though, when we remember what is at stake in identifying a saying as 'Scripture', that Paul would simply add the second saying to the first, if it were not in fact in his mind Scripture.

[8] Writers on inspiration debate the status that should be given to the Bible's self-testimony. For B. B. Warfield, the decisive 'phenomena' of the Bible are its self-testimony over against some apparent conclusions of critical scholarship (B. B. Warfield, *The Inspiration and Authority of the Bible*, Phillipsburg, N.J., Presbyterian and Reformed, 1948, pp. 419–42). For William Abraham, the conclusions reached by 'a natural and honest study of the Bible' should be decisive (Abraham, *Divine Inspiration*, p. 29). This is Abraham's description of critical scholarship, and it is one that contemporary epistemology, stressing the locatedness of every interpreter, would think of as somewhat naive. The recognition that there is nothing inherently 'natural' or 'honest' about critical scholarship, in comparison to other ways of approaching the Bible, makes Warfield's position seem more tenable than it might have done in 1950.

[9] E.g. Trembath, *Evangelical Theories*, p. 6; Abraham, *Divine Inspiration*, p. 93. Both writers assume, with very little consideration of the matter, that *theopneustos* is exactly identical in meaning to the modern English usage of the word 'inspired'. The linguistic and historical dangers of using a human analogy to determine the meaning of the word have been pointed out elsewhere (I. Howard Marshall, *Biblical Inspiration*, Carlisle, Paternoster, 1995, p. 40; Warfield, *Inspiration and Authority*, p. 154).

[10] One of the clearest examples of this research is found in Warfield, *Inspiration and Authority*, pp. 245–96.

[11] It is likely that a few writers on inspiration, particularly in the seventeenth century, did in fact hold to a dictation model of inspiration in the 'boss–secretary' style. Warfield lists the

names of some whom he thinks are guilty, and distances himself from them (B. B. Warfield, *Selected Shorter Writings of Benjamin B. Warfield*, vol. 2, ed. John E. Meeter, Phillipsburg, N.J., Presbyterian and Reformed, 1973, p. 543). Dictation has not been the mainstream evangelical understanding of inspiration.

[12] That would produce a bizarre notion of God's action in the world (see Wolterstorff, *Divine Discourse*, p. 187).

[13] Warfield, *Inspiration and Authority*, p. 83.

[14] William Abraham argues that any stress on the Bible as given word for word by God is 'a carry-over from dictation theory', even if the word 'dictation' is not actually used. (His sights are set on B. B. Warfield's and Jim Packer's doctrine of Scripture here.) They offer, he argues, 'a kind of telepathic dictation without the writer being aware of it' (Abraham, *Divine Inspiration*, pp. 36–37). Abraham's implicit conception of the mode and scope of God's action in the world here is very thin.

[15] See e.g. Colin Gunton's desire to 'dispense with the need to wring equal meaning out of every text' (Colin E. Gunton, *A Brief Theology of Revelation*, Edinburgh, T. and T. Clark, 1995, p. 66).

[16] See J. I. Packer, *'Fundamentalism' and the Word of God*, London, Inter-Varsity Fellowship, 1958, p. 95.

[17] J. L. Austin, *How to Do Things with Words*, 2nd ed., Oxford, Clarendon, 1975.

[18] Searle is an analytic philosopher who develops speech-act theory in a very analytic direction. He has rightly been taken to task for treating the massive complexities of interpersonal linguistic communication as too susceptible to analytic-philosophical analysis. However, speech-act theory can equally easily be developed in a direction more interested in the social and moral dimensions of speech (e.g. Wolterstorff, *Divine Discourse*, pp. 75–94; Vanhoozer, *Is There a Meaning?*).

[19] See note 4 above.

20 A coherent case has been made for viewing written texts as 'speech-acts'. See Mary Louise Pratt, *Toward a Speech Act Theory of Literary Discourse*, Bloomington, Indiana University Press, 1977; Vanhoozer, *Is There a Meaning?* pp. 225–28; Ward, *Word and Supplement*, pp. 90–94.

21 John Goldingay, *Models for Scripture*, Grand Rapids, Eerdmans, 1994, p. 45.

22 Goldingay, *Models for Scripture*, p. 279.

23 Roger Nicole, 'The Biblical Concept of Truth', in *Scripture and Truth*, ed. D. A. Carson and John D. Woodbridge, Leicester, Inter-Varsity Press, 1983, pp. 287–98, at p. 296.

24 Stephen I. Wright, 'The Bible as Sacrament', *Anvil* 19 (2002), pp. 81–87. He acknowledges that the view is not unique to him.

25 Ibid., p. 87.

26 Ibid., p. 81.

27 Ibid., p. 82.

28 See further Vanhoozer's illuminating use of Paul Ricoeur's concept of 'identity' to describe the nature of a speaker's identity with his words and a writer's identity with his text (Vanhoozer, *Is There a Meaning?* pp. 225–26).

29 Quoted in John Calvin, *Institutes of the Christian Religion*, Library of Christian Classics 20–21, ed. John T. McNeill, trans. Ford Lewis Battles, Philadelphia, Westminster, 1960, 4.14.4.

30 Ibid., 4.14.3.

31 Ibid., 4.14.17.

32 It is important to note that the use of 'speech-act' as a controlling concept for the Bible does not represent the illicit importation of a non-theological category into theological description. Instead, it gives us the conceptual apparatus to discern more clearly the view of language to which the Bible regularly bears witness.

33 Vanhoozer, *Is There a Meaning?* pp. 462–63.

Chapter Two

Isn't It All a Matter of Interpretation? Scripture, Truth and Our World

Paul Gardner

D oubt about the truth and authority of Scripture runs deep in this generation. The question 'Isn't it all a matter of interpretation?' indicates the common belief that Scripture interpretation is a largely futile task. This chapter examines first the question of the authority of Scripture, arguing that biblical authority is rooted in the author, God. Such an attitude to authority involves a profound life commitment, and is not determined by the interpretation of any text. Second, it argues that so much emphasis on the 'problem' of interpretation has led to the 'closure' of the Bible for ordinary Christians. Championing the clarity and truth of Scripture, the author then focuses on factors in interpretation which suggest the task is not only possible but is the remit of all Christians. He also gives pointers to encourage the non-theologically trained that interpreting the Bible is both vital and enabled by God himself, who communicates effectively to his people.

Introduction

'But isn't it all a matter of interpretation?' is a frequently heard comment these days as the Bible is studied. What people usually mean is that they think the Bible can be made to mean many different things (which is undoubtedly true). The implication of what they are saying, though, is that any person's interpretation may be as valid as any other, or that there is no way of truly *knowing* anything from Scripture because no one understanding of a passage is better than another. In this chapter I shall suggest that it is indeed possible to understand what God is saying to us in Scripture. Though our knowledge and understanding of God's Word is never comprehensive this side of eternity, interpretation of Scripture is, nevertheless, a possible task because God is the one who enables his communication with us to be effective.

Evangelical Identity

Part of our identity as evangelicals is that we are committed to the authority of Scripture as God's Word written for his people. While written by people of normal human abilities, living in specific cultures at specific times in history, evangelicals believe that these authors were so inspired by the Spirit of God that what they wrote was entirely reliable and reflects not just their own perspective but the mind of God himself on the matters addressed. This is no more than what has been believed throughout most of church history by all churches. Traditionally many, especially evangelicals, have therefore referred to Scripture as 'infallible';[1] that is, as possessing in its nature the entire trustworthiness that we already ascribe to its ultimate author, God himself.

At some stage in our growth as Christians we will all have experienced challenges to this way of thinking about Scripture. Perhaps we grew up as teenagers in one church and then, when we moved to another area, we suddenly discovered there were good Christian people who thought rather differently about some matters that were important to us. Many examples might spring to mind. Perhaps we had always believed the Bible to be clear that baptism is only for adults. Now we discover that some good, gracious and Bible-believing people are convinced that the baptism of infants is biblical. Perhaps we have grown up believing the Bible is clear that women's ministry as 'elders' (incumbents etc.) is encouraged in Scripture. We then find some Christians who are convinced of the opposite. On whichever side of these or other particular arguments we may find ourselves, reactions can take a variety of forms.

First, we must all admit to the temptation to 'dig in'. The 'I am right and you are wrong' position is found in all camps. It is a position that allows no debate. At best it allows a statement of 'my position' (which is right) and 'your position' (which is wrong). The trouble is that ultimately we all know this way of handling such matters is unsatisfying, especially when a wall of division arises between two people both claiming to be evangelical Christians! In some circles rancour develops. Instead of addressing our differences of interpretation, words like 'fundamentalist', 'liberal' or even 'sectarian' (legitimate words in some contexts) now become part of the verbal abuse exchanged.

Second, some people react with self doubt, which can ultimately lead to a degree of biblical scepticism. Faced with differing interpretations they begin to ask, 'How can I know if I am right?' Sadly, this is not some godly expression of humility; rather, it is the sort of self doubt that immediately seeks a justification. Thus it quickly turns into the start of a scepticism about what was taught in the first place back in the 'home church'. Too often this then develops into a broader scepticism about Scripture itself.

There are, of course, many other reactions to encountering this first questioning about how we interpret Scripture. Some will be useful, good and biblical responses, and others will be profoundly proud and unbiblical. It should thus not surprise us that often discussions on matters of interpretation involve discussions about the nature of the Bible's 'authority', of how we can 'properly interpret' the Bible, and how we know what a passage 'means'. Neither should it surprise us if, as evangelicals, these issues arouse passions. Indeed, they *should* arouse passion. If we are committed to serving and witnessing to Christ as Saviour and Lord of all, then we know we are committed to the Christ revealed to us in Scripture. We are committed to the God who has chosen to communicate with us about himself, and about his Son, and about his purposes for this world in his written Word. Differing interpretations of Scripture will therefore be (rightly) disconcerting. They may challenge our thinking about how God's Word is truthful, how it works among us, and its authority.

Since many good evangelical books have been written on the authority of Scripture and its interpretation, my purpose here is limited. It is to point again to the need for us all to be clear on the 'authority' issue and, second, to rehearse some of the issues relating to interpreting the Bible. My desire is to encourage confidence in the Bible for this age in which we live, and to point in directions that may help build that confidence so that we are better able to trust God's Word and thus become more faithful to God himself.

The Authority of Scripture

You have commanded your precepts to be kept diligently.
(Psalm 119:4 ESV)

In some sense anyone who is a Christian must give some degree of authority in their life and in their belief system to the Bible. Ultimately it is only here that we find an account of Jesus and an explanation of who he is, his life and ministry, death and resurrection. Yet we need to be aware that simply to claim that the Bible is our 'authority' does not mean very much. Most heretical sects throughout the history of Christianity have claimed the same.

In modern theological debates, many have a commitment to biblical authority of some sort, but their definition of that authority and how it functions is certainly not the same as that espoused by evangelicals. For example, on matters of sexuality, we need to realize that there are many people who believe that, properly interpreted, the text says what traditionalists have always said it means. However, their view of Scripture itself is such that they can then go on and say either that Scripture got it wrong, or that we now know better.

Here we need to note that the mark of an evangelical view of Scriptural authority does not rest on a specific interpretation of a text or texts. Rather, evangelicals have accepted the authority of the Bible for the life of the Christian community because of the one we believe to be the author. Thus, based on Scripture's own understanding of itself, since what Paul says is truly what God says, we would not allow ourselves to say, 'Paul was wrong.'

In spite of the challenges to such a view of authority (authority guaranteed by the author) most evangelical discussions about interpretation and meaning in the Bible start from this common commitment to the Bible's authority. This Book, a gracious gift from God to his people, is treated as authoritative because the author, God, does not lie (Titus 1:2).[2] In locating the authority of Scripture in the author, God, Christians have sought to imitate Christ himself. For example, Jesus himself assumes the authority of Scripture when he begins statements with the phrase 'it is written' (e.g. Matthew 4:10).[3]

Authority as Pastorally Significant

> Your promise is well tried, and your servant loves it. (Psalm 119:140 ESV)

This approach to the authority of Scripture involves a profound life commitment. Of course, as we shall see, we cannot simply divorce the authority of the text from its meaning.[4] Nevertheless, the evangelical understanding of authority is such that, when a person has 'understood' (or believes she has understood) the passage of Scripture she is reading, she seeks to submit to it rather than ignore it or pretend that she knows better than God's Word.

In the modern debates, this distinction relating to authority can be helpful. We may use similar tools to help us understand the text as we would if we were studying any literary masterpiece, but we would not necessarily feel the need to submit to what we find in other texts. When, as evangelicals, we study Scripture we do so because the authority it carries is the authority of its author, God.[5] As our greatest desire is to worship God and obey him in every area of life so, having heard him address us in his Word, we *live* accordingly, we *obey*, and we are prepared to *change*. Constantly we seek to align our lives and minds to the will of God revealed in his Word. We long to be able to say with the apostle Paul 'we have the mind of Christ' (1 Corinthians 2:16). 'Authority' in this sense carries with it the existential commitment to a life of obedience or submission to the author.

In practice then, when evangelicals hear of theologians who deny, say, the divinity of Christ, or who discount the Bible's teachings on sexual ethics, we may not, strictly speaking, be dealing with issues of 'different interpretations'. Rather, we may have different attitudes to 'authority'. Some will agree with us about what the Bible says, but will indicate they think the Bible is wrong or irrelevant for today. When evangelicals are sometimes heard to say, 'He doesn't believe the Bible,' their talk may be technically inaccurate, but what they are driving towards by saying this may indeed be true; that is, that people have different views of the Bible's authority. Some listen and seek to obey, even if it is countercultural; some do not.

A traditional evangelical view of the Bible's authority is summed up not in what words we use to describe its perfection or inspiration so much as in what we *do* with it. We may struggle with interpreting a verse. We may disagree with someone else about what a passage means but, at the end of the day, if we believe Scripture is telling us something, we shall always seek to obey what it is saying even if that means changing a previous understanding on that matter.

When people resort to saying, 'But isn't it all a matter of interpretation?' they are often finding some excuse not to do what God is asking them to do through his Word. We may need to point this out. Sometimes simply knowing this will encourage us to see that our understanding of Scripture is reasonable enough. We have no need to doubt or become sceptical. Rather, the issue is obedience. It also helps remind us that we all have the sinful tendency in our minds to seek any excuse not to obey what we realize is actually quite clear in the text.

Authority and Interpretation

However, while the issue of 'authority' is the first and most critical matter to address, the next is the question of interpretation. The problem is specially highlighted when we encounter someone with the *same* view of authority, with the *same* desire to be obedient to what God says, yet who understands what God says in different ways.

What we then discover as we work with other Christians is that, precisely because we do not properly 'think God's thoughts after him', because we are sinful fallen creatures, our ability to understand God's Word is fallible. While Scriptures are inspired by the Spirit of God so that they truly reflect the mind and intention of God in language that communicates, we do not always have the 'ears to hear'.

This week, during breaks in writing this chapter, I have prepared a talk for a family service on the parable of the sower (Luke 8:4–15). In this parable Jesus talks about hearing and understanding. Note that understanding here is not described as intellectual comprehension so much as in terms of obedience and lifestyle. The seed, the Word of God, is sown. It is the fruit that will reveal whether the Word has been heard. The parable gives a good indication of how much can come in to distort and upset that 'hearing' in the lives of sinners. Their context may make the hearing difficult; for example, 'life's worries' or their culture of 'riches and pleasures' (Luke 8:14). Their religious presuppositions or background may make it difficult for them to hear and so believe and be saved (v. 12). What a person hears may not be fully heard, and so when someone challenges their belief or even persecutes them for their understanding, they fall away and give up on it (v. 13). On the other hand, says Jesus, hearing is actually possible. It is a hearing that is 'given' (v. 10). As we discover from other Scriptures, this hearing is enabled by the author himself, by the Spirit of God. But more on this later.

The Authority Gap

Sometimes people are not really interested in carefully interpreting Scriptures, they are only interested in restating what they already believe. We have all been guilty of this from time to time, sometimes for the best of intentions. For example, we want to withstand the attacks on a biblical position from a person who clearly has a different view of biblical authority from our own. This is the 'dig in' approach mentioned earlier. While it is understandable, in the end it is actually *reducing* biblical authority rather than affirming it. It is important that evangelicals not only *do* but are *obliged* to treat the matter with the utmost care precisely because of the authority they invest in the Word of God. While the processes of interpretation in many church Bible studies may not be the best, this is why evangelicals are known for their Bible studies: we really do want to know what God is saying to us as we learn to live, think and worship with our whole mind, body and soul.

Nevertheless, we need to recognize (and this is the heart of the problem of interpretation) that the further we move from the text itself and the author-guaranteed meaning the bigger becomes the authority gap.[6] When a teacher relates to you what he thinks God's Word is saying, he does not speak as God. He speaks as one who has studied what God has said, who has weighed Scripture with Scripture, who seeks to live in obedience to the Scripture, yet he is still not God. The interpreter is fallible. The authority gap is there. We are therefore inevitably going to have to study together and discuss together. So the work of interpretation does need to be done, but it is *not* an impossible task!

Much modern work in hermeneutics has implied and sometimes stated the opposite. Undoubtedly there is a 'crisis of confidence' among scholars concerning biblical interpretation.[7] The advent of postmodern literary theories following hard on the heels of decades of an all-pervasive historical criticism, has indeed taken its toll even among many evangelical writers. Sadly this has had a debilitating effect especially on pastors and teachers in the church. It is not much wonder, therefore, if congregational members and even new Christians find themselves confused and wondering whether anyone can really understand or interpret the Bible, or whether any one person's view is as good as any other.[8] One of the main ways of working through the issue of the 'authority gap' is to enable and encourage the 'ordinary Christian' to read the Bible for him or herself. In other words, working our way through these issues requires the exact opposite of what happens in so many churches where *less* rather than *more* attention is given to the Bible.

A 'Closed' Bible Must Be Reopened

> The unfolding of your words gives light;
> it gives understanding to the simple. (Psalm 119:130)

Seen from a different angle, the situation in our day and age has parallels to that existing in the medieval Roman church. There the Bible had effectively been relegated to the status of a 'closed' book known only to the elite teachers of the church who had studied theology and knew Latin. Today in some circles the Bible might as well be a 'closed' book. Does everyone have to understand the complexities of postmodern hermeneutical theories in order to access Scripture? For some, the book has once again become the privileged domain of an elite.[9]

The way back into this 'closed book', for those who believe that the Bible is for 'ordinary' Christians to understand, is often to engage in a form of interpretation in which really the Bible becomes a series of 'proof texts'. Here the same great truths the reader has always believed are seen to emerge from almost all passages that are read. The danger is, of course, that God's Word has become static, like a textbook. There is not a lot of scope left for the Word of God to be 'living and active. Sharper than any double-edged sword . . . it judges the thoughts and attitudes of the heart' (Hebrews 4:12). Such a reader will look for verses that address a relevant life issue, and lift them straight from the biblical context to his own context without regard to history, use of language, flow of the Bible as a whole, the genre of literature and so on.

Others attempt to re-enter this 'closed book' by using the Bible as little more than a 'jumping-off point'. The text becomes a launching pad for people to speak their views on a matter of relevance and importance. This way forward is actually found both among so-called liberals as well as among the most committed of evangelicals. For liberals, the 'spiritual experiences' the text leads us to are more important than whatever an ancient text might say. For evangelicals, it is as if the Holy Spirit uses the Scripture simply to help us dig deeper into our *own* wells of experience and spirituality to understand meaning for today. Here the original meaning of a text, the context, the history, even the discussion about genre, all once again disappear. What matters now is whether the Bible has generated 'spiritual experiences'.

There are many other routes by which 'ordinary' Christians, who have not been trained at theological college, will want to reinstate the Bible in their lives. These different approaches are symptomatic of the gulf that has been formed between the theologians and millions of normal Christians. Often the elite are damning and full of disdain for such 'naive' readings of the biblical text as those they see in Bible study groups. If such people should dare to suggest that a theologian does not appear to be 'biblical', they are simply told they haven't understood the complexity of the interpretation of this or that passage. People come to assume that only 'theologians' can do this work. Of course, what is then forgotten is that the Word of God in Scripture is for *all Christians*. Some have failed to grasp the need to link the academy with the church.

In a world of increasingly specialized study, we need many more pastor-theologians who can teach and preach using the best tools available but then model a better handling of Scripture that others can imitate as they reach its meaning for today. The Bible must be wrested out of the hands of a new elite and placed firmly back in the hands of normal Christian (and non-Christian) people.

Reopening the Bible

The clarity of Scripture

> Your word is a lamp to my feet
> and a light for my path. (Psalm 119:105)

We need to start with the evidence of Scripture itself that it is 'clear', for it assumes within itself that understanding does take place as God's Word is read. The use of the phrase 'Do you not know?' in the Old Testament, on the lips of Jesus, and in the writings of Paul, carries almost a sense of despair from the speaker or writer to the one reading. The writer implies that a certain truth was surely self-evident as people read what had been revealed by God in the past.[10] When handling the law, it is assumed that the writings of Moses are sufficiently understandable that they can be taught to children and even discussed with them! (Deuteronomy 6:6–7). The command to meditate on God's Word day and night assumes that the Word can be understood and will be of genuine value to the reader (Joshua 1:8; Psalm 119:97). Scripture even enables the *simple* to rise above the teacher! (Psalm 119:99, 130).

As we pause to remember that the Bible belongs to the 'ordinary' reader who has trust in God who speaks truly in Scripture, we must also remember that this Word is active. It is for every faithful believer and produces wisdom but also produces changed behaviour and changed emotions. Psalm 19:7–11 (NIV) reminds us:

> The law of the LORD is perfect,
>> reviving the soul.
> The statutes of the LORD are trustworthy,
>> making wise the simple.
> The precepts of the LORD are right,
>> giving joy to the heart.
> The commands of the LORD are radiant,
>> giving light to the eyes . . .
> The ordinances of the LORD are . . . more precious than gold,
>> than much pure gold . . .
> By them is your servant warned;
>> in keeping them there is great reward.

Reopening the Bible for all and recognizing its value for all is essential if we are to remain faithful to the author himself. The essential clarity of Scripture must be reaffirmed. We must also note that the Bible assumes that God will bring about his ends as understanding takes place.[11] Paul thanks God that the apostolic teaching has been accepted as the Word of God ('which it truly is') and that this Word has been 'at work' among those believers (1 Thessalonians 2:13).

The clarity of Scripture should humble the academy, as it is remembered that the claim of Scripture itself is that the ordinary person will understand. It leads to salvation and it speaks to the life of obedience – the practice of the Christian life – but, above all, it gives us the only true account of Jesus, our Lord and Saviour.

Whatever problems we may feel we have with understanding the Bible, it should not surprise us that essentially it is *clear*. The ultimate author is God, who communicates with his people. He introduces us in his Word to Jesus and draws us into relationship with him. All relationships are enhanced and strengthened as verbal communication takes place. Words speak to us. If the words are not trustworthy then the relationship will not grow.[12] Our joy is that we are dealing with our Saviour God who *is* trustworthy and whose words are therefore trustworthy.

There are times when I communicate badly with my wife and so fail her. But our ever deepening love for each other depends on the clarity with which we communicate with each other. How much more true is this as we deal with the Sovereign of the universe? The great difference between our human communications within relationships and God's with us is that there is a 'divine competency' in God's communication. Thus it is not just that God communicates what is true and does so in writing through human authors in Scripture, but that he ensures he has communicated properly because his Word achieves its goal. When God communicates on any matter he does so competently, effectively. His Word is a 'lamp' to our feet. There is no doubt that without Scriptures that can be understood we have a serious problem! As Craig Bartholomew has put it, 'The God and Father of Jesus Christ who speaks and addresses us through the canon of Scripture by the Holy Spirit is utterly central to Christianity. Without the voice of the Living God addressing us through Scripture, Christianity collapses into so much empty rhetoric, and the world is left without the redemptive, recreative Word of God.'[13]

The truth of Scripture

> The sum of your word is truth. (Psalm 119:160 ESV)

The truth of Scripture and its reliability is examined in detail in Tim Ward's chapter in this volume. The need to place ourselves within that truth and to hear and follow it is developed in Edith Humphrey's chapter. Here it is enough to reiterate that God as ultimate author is trustworthy. The Spirit-inspired process of inspiration has guaranteed that God's self-revelation is as trustworthy as God. His Word is an extension of him – his voice, if you like. The human authors were enabled adequately to reflect God's revelations (2 Peter 1:21).[14] Our task is to respect the Word we are seeking to interpret as we would if Christ were here speaking to us.

Differences of interpretation: it was ever thus!

> Your testimonies are righteous forever; give me understanding that I may live. (Psalm 119:144 ESV)

Differences of interpretation and arguments over meaning are not something new. Take, for example, the very serious differences between John Wesley and George Whitefield. They differed over a number of important theological points, yet both argued passionately from Scripture. They spoke together around Scripture and Whitefield later still trusted Wesley with some of his 'flock' when he went abroad with the gospel. But the problem of interpretation is also to be found right back in Scripture itself. For example, in Mark 4:10–13 the disciples do not understand the teaching of Jesus! (See also John 8:27; 10:6.) In our church today differences of opinion on the meaning and interpretation of Scripture still exist.

It is worth noting, however, that the fact that Scripture may be said to be 'clear' does not mean that agreement on interpretation will always be reached. However, as Wayne Grudem notes, 'it does tell us something very important – that the problem always lies not with Scripture but with ourselves . . . we also recognize that people often (through their own shortcomings) misunderstand what is clearly written in Scripture'.[15]

So, we desire to reopen Scripture. We are committed to the clarity of God's Word for us even in today's world, but we recognize that faithful believing people do differ on the interpretation of some passages. We also discover that it is hard to interpret because of our own blindness and shortcomings. So we return to the question of how the 'ordinary reader' is to interpret the Bible.

Interpreting the Bible for Us All

Many never realize that understanding the Bible gets easier the more we read it and the longer we are Christians. Learning to understand the Bible better is part of our spiritual growth and maturing as Christians. In looking at a passage that we have understood 'clearly' before, the maturing Christian may now see for the first time that it applies to himself! We may discover that a teaching of Scripture that seems so culturally conditioned in a way that is irrelevant to us, has much to teach us about how we should live today. Texts that seemed somewhat obscure to us before may now be seen as very valuable. After listening to a scholar talk of the theological or historical or geographical, or sociological background to a book or text, things will suddenly make more sense or 'come alive' as we understand better. This growing and understanding process will continue until we see 'face to face' (1 Corinthians 13:12). Whole books have been written on how to interpret the Bible and how Christians can mature in this area,[16] and it is well worth the effort to work on this. However, even as we do this we are aided by the author. We have been given the Holy Spirit of God.

God's Interpreter: The Holy Spirit

The Holy Spirit, who is God with us until we 'see face to face', is the interpreter of his Book. Sometimes his particular role in helping us understand his Book has been underplayed. The Holy Spirit, who has divinely inspired the authors so that what they give us in Scripture is truly theirs (human) but also truly what God intends for his people (divine), is the one who 'leads us into all truth' (John 16:13). The Holy Spirit is not some 'tool for interpretation', but is the personal God who works in the life of the believer, imprinting what is *already* God's Word on hearts and minds. Thus we not only read a page of Scripture as an ancient text, but understand it, at least at some level, as *God's Word*, and begin to recognize how it should be applied in our lives.

The work of the Spirit should thus be traced from 'inspiration' (he ensures the trustworthiness of the text), through to the eye-opening process that enables us to see what God is saying (rather than simply reading a story that seems irrelevant), through to the internalizing of that Word as God changes us or moves us or challenges us. This work of God's Spirit involves much more than simply helping us 'understand'. Here, through the work of the Holy Spirit we have access to 'authorial intent'. The Spirit enables us to see that in the words, sentences and paragraphs themselves we encounter the author. He sensitizes us to the author's perspective. He enables us to see that even the things we don't like, or find strange, are what God intends to be read by his people throughout history as part of his self-revelation. Ultimately the Spirit therefore helps us *understand* the mind of the Lord (1 Corinthians 2:16).

However, the Spirit does more for he also empowers this Word of God to produce God's desired effect in our lives. For example, if the Spirit has helped us understand the plain meaning of the text 'You must not steal', he also enables us not to steal! In the emotional cadences of the poetry of Psalm 116 we find the Holy Spirit helping us understand something of the crisis through which the poet has been. The poet nearly despaired (v. 3), but he was rescued by God and desires to say 'thank you' to the Lord (vv. 12–19). First, the Holy Spirit will help us understand the actual God-intended words. We see the spiritual conflict going on in the psalmist's mind. We hear of his affliction. We learn of the saving God, and are moved to tears and to joy with the poet (surely all part of what God intends us to understand as we read the text). But the Holy Spirit, building on that Word, and *not* independently from it, also helps us see how to follow this faithful poet in our own lives. Thus he asks us, but also *enables* us, to respond as the human author responds when we too are faced with similar situations. We also come to understand how the Lord has 'delivered my soul from death, / my eyes from tears, / my feet from stumbling'. The Spirit enables us to say God's intended words (given us through the poet) and make them our own, so that we too can say, 'I will lift up the cup of salvation / and call on the name of the LORD.'

Thus the Holy Spirit helps us *become* biblical, that is, Christlike. To put it in modern jargon, the author is present to enable and empower reader-response. Through the work of the Holy Spirit in our minds and hearts, we find that the Word of God can be understood but can also be followed. The Word itself turns out truly to be 'a lamp to my feet / and a light for my path' (Psalm 119:105).

The Holy Spirit thus enables us to move beyond statements like 'It's all a matter of interpretation' to show us that God's Word is true, that it communicates properly and clearly, that we as sinners can distort it or not understand it, ('conviction': John 16:8), and that the Spirit-endowed reader will be led ever more deeply into all truth (John 16:13). The one who enables spiritual growth in the people of God uses God's words so that we may grow to have the mind of Christ.[17]

Some Pointers for All Christian 'Readers' of the Bible

As we seek to reopen the Bible for ourselves or as we teach others, there are some basic and yet useful points we should always keep in mind as we interpret Scripture. While they are obvious for many, they are not so for others and especially leaders need to help new Christians on this. For those who have become sceptical of biblical truth and the possibility of interpretation, these 'basics' need to be revisited or the lie that God's Word cannot be understood will be perpetuated.

1. *We approach the Bible with trust and commitment.* Whether scholar, preacher, or new Christian, our doctrine of Scripture depends on our doctrine of God.[18] We trust our God whose nature includes the following: he is personal, omniscient and king. He is also transcendent and eternal spirit. He is faithful and he speaks.[19] *We trust the author.* This is why the Bible talks of the God who is *faithful.* We should therefore approach his Word with the same commitment that we have to the author and with the same trust. As a person he speaks to us in Scripture. 'Can the words of human authors convey divine truth? The answer is yes, if and when God chooses to use human words to communicate what he wants

to say to people.'[20] He can do this because he is transcendent and has the authority and power always to achieve his ends.

2. *We approach the Bible with humility.* The problem for us all, which is part of our sinful nature, is that we see things through our own glasses – as we want to see them. We need to be truly humble as we read. We need God's forgiveness and help so we can stand back to some extent from our own world and our own preoccupations and hear what God's pre-occupations for us really are. For those who are 'professional theologians' there is the additional temptation to a pride which comes from feeling that we 'know all about this', or that we now have better information than the writer of the particular book of the Bible did. We may be tempted more than many to adopt a position of arrogance with regard to the text. Yet in these texts of Scripture we come to the self-authenticating Lord and should sit humbly at his feet trusting and listening. As Vanhoozer has so clearly put it, 'We do not yet have absolute knowledge. Yet we do have adequate knowledge, enough to respond to the overtures of the Word. Our first reflex upon being addressed should be trust.'[21]

3. *We approach the Bible prayerfully.* We need to ask God to enable our reading by his Holy Spirit. We need to pray that, as we read, we shall understand and be able to carry out our part in the will of God.

4. *We first seek the 'plain meaning' of the text.* Too often Christians are fearful of the Bible. They find language, ideas, history, images, even genres of literature that they have not previously encountered. Christian leaders must remind people that the 'plain meaning' of any text (let alone the biblical text) is usually the right one. While we need to point out this may not *always* be so, it is a good enough principle for us to encourage all people that they can indeed read the Bible, find it to be reasonably clear, and understand it. We must also insist that reading more Scripture will help us

become accustomed to its ways of communication, its different genres of literature (poetry, narrative etc.). The more we read, the more we will find 'plain'. Let's make sure people see that this is not as complicated as it sounds. How often have we seen new Christians rapidly changing their whole lives around, not because of some sermon, but simply because they have started reading the Bible for themselves.

5. *We must read the whole of Scripture.* Because we believe the Holy Spirit has inspired all the biblical writers, we shall find that reading the whole Bible makes 'understanding' much easier. There is a need to recover a good sense of 'biblical theology'. The more we encourage people to read the whole of Scripture the more they will, for themselves, begin to see the many links between passages and books, links which remind us that we are worshipping the God who is 'the same yesterday, today and forever'.

6. *We must read in context and take account of the type of literature.* Too often Christians have learned how to provide 'proof texts' for particular teachings or for descriptions of how we should live. This is not wrong provided the so-called proof text has been properly understood in its context and is a true summary of the matter. But often such texts are not that. We need to help people to read whole poems so they *feel* the emotions and concerns of the poet. We must help people know that a book like Revelation is in a more or less unknown genre of literature and so give them some tools to help them begin the process of understanding and of applying the Word to themselves. For many Christians, reading the Bible seems to be rather two dimensional. Placing Scripture in its context and helping people know the adjustments we make as we understand different types of literature are important. Indeed, the higher the view of Scripture, the more important this work really is. My personal conviction is that the genre itself is inspired of God; that is, that he chose to have this part of his communication in poetry or prophecy or command or narrative and so on. If he chose the one rather than the other, then

it should not surprise us that the genre is significant when we seek to understand what God is saying to us.

7. *We read Scripture as members of God's church.* We have talked largely thus far about encouraging individual Christians to be able to reopen the Bible. But we easily forget that God has placed us in an international Christian community in which his Spirit has been and is at work. Learning from other Christians who, past and present, have examined the same Scripture, is sometimes hard work. But this is what the Holy Spirit expects of us as he works among his people, and they need to know that the interpretation of Scripture will usually be helped by referring to the church. While we must not err on the side that says the church's interpretation is always authoritative,[22] we should be slow to change what has been received for many centuries. This is why so many ordinary Christians who have looked at 'plain meanings' of the text have found it strange when their understanding has been deeply challenged by some individual scholar, especially on matters of doctrine or life. While we should always be prepared to be challenged, we must insist that, in this sense, 'It is *not* all a matter of interpretation.' Godly men and women over the centuries have already addressed most of the issues that we have to address today. At least they have discerned biblical principles that speak to us today. We must not lightly put this aside. The principle of 'private interpretation' must always be tempered by consistency of biblical thought, and consistency of the church's witness to the meaning of the text.

It is important therefore to encourage people to discern godly teachers who can help keep us from error, and who can relate a passage to its historical or sociological context and help 'bring it alive'. Such teachers can help explain exegetical, linguistic and translation problems, and point us to books to read to help us learn still more, so that when we next come back to a passage we learn further what God wants us to hear.

Conclusions

'It's all a matter of interpretation' is normally on the lips of those who do not want to understand a text in a particular way, or who do not like what they hear. It becomes therefore a statement about Scripture itself. Roughly translated it means that because the Scriptures can be made to mean many things, and especially because Christians sometimes disagree, there is little point in the whole exercise of reading Scripture.

My contention is that the church has often brought this state of affairs upon itself. The Bible has in effect become a 'closed book'. Especially among some teachers there is often an arrogance, an attempt to suggest the Bible does not mean what the 'plain meaning' seems to have suggested for hundreds of years. I have suggested that there is a desperate need to 'reopen' the Bible for the 'ordinary reader'. Good hermeneutics must be done, and such work, whether it involves exegesis, careful genre criticism, historical criticism, insights from the social sciences and so on, is all very useful indeed. It will be done by scholars, and it should be mediated to theologically educated church leaders, and in turn to congregations who will be able to understand and apply Scripture more accurately as a result.

The complexity of modern hermeneutics has received such prominence that the academy itself has come to believe the ordinary reader will never 'crack the code'. Evangelicals must be at the forefront of recovering the open Bible as they were at the Reformation, in the days of Wesley and so on. We must insist that the Bible can be understood and that the believing person has the greatest interpreter of all right present with him or her – the Holy Spirit. We must insist that the authority of Scripture is complete, for it carries the full authority of the author, and that the intention of the author is not as obscure as we might think.[23] This is because the author, present with us by his Spirit, guarantees authorial intent and helps us to grasp the Word and act upon it.

That all this must be done in a spirit of great humility, as fallible interpreters standing before an infallible text, must be said again and again. But we must also insist that our fallibility does not mean we cannot 'know' anything. As Vanhoozer puts it, 'I am seeking a degree of interpretive confidence somewhere between pride and sloth – the humble conviction *that stands firm*, even while acknowledging that it is rooted on earth rather than looking down from heaven.'[24]

When this is done, when we believe we understand what Scripture has said, we must act on it and live by it and let God's Word change us where he would have us change. This is humble submission to a text, yes; but actually to the author of the text. God's spoken and written Word brings forth its own fruit, and we must be open and receiving of that truth as the Holy Spirit lives in us. The Spirit's power is vital in this, not to make us into new figures of 'authoritarian power'; much the opposite. The Holy Spirit's power is most seen in our weakness. He is the one who lifts us up when God's Word has chastised us. He keeps us humble and open to God speaking to us. He enables us to hear the challenge but empowers us to change our lives that we may eventually come to 'have the mind of Christ'. As has been said, 'the most profound kind of understanding . . . has to do with cultivation of the ability to follow the Word of God, not just on our reading but in personal response to what we have read . . . understanding is our ability to follow the Word'.[25]

Notes

[1] See Tim Ward's discussion (ch. 1) on 'The Bible, Its Truth and How It Works' for the usefulness or otherwise of such words to describe Scripture.

[2] Few evangelical writings on hermeneutics investigate the all-important relationship between interpretation, meaning and biblical 'authority' itself. An outstanding exception is Kevin J. Vanhoozer, *Is There a Meaning in This Text? The Bible, The Reader and the Morality of Literary Knowledge*, Leicester, Apollos, 1998. Also B. Corley, S. Lempke and G. Lovejoy, *Biblical Hermeneutics: A Comprehensive Introduction to Interpreting Scripture*, Nashville, Broadman and Holman, 2002.

3   Tim Ward (ch. 1) develops this view of authority and examines the nature of 'inspiration'.

4   'Authority without meaning is a merely formal and empty principle' (Vanhoozer, *Is There a Meaning?* p. 44).

5   Linking authority with the author inevitably leads to discussions about the link between authorial intent and grasping the meaning of what has been written. Other questions such as 'Did the author only have one intention in what he said?' also become significant. See two introductory books on these matters that take different evangelical perspectives, M. Silva and W. C. Kaiser, *An Introduction to Biblical Hermeneutics: The Search for Meaning*, Grand Rapids, Zondervan, 1994; and M. J. Erickson, *Evangelical Interpretation: Perspectives on Hermeneutical Issues*, Grand Rapids, Baker, 1993.

6   See Grant Osborne, *The Hermeneutical Spiral*, Downers Grove, InterVarsity Press, 1991, pp. 8ff.

7   The Scripture and Hermeneutics Seminar, headed by Craig Bartholomew at Cheltenham and Gloucester College of Higher Education, is one of a number of groups of specialist theologians providing excellent work on hermeneutics. See their first volume of essays, *Renewing Biblical Interpretation*, eds C. Bartholomew, C. Greene and K. Möller, Carlisle, Paternoster, 2000. Also, R. Lundin, C. Walhout and A. C. Thiselton, *The Promise of Hermeneutics*, Carlisle, Paternoster, 1999.

8   On communicating Christian commitment to 'truth' in the modern world see 'Obeying the Truth in a Network Society: The Problem of Truth in a Changed Society' by Graham Cray (ch. 3).

9   For analysis of some of the influences here see A. C. Thiselton, *New Horizons in Hermeneutics*, London, Marshall Pickering, 1992; esp. pp. 531–35.

10 E.g. 2 Chronicles 32:13; Isaiah 40:21; 1 Corinthians 6:2ff.; and on the lips of Jesus, John 3:10 etc.

11 More technically, Tim Ward describes the effects of texts (speech-act) in the last section of Chapter 1.

[12] P. Jensen, *The Revelation of God*, Leicester, Apollos, 2002, pp. 25–6.

[13] Bartholomew, *Renewing*, p. xxiii.

[14] 'Divine competency' provides one answer to one part of the so-called intentional fallacy. For a detailed and readable response to these and other objections to this position see R. H. Stein, *A Basic Guide to Interpreting the Bible*, Grand Rapids, Baker, 1994.

[15] W. Grudem, *Systematic Theology: An Introduction to Biblical Doctrine*, Leicester, Inter-Varsity Press, 1994, p. 109.

[16] Among the most accessible is G. D. Fee and D. Stuart, *How to Read the Bible for All It's Worth*, London, Scripture Union, 1982.

[17] See *The Holy Spirit and the Bible: The Spirit's Interpreting Role in Relation to Biblical Hermeneutics*, Paul E. Brown, Fearn, Mentor, 2002.

[18] Most older expositions of the doctrine of Scripture insisted on this. Recently the position has been defended for the modern context by Vanhoozer and others. Their analysis of problems faced with an entirely 'propositional' approach to revelation or, on the other hand, by a Barthian approach with its stress on 'prophetic' revelation experienced as God's Word only to those of faith, or even a more 'personal-relational' approach to revelation locating authority back in the church, is hugely helpful to us all. See Vanhoozer's *God, Scripture and Hermeneutics: First Theology*, Leicester, Apollos, 2002. On the 'Centrality of the Doctrine of God' see pp. 141ff. Evangelical scholars must revisit the tendency to look to K. Barth for all our answers to the nature of biblical word-revelation. Cf. Vanhoozer, *Is There a Meaning?* pp. 132–58.

[19] On the nature of God in relation to God's communication in Scripture see E. J. Schnabel, 'Scripture', in *The New Dictionary of Biblical Theology*, Leicester, Inter-Varsity Press, 2000, pp. 34–43.

[20] Ibid., p. 37.

21 Vanhoozer, *God, Scripture and Hermeneutics*, p. 230. Further developed on pp. 360ff.

22 There is always a danger that an interpretive tradition can be placed *over* Scripture. See Vanhoozer, *Is There a Meaning?* pp. 316–17, 'consensus alone does not guarantee correctness of interpretation'.

23 For further on how 'intention affects meaning' see Kaiser and Silva, *Search for Meaning*, pp. 34–45.

24 Vanhoozer, *First Theology*, p. 230; my italics.

25 Ibid., p. 228.

Chapter Three

'Obeying the Truth in a Network Society': The Problem of Truth in a Changed Society

Graham Cray

Monumental change has taken place in the way modern humans understand Truth. In some quarters it has been reduced to 'my truth'. This chapter argues that in a fallen world truth is rooted in both revelation and redemption. It is high time to leave the term 'postmodern' behind, and instead view twenty-first-century society as 'the network society'. Today the dominant value is individual consumer choice, and both truth and identity are assumed to be constructed by these choices. After examining three Christian responses to the network society, we are called to confront this society with the stumbling block of creation and of the cross.

Introduction

In the later decades of the twentieth century it became clear that something had changed about truth, or rather about the way truth was being understood. Although most people carried on their lives with an assumed framework of truth, it became harder and harder to argue for the truth of any particular viewpoint. At an intellectual level this represented the demise of an understanding of truth that has its roots in Plato.[1] At a popular level, rather than truth being the sure foundation for human life, truth claims were increasingly seen as power plays, to be greeted with irony or scepticism: 'The Truth' became many truths, as global electronic communications and increased mobility made most people aware of the great variety of truths on offer. At the same time Western consumer society reduced commitment to any worldview to something parallel to a supermarket shopping exercise, where 'The Truth' was increasingly reduced to 'my truth'.

We should not underestimate the scale of these shifts. They are of huge importance to the church and to its mission. Evangelicals have reacted and responded to them in a number of ways; but before considering these it is important to outline some key elements of a biblical understanding of truth. This is not to short-circuit any arguments about the possibility or otherwise speaking of 'The Truth' today. It is simply to recognize that everybody argues from somewhere, everybody believes in order to understand, and evangelical Christians start with Scripture.

The Biblical Framework for Understanding Truth

Whatever crisis the Western understanding of truth may be undergoing, the biblical understanding of truth far predates Plato.[2] In fact Christians claim that the roots of their understanding of truth predate history itself! The starting point is 'In the beginning God ...' The existence and consistent character of the Creator provides our starting point. Humans, we believe, are a distinctive and unique part of the Creator's creation. Made in the Creator's image, sufficiently like him to be able to relate to and communicate with him and to exercise responsibility for the earth in his name. At the same time we are sufficiently unlike him to need, by our very created nature, to depend upon him and to live under his loving authority. Truth was to be embodied in a way of life arising directly out of a living relationship with God.

If the story had ended as it began, there would never have been a crisis over the nature of truth. But the story did not end there. We are fallen creatures who have doubted our Creator's love, disobeyed his commands and rejected his authority. As one result among many we have a crisis of truth and knowledge. Our rebellion against God has distorted our capacity to grasp truth. We suppress the truth we do not like and go in search of something that matches our desire for autonomy (Romans 1:18–25). Our fallenness has also resulted in broken relationships with our fellow humans. Truth becomes a weapon in battles of power. The commitment to truth that was given to us for our stewardship of the earth is reforged as a weapon to use for our own ends. In our own culture, in recent decades, all of this has been ruthlessly revealed by the scalpel of postmodern criticism.[3] Only too often fallen creatures turn truth into power plays.

However, mercifully the story has not stopped there either. The deepest Christian foundation for truth is Jesus Christ. 'And the Word became flesh and lived among us, and we have seen his glory, the glory as of a father's only son, full of grace and *truth* ... grace and *truth* came through Jesus Christ' (John 1:14–17 NRSV; my emphasis). In a fallen world truth is rooted in both revelation and redemption.[4] The one through whom and for whom the world was made stepped into it to reveal his and our true nature, to die to bear the full consequences of our rebellion, and to break the power of sin that makes us distort the truth and deceive ourselves. Fallen humans have no final grasp of truth apart from *both* revelation and redemption. In the work of Christ these two are fused into one. It is by his saving work (incarnation, atonement, resurrection and ascension) that he reveals the truth and makes it possible for us to be grasped by it.

This does not mean that humans can have no grasp of truth at all apart from Christ. We are still made in God's image. Our fallenness has marred every aspect of our being, but it has not removed the evidence of the Maker's handiwork. The world is still full of his wonders and order. The very revelation of himself through his Son and by his Spirit contributed to the emergence of scientific knowledge.[5] But as a result of the fall we suppress truth we do not like, rather than are absolutely incapable of seeing it. We have a problem with knowing the truth, but even when we know it we have a problem with obeying it. From our desire to be independent of God we create cultures in our own image, and these cultures (called 'the world' by both Paul and John) blind us to Christ (2 Corinthians 4:4). This chapter addresses the changing nature of truth in recent history and contemporary Western society. Any critique that claims to be biblical must be true to this basic framework.

Truth in the Network Society

Human beings rarely, if ever, believe anything for purely intellectual or theoretical reasons. They believe if their experience of the way the world seems to be backs up a proposed explanation of it. This is what sociologists call a plausibility structure. 'Ideas and world views are maintained by social support. They are culturally embedded in community.'[6] 'The power of any culture is measured by the extent to which its formulation of reality seems "natural".'[7] If we are to engage our society with the truth of the gospel we need to understand how our society views truth. In particular we need to understand why some views of truth seem 'obvious' or 'common sense' and go largely unquestioned within our particular culture.

We have been going through a major change in culture. There have been substantial theoretical disputes over the appropriate name for our era (Late Modernity, High Modernity, Postmodernity etc.) But more important than the name, has been the fact that all the major theorists have identified the same characteristics of the emerging society. All have recognized the same overall direction of change; the disputes have been over the degree of continuity or discontinuity. All recognize that we have moved from an industrial society to an information one, from an era that found its identity in production to one that finds its identity in consumption, and where consumerism and shopping act as a metaphor for the way we make life choices. Finally, we have moved from the age of the nation state to a globalized world.[8] The combination of these three have created a new social structure.

I believe it is time to leave 'postmodern' terminology behind. It has had value, but it inevitably points to a move from a previous era, while having no capacity to name or describe the new social order now established. My own preference is for 'the network society'.[9] Electronic networks make an unlimited supply of consumer choices available on a global scale. The dominant value becomes individual consumer choice. Both truth and identity are assumed to be constructed by these choices. The World Wide Web becomes a metaphor for an ever-expanding range of personal choices and combinations to make a temporary worldview. There is no Truth, only 'my choices'. It will not be possible to avoid words like 'postmodern' or 'postmodernity' in this chapter, but I believe they have reached their sell-by date.

Another helpful metaphor for our current society is the transformation from solid to liquid. If we are in the latest stage of modernity it is 'liquid modernity'.[10] In a 'liquid world' there seems only to be 'liquid truth'; truth that fits for now – meaning, keeps moving. Words mean what they seem, or what we want them to mean. Attempts to claim any foundation for truth or morality are 'opinions' which open up 'gulfs' between those of different views. Truth is seen not so much as relative, but as constructed. It is hard to hold on to Truth in a liquid world.

The network world has gone beyond an initial recognition of pluralism (the reality that there are competing truth claims), to relativism (that no truth claim can claim superiority over any other) and is now settling on constructivism (the claim that truth is something we construct to help us through life). The final move is from realism (the truth is out there to be found) to constructivism. Taken to its extreme this is an atheistic epistemology. The American philosopher Richard Rorty was explicit about this when he wrote, 'We need to make a distinction between the claim that the world is out there and the claim that truth is out there . . . The suggestion that truth, as well as the world, is out there is a legacy of an age in which the world was seen as the creation of a being who had a language of his own.'[11]

The distinction is clear: either truth exists because there is a Creator who communicates, or truth is no more than a human construct.

Constructivism seems 'common sense' to many people who have never read philosophy, nor heard of the term. A multichoice consumer world, with many competing truth claims makes it seem 'obvious'. As a result it goes unrecognized and unquestioned. In such a culture claims about 'The Truth' are seen, at best, as expressions of ignorance and intolerance, at worst as cynical power plays.

Evangelical Responses

Evangelicals have responded to this changing context in three different ways.

Is the future more of the same?

The first has been a failure either to see that there is a problem, or to grasp its significance.

The evangelical movement took shape as a gospel response to the Enlightenment era.[12] It did so because to be biblical is to be missionary. In the New Testament the first generation of Jewish believers were called to take the good news of Christ to the Gentiles, without requiring Gentile converts to become Jewish in culture (circumcision, food laws etc). So, in the eighteenth century, biblically rooted Christians such as Jonathan Edwards, John and Charles Wesley and George Whitefield, evangelized the culture of their day, engaged with its thought forms, and used its means of communication and transport to further the gospel. The result was evangelicalism as we know it: a serious attempt to stay rooted in Scripture and the historic gospel while genuinely engaging with the thought forms and culture of the time.

Every engagement between gospel and culture walks a fine line between irrelevance (failing to communicate at all) and syncretism (allowing the culture of the day to reshape the gospel and eliminate its challenge). In my view our evangelical forebears negotiated that challenge very well. However, once an appropriate missionary practice has been established, there is always the danger that the emphases and habits, which made up that practice, get confused with the scriptural gospel itself.

To repeat the great truths of the gospel, just as we heard and responded to them in one era, is not necessarily to have faithfully communicated them in a new era. For example, my generation of evangelicals responded to the gospel as it was proclaimed as a series of doctrines – creation, fall, redemption and so on. As Don Carson has pointed out, 'the good news of Jesus Christ is virtually incoherent unless it is securely set into a biblical worldview'.[13] The network society is largely biblically ignorant, disbelieves any claim to absolute truth and treats all competing truth claims as raw materials for a personal worldview. Gospel preaching in such an atmosphere has to begin with the telling of the story of God in Christ, not a systematic presentation of Christian doctrine. We start much further back than in a more biblically literate time. It is not necessarily faithful to stay the same! If one form of evangelicalism, with an emphasis on the written Word of God might be in danger of being too rationalistic in its presentation of the gospel in the network society, the other major contemporary form, which emphasizes the work of and experience of the Spirit, may steer too close to the network society's reduction of everything to a sensation. Word and Spirit must be held together. Classic evangelicals and charismatics need one another.

Is the future post evangelical?

Another response has gone under the name 'post evangelical'. The expression formed the title for an influential book by Dave Tomlinson.[14] The strength of Tomlinson's argument lay in his cultural analysis: 'My thesis is that post evangelicals are influenced by a different culture from the one which helped shape present-day evangelicalism.'[15] He spelled out many aspects of the cultural shift from a modern to a postmodern era. In particular he articulated the concerns of many young adults in evangelical churches who felt that their churches and tradition no longer addressed the world as they knew it, or even their own pastoral and liturgical needs. This is not the place to give an in-depth response to Tomlinson. His book was important and deserves a more nuanced and detailed response than can be given here.[16] In summary however, his cultural analysis was better than his proposals for change, and his assessment of modernity and the evangelical church was sharper than his critique of postmodernity. He saw evangelicalism as coming into being at the time of the Enlightenment rather than as going through an appropriate missionary transformation. As a consequence there was as much ambiguity in the book about 'post' evangelical as there has been in sociological literature about 'post' modern. Both words can imply a degree of continuity and change, or can imply leaving behind and departure. The reality was that some of those attracted to Tomlinson's thesis were on the way out of evangelicalism, while others saw the book as an opportunity to renew their tradition. Precisely because of this ambiguity I believe the 'post' word needs to be left behind.

The same subject issues were addressed by David Hilborn (now Theological Advisor to the Evangelical Alliance).[17] Hilborn recognized the shift in cultural eras and its implications for evangelicals, but he had a stronger critique of postmodernity. He called for a 'postmodern evangelicalism'. In other words, a transformed evangelicalism, true to Scripture, which engaged with the postmodern world (the network society as I wish to call it), just as our spiritual forefathers engaged with the Enlightenment era.

Can there be a postmodern evangelicalism?

A third option remains. It recognizes the significance of cultural change. It is open to the suggestion that new cultural eras require a new engagement of the gospel with society as it is, not as it was. But it also has a sharp biblical critique of the network society.

So what do evangelicals have to do to take seriously the challenge of truthful gospel proclamation in a new era? In particular, what are the key changes in the contemporary understanding of truth that we must address?

Scientific Certainty to Artistic Appreciation

The Enlightenment era opened up a great flourishing of science. Scientific knowledge began to be regarded as the only 'true' knowledge. Objective knowledge was set over against and valued above the subjective. If something could not be proved it should not be believed, except as a private opinion. Religious belief was compartmentalized as a purely private matter, to be kept out of public debate. In response evangelical apologists set out to prove the claims of their faith. In part this was both right and unavoidable. If the resurrection of Christ took place in history, then historical method could and should be used to examine and give evidence that supported it. However the very division of knowledge into objective and subjective compartments needed challenging from the beginning. It was a kind of reductionism or 'nothing buttery'. If scientific knowledge ate up other forms of knowledge at one time, the reverse is now the case. Artistic knowledge, particularly in the form of literary theory has tended to devour all other knowledge. The meaning of any 'text' has come to be the invention of the interpreter. An underlying divide between subjective and objective still controls the way many people understand truth. It is simply that the pendulum has swung from one extreme to another.[18] A biblical response must begin with the recognition that ultimate truth has been revealed in and as a person. If the incarnate Christ is 'The Truth' then truth is multidimensional and integrated. It is personal and relational, it has elements of the subjective and of the objective; but its solid, underlying reality is that God has spoken through his Son.

History and poetry

A further distinction has been made between literal and poetic truth. Evangelicals are sometimes accused of a wooden literalism in their interpretation of Scripture, while post evangelicals emphasize the poetic nature of scriptural truth.[19] Again the distinction is an artificial and unhelpful one. Some of Scripture is poetry; some is parable (don't expect to discover the 'actual' inn where the good Samaritan took the man who fell among thieves); some is prophecy; but some is history and needs to be treated as such. The resurrection may be a metaphor for many things, but it is of little help if the historical Christ never rose from the dead!

It is true that evangelicals of an earlier generation, myself included, tended to treat Scripture in a rather one-dimensional way. But one of the great gains in more recent evangelical treatments of the doctrine of Scripture has been the recognition of the significance of different literary genres for biblical interpretation. Poetry is to be interpreted as poetry, history as history. This is evidenced across the evangelical spectrum and among both those for whom 'inerrancy' is an essential category and those for whom it is problematic.[20]

Story and doctrine

The same applies to the contemporary emphasis on story over doctrinal proposition. Doctrines are explanations of the meaning of the biblical stories. Much of Scripture is indeed in story form, and contemporary culture favours stories. It is also true that a previous generation of evangelicals tended to turn stories into propositions, as though we were only at ease with Scripture when it looked like Romans. Now we often find it necessary to preach the epistles by telling the stories that lie behind them. We have to start further back because most people outside the church no longer know the stories. Nevertheless, biblically based doctrines are a clear element of Scripture and are essential for a grasp of the gospel. They are the true meaning of the stories. It is little use to know the story of the death of Christ if I do not know the doctrine that he died for my sins.

Reason and rationalism

The fact that the Enlightenment era tended towards rationalism is no reason for Christians to despise reason. God gave us minds; they matter and he expects us to use them. The difference is that Christians believe in order to understand, rather than only believe what a narrowly defined reason can prove. In point of fact all people believe in order to understand; it is the way God-given reason works. Our culture's loss of trust in scientific 'objectivity' has led to an equal *naïveté*. As one Muslim scholar has written, 'postmodern seekers have no moral discernment simply because there are no criteria for discerning good from evil. In postmodern times belief in everything from aliens, witches, dead and alive pop stars, charismatic leaders to the ideology of the X Files is mushrooming.'[21] Reason that is submitted to the gospel is a vital, critical tool for our times.

Certainty and assurance

The 'post evangelical' debate made much of evangelical commitment to certainty. It is true that our evangelical forebears, caught between an increasingly sceptical science and an equally sceptical biblical criticism, focused their apologetic on the matters that Christians could be certain of. As shown above they developed the best proofs they could in support of their beliefs. What else should they have done? These were the issues of their day and the gospel was at stake in their culture. However, the evangelical distinctive since the Enlightenment has been assurance, not certainty.[22]

Biblical Christians have the assurance of salvation, not the certainty that our every interpretation is accurate. This assurance frees us for mission. We accept that we know in part, but know that we are fully known and loved. We trust the 'objective' revelation of God's saving acts in history, which we have been given in Scripture, and we experience the personal and 'subjective' witness of the Holy Spirit.

Exegesis and hermeneutics

The interpretation and application of Scripture remains central to evangelical faith. We are as committed to it as we ever were, but generally acknowledge that it is a more complex task than we used to realize. The preparation of a sermon was once seen as a simple matter of exegesis. Understand the passage as best you could in its original context and apply it to today. Now we know that there is another perspective to take into account, our own assumptions and biases as interpreters. Bonhoeffer is alleged to have pointed out that we read the Bible 'for ourselves, not against ourselves'. The new discipline of hermeneutics exposes this capacity very well. It is an uncomfortable friend rather than a sworn enemy of those committed to biblical truth. It provides supporting evidence for a healthy doctrine of sin. Nor is this new to Anglican evangelicals. It was introduced by Anthony Thiselton at the second National Evangelical Anglican Congress in 1977 and he has remained an expert in the field.[23] Whether or not evangelicals have taken all this to heart is a different matter. Nevertheless some one-sided understandings need to be resisted. As Thiselton points out, it is one thing to recognize the capacity of the human heart to bend interpretation to our own ends. It is another thing altogether to claim that all claims to a true interpretation are power plays, or that the intention of the original author can be ignored. There are real limits to the possible meaning of any text.

Perspectives and relativism

Relativism seems 'obvious' to many people today. They do not act as though everything is relative, but the multiple-choice networked world of possible and competing truths makes any exclusive truth claim seem intolerant. On this issue contemporary theory is partly right and partly wrong. All seeing and knowing is perspectival. We can only see from where we stand. Humans have a capacity for self-detachment and self-analysis, but that is not the same as being able to step out of our skins. What we see depends in part on what is there, in part on where we stand and in part on what we hope or expect to see. The Enlightenment expected scientific reason to operate as a 'spectators' gallery' outside the world, objectively analysing from a distance. But we cannot step out of the universe and there is no spectators' gallery. But this does not imply relativism. Relativism only follows if every viewing point is as good as any other. But reality is that there are places to go for the best views. The Christian claim is not that we can step out of our skin, but that God in Christ stepped into it. Truth was revealed through the incarnation and death of the one through whom everything was made. If we look from his perspective, having the mind of Christ, we can trust what we see.

Two Stumbling Blocks: Cross and Creation

But relativism is not the most powerful opponent to the concept of truth. As has already been said, that rests with constructivism. Truth is seen to be relative *because* it is made up. The gospel calls men and women to obey God. Paul speaks of 'the obedience of faith' at the beginning and at the end of his exposition of the gospel in Romans (Romans 1:5; 16:26). In all cultures fallen people reject and resist that obedience. Cultures may change, but the human heart does not. In its insistence that identity is a human construct, the network society values the freedom to avoid identity above the drive to find or establish it. 'The hub of postmodern life strategy is not identity building but avoidance of fixation.' 'Keep the options open.'[24] Many Western human beings run from any hint that they might be answerable to anything or anyone beyond themselves. Kevin Vanhoozer describes the philosophers who deny any fixed meaning as 'the Undoers'. He suggests that this theory may itself be a device to avoid accountability and the possibility of change:

> Despite their alleged concern for the other ... Undoers have difficulty encountering the other. How can the postmodern critic really be said to respect the other if the other's presence is always deferred, if what the other says is always undecidable? ... Might it be that despite the rhetoric about ethics, postmodern critics actually are afraid to meet the other? And what else is encountering the other but the fear that the encounter may change us, the fear that we may be 'undone'?[25]

Constructivism avoids the question 'Who is it (i.e. what is the identity of the person) who makes these identity- or truth-constructing choices?' Richard Rorty claims that 'there is no centre to the self',[26] and as a challenge to the Enlightenment understanding of a totally fixed 'centred self' he is partly right. The Christian response, however, must point to the self-deceptive nature of human sin. Miroslav

Volf has written a splendid reply to Rorty's point, based on Galatians 2:19–20:

> Though the self may lack an 'objective' and 'immovable' centre, *the self is never without a centre*; it is always engaging in the production of its own centre ... Whichever way the centring takes place and whatever its result, the self should be de-centred, claims Paul ... then a re-centring of that same self can take place. The centre is Jesus Christ crucified and resurrected who has become part and parcel of the very structure of the self ... At the centre of the (new) self lies self giving love.[27]

The postmodern self seeks to construct identity while evading answerability. The only Christian response is the stumbling block of the cross.

It is important not to overreact. We are constructivists but we are constructivists under licence:

> It is the distinction of the human creature, created in the image of God, to be called to exercise its created destiny in *finite* freedom ... Where it interprets itself as absolute self-created freedom and denies its character as gift, it falls into a bondage from which it can find no escape.[28]

The world is not without meaning; it is laden with it. Only our sin stops us seeing it (Romans 1:18–23). The commission to be stewards of the earth means that we are to construct cultures in which our identity as God's children can thrive, and in which our rational and imaginative powers seek out God's truth. But it may be that before we challenge our fellow members of the network society with the stumbling block of the cross we must challenge them with the stumbling block of creation, for the truth is that we are creatures whose identity is found in our Creator's purposes.

For several centuries evangelical Christians battled for biblical truth in a culture shaped by the Enlightenment. Now we do so in the network society. Not all of the tactics and strategies of that earlier time are still appropriate. New issues are being raised and new responses are being developed. What links the two eras is the vital nature of the task and the bedrock of scriptural truth.

Notes

1   Peter Hicks, *Evangelicals and Truth*, Leicester, Apollos, 1998, chs 2, 3.

2   Plato lived from 428 to 348 BC.

3   In particular in the work of Derrida, Foucault and Lyotard.

4   See Stephen N. Williams, *Revelation and Reconciliation*, Cambridge, Cambridge University Press, 1995.

5   See Christopher Kaiser, *Creation and the History of Science*, London, Marshall Pickering, 1991, part 1.

6   Andrew Walker, *Telling the Story*, London, SPCK, 1996, p. 124.

7   James Hunter, 'What Is Modernity?' in *Faith and Modernity*, eds M. Sampson, V. Samuel and C. Sugden, Carlisle, Paternoster, 1994, p. 13.

8   For an introduction and overview of the sociology see David Lyon, *Postmodernity*, 2nd ed., Buckingham, Open University, 1999.

9   See Manuel Castells, *The Rise of the Network*, 2nd ed., Oxford, Blackwell, 2000.

10 See Zygmunt Bauman, *Liquid Modernity*, Cambridge, Polity, 2000.

11 Richard Rorty, *Contingency, Irony and Solidarity*, Cambridge, Cambridge University Press, 1989, pp. 4–5.

12 See the work of David Bebbington. In particular 'Evangelical Christianity and the Enlightenment', in *The Gospel in the Modern World*, eds Martyn Eden and David F. Wells, Leicester, Inter-Varsity Press, 1991.

13 D. A. Carson, *The Gagging of God*, Leicester, Apollos, 1996, p. 502.

14 Dave Tomlinson, *The Post Evangelical*, London, SPCK, 1995.

15 Ibid., p. 8.

16 See my 'The Post Evangelical Debate', in *The Post Evangelical Debate*, eds Cray et al, London, SPCK, 1997.

17 David Hilborn, *Picking up the Pieces*, London, Hodder and Stoughton, 1997.

18 For Christian challenges to the objective/subjective distinction see N. T. Wright, *The New Testament and the People of God*, London, SPCK, 1992, pp. 44–46; Fraser Watts and Mark Williams, *The Psychology of Religious Knowing*, London, Geoffrey Chapman, 1988.

19 Tomlinson, *Post Evangelical*, pp. 87–90.

20 E.g. see both The Chicago Statement on Biblical Inerrancy, and John Goldingay, *Models for Scripture*, Grand Rapids, Eerdmans, 1994.

21 Ziauddin Sardar, *Postmodernism and the Other*, London, Pluto, 1998, pp. 265–56.

22 D. W. Bebbington, *Evangelicalism in Modern Britain*, London, Routledge, 1993, pp. 42ff.

23 See Anthony Thiselton, *Interpreting God and the Postmodern Self*, Edinburgh, T. and T. Clark, 1995; also Kevin Vanhoozer, *Is There a Meaning in This Text?* Leicester, Apollos, 1998.

24 Zygmunt Bauman, *Life in Fragments*, Oxford and Cambridge, Mass, Blackwell, 1995, p. 89.

25 Vanhoozer, *Is There a Meaning?* pp. 186–87.

26 Rorty, *Contingency*, pp. 83–4.

27 Miroslav Volf, *Exclusion and Embrace*, Nashville, Abingdon, 1996, pp. 70–71.

28 Christoph Schwöbel, 'God, Creation and the Christian Community', in *The Doctrine of Creation*, ed. C. Gunton, Edinburgh, T. and T. Clark, 1997, pp. 167–68.

Chapter Four

Biblical Confidence in Youth Ministry

Dave Fenton

This chapter, in the light of the author's long-term experience in youth and children's ministry, wrestles with the problem of declining numbers of young people involved in churches. The impact of the Bible on modern Christian youth work is examined as is the question of 'relevance'. The chapter challenges youth leaders to be faithful to God's Word and to re-examine the purpose of church-based youth ministries. The church is urged to take to heart the training of youth leaders and to recognize the biblical injunction for one generation to pass on the torch of God's words and works to the next.

Introduction

The church clearly has a problem. Peter Brierley's excellent work *Reaching and Keeping Teenagers* gives us the statistical rationale for something we know already: young people are leaking from the church at an ever increasing rate and with it there is an evaporation of confidence in biblical youth ministry.[1] It is very natural that we should be concerned about the situation because many of the young people come from families we know and love. We may ask how that beautiful seven-year-old child who was once so enthusiastic about going to Sunday school could be so different now. The church no longer has anything to say to him and he wants out. What follows is a personal reflection on the issues involved and how we need to respond to the situation we now find ourselves in.

A Long-term Problem

In the mid-eighties a report published in the Sheffield diocese revealed the huge numbers of young people who had been confirmed but who had decided that the church was not for them by the age of 18. The problem is not confined to the Anglican Church; many other denominations have seen significant reductions in their youth numbers. Perhaps because it is realized that young people enjoy a crowd, the answer to the problem has been sought in areas outside the walls of the church. The emergence of the 'Youth Church' phenomenon has been significant and has often been the result of frustration on the part of youth workers and the refusal of their churches to consider more youth-friendly models. I understand the frustrations of such people but the end product raises questions. Are we to have a church made up of very narrow age bands all locked into their own cultural milieu? The concept of one generation passing on truth to another becomes nearly impossible with wisdom and maturity being in very short supply. Perhaps this should be a last-resort solution when all other possibilities of working in an all-age setting have been completely exhausted. This does not rule out the possibility of young people being taught in their own group within the context of an all-age church.

Some have seen the parachurch movement as the solution. There is great value in young people gathering in a large group (I have been involved with such things for many years) but it is not a substitute for the local church. Inevitably, large groups generate a certain type of atmosphere and young people can be frustrated when that atmosphere cannot be replicated in their youth group. Events like Spring Harvest, the Keswick Convention, and Soul Survivor can be a great source of encouragement but they could actually be the cause of the drift from church life unless they are very clearly and obviously supporting local church ministry. Large events have a place but it is not possible to get all one's food from that source. Turkeys are great at Christmas but if every meal was a Christmas dinner we would be unhealthy. So we must return to the central problem. What should good local church youth ministry look like, and what should be its foundational principles?

Theology of Youth Ministry

What does the Bible say about young people and what does it say about our ministry to them? It certainly doesn't contain a book or even a chapter about the topic that would become the basis for all our principles and practice. Adolescents were not identified in the same way as they are in our culture, but the Bible does insist that our God is the God of the child. Jesus encouraged children (Luke 18:15–17). Paul clearly established household churches (Acts 16:30ff.) that would almost certainly have included children, and he was concerned about Timothy as a young man. In both 1 Timothy and Titus young leaders are a significant grouping. Steven Hale in his paper to the Oxford youth ministry conference in 1997 helpfully lists some of the starting points for youth ministry. He suggests that historically youth ministry has roots in one of the following areas:

1. Developmental theories
2. Sociology – youth in society
3. Theological / biblical perspectives
4. Practical youth ministry
5. Christian education

Most youth ministry would be a combination of such ideas and most would have a particular style that would have its emphasis in one of these areas.

One of the key areas we have neglected has been the developmental understanding of our young people. What should we expect them to be like at a certain age and do we recognize characteristics as they emerge? It might save us a lot of grief if we understood young

85

people a little better rather than assuming their behaviour is yet another sign of deliberate disobedience. But that is no basis to impart to them the truths of God.

Again sociologically it is good for us to understand the society in which our young people move. But this is as much shifting sand as developmental theories that come and go with the sands of time. Likewise it is good for our young people to serve in practical ways and to be educated, but we are really left with the biblical perspective as the only piece of rock in a world of ever shifting quicksand. If, as evangelicals, we take a high view of Scripture, and truly believe it is God's Word for every generation, what else can we do except pass on its truth to those who are young? It would be irresponsible to fail in our duty to pass the sufficient, infallible and inerrant text of a book written by God on the grounds that a few of them got a bit bored in our Bible class.[2] If we accept that the ministry of the Word is one poor beggar telling another one where to get bread, it is almost cruel not to pass that on to enable our young people to survive. Of course we should reflect with them about everyday issues and give them all the survival skills we can muster. But are these just survival skills that can, if we're not very careful, make young people dependent on their youth leaders rather than on God and his Word? An explorer needs tools for the rough country, which she has learned in the classroom but has to work out in the field. And what better lesson can there be than what God has said, applied in a way that young people can understand?

What Is the Purpose of the Bible?

Some would argue that evangelical Christianity has moved on beyond the Bible. The last two verses of John's Gospel would appear to say that we have been given all we need to know. Let us examine some of the Bible's teachings and consider, as we do, whether they are relevant to young people. The message brings us

1. *Salvation (1 Corinthians 1:18).* The Bible is the story of how God reaches out to and saves his people.[3] From the fall in

Genesis 3 to the city of Revelation 22, it is about restoring God's people to relationship with him.

2. *The central gospel truth of Jesus' death (1 Corinthians 2:2).* Is this bit too unpalatable now or have we missed the fact that young people like to be told the truth as it really is and not some watered-down version of the truth?

3. *God's power and wisdom takes us beyond the realm of man's wisdom (1 Corinthians 2:4–5).* Have we not spotted that young people are cynical about institutions (including the church) and do not give much credibility to human wisdom? So let's talk about the fact that there is a greater wisdom and a greater power which can only be found in God's Word?

4. *'Teaching, rebuking, correcting and training in righteousness so that the man of God is thoroughly equipped for every good work' (2 Timothy 3:6–17).* One of the themes of the Old Testament wisdom literature is just this. Young people are immature and need something that will make them more like Christ. God's Word taught and modelled by their leaders is the only way.

There are many other purposes. The Bible is a sword to fight against the evil in our world (Ephesians 6:17). It is the book that reveals Jesus to us – his character, his actions and his words. And so much more. Would we send an army into battle with no armour and empty handed with nothing to fight with? Our failure to teach young people the Word of God is equally negligent. It may be that we have found it difficult. It's easier just to chat to them and get to know them. I certainly have no problem with the relational aspect of youth ministry – it is vital. But our failure to help them learn God's truth is equivalent to sending an explorer into an infection-filled jungle with no jabs – we simply wouldn't do it.

Making the Bible Relevant

In one sense we don't need to make the Bible relevant because it already is. But there have been times when those teaching young people have effectively masked God's truth by teaching it in a way that simply doesn't cut much ice. I would never claim that all of my sessions with young people have been wonderful, but I think I know when they have stood a better chance. To caricature only gently, we must admit that there is a bit of tradition around that says the most essential thing about youth teachers is their ability to relate to their audience. As long as they can chat with the group and drop in enough 'cool' words and illustrations drawn from the Australian TV series *Neighbours* then all is well. My experience would suggest that the key point in any communication is good preparation. Again, one hears worrying statements that last minute, informal presentation is almost more holy than something that has been given careful preparation. Time spent in understanding the Word of God is good not only for our own spiritual development but also means that what we communicate is God's Word not our wisdom.

The context of a passage needs to be understood and can, if presented well, become both a good introduction and a means of understanding what God is saying in the passage. I worry about the view that communicating God's truth can be replaced by a talk based on human wisdom or the latest cultural mood swing. *Key to the whole exercise is good application.* Of course any teaching session must contain this and it could be that young people who walk away from our youth groups do so because of the failure of their leaders to engage with real issues.

The Bible is full of God's view on sexuality, but failure to teach this clearly has left many young people with the feeling that the Christian faith has little to say in such crucial areas. It is a huge challenge and one that needs a great investment of time in the training of youth leaders, but the failure to communicate God's agenda in the lives of young people leaves them vulnerable to being 'blown here and there by every wind of teaching' (Ephesians 4:14).

Some have tried to teach young people in a kind of 'watered down' sermon style – 'all they need is a good straight talk and all will be well'. Most of us know that doesn't work. So there is a need for good research that will help us understand the mind of the young person as well as effective ways of communicating. Some of the work done by the Damaris Trust in Southampton with their Connect Bible Studies helps us to see that it is possible both to engage with the culture and be faithful to Scripture.[4] At the heart of communicating truth to young people is a teacher who has a passion for God's Word. They truly are those who 'meditate on it night and day' (Joshua) and who, when they talk with young people, have a singular aim to communicate what God is saying from his Word. For some this may mean more time spent in the Word. It is essential that we do everything we can to understand what we are talking about in both the context and the meaning of the passage so that we can truly teach the application of God's Word in a relevant way.

Purpose of Church-Based Youth Ministry

This teaching model needs a framework in which to operate. Young people will question what their leader says. Throughout, we must remember that we are not in this work for popularity (a big issue for some youth leaders); we are in it to please God (1 Thessalonians 2). My main concern at the end of giving a talk is whether or not the talk spoke truth, not necessarily whether it was well received and notched me some points on the popularity scale. We should not deliberately seek to be unpopular but we should always seek to be faithful to God's Word.

What is the framework for such ministry? It has to be the local church. When teaching occurs it is always vital to say to young people that there is no such thing as a silly question. If it's a genuine question, then ask and I will try to answer it. I have known issues rumble on for months in the minds of young people. There needs to be a context in which their question can be aired, and, if necessary, time after time. In spite of good teaching in large annual festivals, there is no replacement for the faithful youth leader who is always around to deal with all the difficult questions. So what is the purpose of church-based youth ministry? It is certainly much more than a babysitting club while the adults have a blessed time in the 'main event'. I am now a minister to all ages, still teaching our young people on a regular basis (though not as frequently as I would like to). I would urge church ministers who employ youth ministers to keep up this contact with young people and still to involve themselves in some teaching of the young people. Don't draw back from the youth. Keep your 'hand in'. Get to know the young congregation who will be your 'older' congregation in a few years. Meanwhile, I believe we should help young people to

1. *Become Christians.* Let's not be surprised if a young person comes into our group. Sometimes we treat them like Klingons from a starship! But as they come in, part of our function is inevitably an evangelistic one. Youth ministry today is missiological and we must stop thinking of it as a pillar of the institution. We should not be afraid to make clear the steps to becoming a Christian. This will often be a good review for our whole group but will challenge people who are without Christ. They need to know the gospel, God's story of death and resurrection, so we must teach it in such a way that its true meaning is clear.

2. *Grow as Christians.* I sometimes marvel at Christians who think that their young people will somehow grow and develop as if by some kind of holy magic. To grow, food is needed. We all need to get to know God better, as we are reminded in 1 Corinthians 2 (to know his mind). At this point there is a danger that young people go looking for new experiences without realizing or being told that God has taken the trouble to write down what he thinks.

3. *Live as Christians.* Young people often find the world confusing. They see it as a world with conflicting standards and in which there are few moral absolutes. To state it at its simplest, what would any of us do if we saw a crawling baby approach an open coal fire? Would we seriously say, 'I will let you go on into the fire and let you find out how hot it is and see what damage it does – I'm sure you will learn from this experience.' Because we love them we either shout a warning or grab them or go out immediately and buy a new fireguard. We take some preventative measure to save them

from harm. It must be obvious to those of us who work with them that young people *want* to hear what God's boundaries are and how to keep to them. We need to help them deal with their pressures and the issues that confront them – we must 'scratch where they itch'.

4. *Serve as Christians.* We wait too long before we involve young people in service in the local church. You almost need a pension book before you can possibly serve on many committees. My plea is that we use young people in almost any service team the church has. I don't know who said this but it is relevant here. 'We must stop regarding church as the remains of a great movement whose heyday was in the nineteenth century. We must see ourselves as the small beginning of what God is going to do in the years ahead.' Churches have experimented with this kind of thing. If they have failed, it could be that they failed to prepare the young person with any kind of mentoring or training or that they failed to teach that a fundamental value for a Christian is a servant-hearted approach to ministry.

Church Structures: New Models

I have often visited churches where many good things are happening in their work with the under-eighteens, but the work is heavily departmentalized and each section is firmly in control of its own work. Any offers of cooperation are greeted with hostility because 'This is our patch.' Just to correct some false theology – it is not 'our patch' but 'God's patch'. The need to see the whole of the work in the local church in a seamless way is of paramount importance. Lone rangers in charge of small age bands do not help anyone to see the big picture. Whatever the size of the church, somebody should be looking after the whole of the programme.

This is truly vital because we need to be extremely careful about our plans for the growth and development of children and young people in our care. It matters what we teach them and how we teach it. There needs to be a plan and each department of the work needs to know how it fits into the plan. It's important that the biblical narratives are familiar to our children and this is something that can be lost if we overplay the thematic approach in our teaching plan. It is not good enough exclusively to lean on published material (these booklets can be extremely valuable), but we all need to plan a balanced diet for our children. I'm not suggesting a particular story should be visited only once, but if the narrative is well known, further lessons can be drawn out in older groups. We need to ensure that all of the key figures in God's dealings with his people are given the right exposure. The story of Joseph is a great story and should be approached in that way with young children. But the lessons of his dealings with Potiphar's wife lead naturally to different styles of explanation for different ages. Starting with a level of familiarity will help us later to teach that passage to teenagers in a more relevant way.

That particular story, of course, raises another issue. The issue of morality is a difficult one for our young people. Their culture is screaming a different set of values at them to the ones we would love them to adopt. If we fail to teach on these issues clearly, our young people will think, quite rightly, that our contact with the real world is minimal. Without resorting to out and out sensationalism, we need both to teach and to model to our young people that these are biblical values and that they are built on a solid foundation. In my own teaching ministry I have lost count of the number of young people who have reacted badly to talks I have given! They tell me the kind of biblical behaviour I am teaching is impossible in the modern world, only to come back to me, some time later, and admit that it is the *only* way to live in a modern world!

As well as the systematic teaching of doctrines and books we must engage with the issues of our day and help our young people to see that biblical values are relevant to our world today. And this is not all about solid wall-to-wall teaching in the back rooms of churches. In thinking about youth ministry we must be thinking about social activities. Sadly, we segregate these two types of activity. During one of our open youth club nights, a whole group of us was involved with a night walk across the Peak District. We knew most of the young people who were with us but one student was unfamiliar. I just said, 'Hi. How are you doing?' and without any further pleasantries she said, 'Do you remember that talk you gave in the youth club the last time I was here?' The five-minute talk had been delivered about five years earlier but she had remembered most of the details of it – I could remember nothing of the talk. It must have been one of my less memorable efforts.

Teaching should be coupled with a good programme designed to create relational situations – where we can meet and talk with young people. I once spent an afternoon jumping off the sea wall at Exmouth with four lads (they had shovelled all the sand off the road into a huge pile below the promenade). It was great fun but it gave me a chance just to hang out with those lads and close friendships developed.

It is important to take time to think about these matters in our own situations. If we're in a medium to large church these things I have mentioned can be done. If we're in smaller churches it may be better done in cooperation with another fellowship. I remember going to a small church somewhere in Yorkshire. They were very apologetic that only four young people had turned up to this evening. But we ate some great food, put on a video and talked about it. Some years later a faithful couple had the joy of teaching the Bible there to a group of 20 week by week and seeing them grow in their walk with God. Recreational settings so often produce opportunities for gospel and biblical explanations of subjects that have been covered in teaching perhaps even weeks earlier.

Youth Leaders and their Roles/Attitudes

We have developed a bit of a stereotype in our picture of a youth leader. He or she has to speak in a certain way, lacing their conversation with an appropriate number of cool words and youth-culture sayings. Now it is important we have some knowledge of the culture in which young people live, but we stopped feeling like they feel when we passed the age of 19. So we can never again be 'cool' in the eyes of young people because we are now classed as non-understanding adults. Why then do some of our youth leaders try to go on acting like teenagers and looking foolish? It almost becomes a race to see who can be supercool. In my experience, what young people need is a variety of people who model different stages of life. That is the beauty of the all-age church – all those people are around.

The finest thing we can show our young people is that Jesus living in us has made a deep and lasting difference to our lives. When we come up against a problem it is to God's Word that we look. We need to be men and women of the Book so when our young people come to us full of questions, our answers are what God says rather than our latest opinion. That opinion will be more likely to be true if it comes from God's Word. If we model the view that there is little value in God's Word, or in preparing our talks, then our young people will gain the impression that the Bible matters very little. Yes, we must cultivate good relationships with our group members, but, if we are to develop the incarnational model, we must develop it to its fullest biblical extent. John 1 says Jesus came and dwelt among us, but there are many chapters in the same Gospel where Jesus *taught* his disciples. He seemed to cram in as much as he could so they would *know* the truth. I believe this task is urgent. Not in the sense that every time we meet our young people we provide no time even to exchange a greeting or have a laugh, but rather that they should see in us the passion to communicate God's truth to them.

It must also be said that if we 'talk the talk', we must 'walk the walk'. Over the years I have had problems with this idea. Some youth leaders take their 'getting to know you' bit to such an extreme that they would go anywhere and do anything to keep their relationship with the young people in the group. I hope we still do exciting things in our groups but we need to be careful. If we teach some truth we need to remember that we can very easily demolish all the good we've done by one false or inappropriate piece of behaviour. Let us be on our guard. Let us be the people of God in whom, when young people look at us, they will see God at work. They should see this as they watch what we read, how we speak to people, what we watch on TV and at the cinema, and how we handle our relationships. If we keep our own spiritual disciplines, then young people can at least see how it's done even if we know we are far from perfect.

Training

Much of this work is hard. It demands a great deal of stickability. It can sometimes be extremely discouraging. At times like this it is good to return to 1 Thessalonians 2. We are trying 'to please God' not men. Be very careful not to deliver your session in order to please your young people. We know which buttons to press and we press them until our fingers ache! I have heard humour used in this way – a brilliant presentation rivalling Morecambe and Wise for its humour content but an hour later it is hard to remember what was said. Humour can be a powerful weapon in careful hands and can transform a talk. But we are there for God and all communication aids must be used wisely.

It is clear from all these personal reflections that developing our skills in this area of Bible teaching is absolutely vital. How do we sit down and prepare a talk and then build a session around it that has cohesion? How do we find out what is the key message of a chapter of the Bible that someone has given us to present when we don't have a clue where to start? It would be good to see those denominations leaking young people at an alarming rate invest more time in training their youth leaders. There is a job to be done for youth workers. It is good to see some theological colleges developing courses for youth ministry, but where is the church's commitment to this through the funding of students and pastoral support?

This support is vital for full-time youth workers whose enthusiasm can quickly evaporate after the honeymoon period of their appointment. It is tragic to see 'full timers' become quickly discouraged because they are given little support. The assumption is made that their arrival in the church will signal the end of the drift away and all will now be well. Experience suggests this rarely happens. The process seems to involve considerably more graft than that!

Let me not finish before mentioning that noble band of people who turn up week by week (having been working at their secular employment all week) and who simply 'get on with the job'. I have deep admiration for such people and I believe they are the most under-resourced people in our church teams. If they are going to help with the programme why do we recruit them and then give them a life sentence (or death sentence) to teach young people for the rest of their time on the planet? I am now involved with a ministry team at a major church but often long for the days when this kind of training will be readily available up and down the UK. Even some simple teaching on planning sessions could be invaluable to many people.

Conclusion

So, does the youth scene in the UK discourage me. Some days, yes, but I believe in a sovereign God and in the power of the Spirit to accomplish his purposes. There are many needs but the key point remains: God has given us his Word – he is a revealing God. What right do we have either to decide that we will replace God's Word with our own wisdom or that we will deprive our young people of what the God of the universe has said. Yes, I worry about youth ministry becoming a profession, if the development and promotion of the individual becomes the main objective. However, there is a long Judaeo-Christian tradition that it is the responsibility of one generation to pass on to the next generation the truth of God. Failure to do that leaves our young people like people open to being blown around by every wind of strange doctrine or practice that comes along.

One final anecdote – A young man came up to me at the close of a Spring Harvest week. He said he was a Christian but admitted that he came to the first meeting thinking that the Bible teaching would be incredibly dull and boring. But that guy stuck at it for the week and thanked the team at the end by saying that he had never before realized how relevant the Bible was to his life. I passionately believe that this is the way to expand our dwindling groups – if we bring God's Word face to face with our youth culture, there may be some sparks but there will be life change. We must not lose our battle. Teach the Bible for all it's worth.

Notes

[1] Peter Brierley, *Reaching and Keeping Teenagers*, Tonbridge Wells, Monarch with Christian Research Association and CPAS, 1993.

[2] See Tim Ward's helpful discussion of these words in his article 'The Bible, Its Truth and How It Works' (see ch. 1).

[3] Note the way Chris Wright develops this in his article in this volume *Truth with a Mission: Reading Scripture Missiologically*: 'Mission is not just one of a list of things that the Bible happens to talk about, only a bit more urgently than some. Mission is, in that much-abused phrase, "what it's all about"' (see p. 223).

[4] Connect Bible Studies, Southampton, Damaris Trust, 2000.

Chapter Five

Kairos and *Chronos:* Meditations on Revelation, God's Word and God's World

Edith Humphrey

E dith Humphrey opens her chapter by looking at the nature of divine revelation: God has revealed himself not only through creation but primarily through the Scriptures. She challenges the reader to hear the inspired words faithfully, especially when the words 'mystery' and 'complexity' are bandied about. These terms are often inappropriate, as much Scripture is clear and must be understood in the plain sense conveyed. Yet we should always approach the Bible's words humbly. Furthermore, the author makes a plea for the church to take on board the variegated nature of the cultures that compose its membership on the one hand – while always remaining true to the absolutes of Scripture on the other.

The Wonder of Revelation

We begin by acknowledging that theology can never be an exclusively human activity if the God about whom we are thinking is One who communes with us.[1] While it is clear that we use these human minds and human tongues to think and to speak about God, theological activity is fruitless if, in the first instance, it springs from human effort. An appropriately humble theology will both acknowledge our feeble condition and the incompleteness of our attempts to approach God, and affirm that, in the first instance, God has made himself[2] known and continues to do so (Matthew 11:25; Luke 10:21). Revelation, then, is the category by which we acknowledge God's initiating love, action, word and imparted vision of reality to us.

Revelation with community in view

'Revelation' means, then, that our understanding of and relationship with God springs from his own initiative. The style of this self-revelation within the Hebrew Scriptures and New Testament has been predominantly the showing of God to his whole community, even where particular people are approached. (What follows is therefore a self-conscious attempt to speak from *within* the Christian tradition, although I do not intend to confine the arena of God's revelation in any way: God is free, and can make himself known as he wishes and to whom he wishes.) Revelation, within Israel and the church, has been consistently understood as the showing of God 'to us' and not merely 'to me'. The covenants, or special ties, made between God and humanity have involved groups, so that individual*ism* is excluded. The primeval narrative of Noah speaks of a covenant made with Noah and his family that involved not only all of posterity, but the entire created order. The covenant with Abraham embraced his offspring through Isaac, but also declared the interconnected blessing of the whole world. The covenant with Jacob (Israel) particularly involved Israel, yet the prophets speak of Israel's vocation to be a 'light to the Gentiles'. In Isaiah, too, the promises made about David's eternal throne are seen as conferring blessing on all the nations, who are envisaged as streaming to worship at Zion. The new covenant, too, is made with a community in view: 'this is my blood of the covenant, which is poured out *for many*' (Matthew 26:28 NRSV; my emphasis). This promise about God's new humanity is interpreted by St Paul and the seer John as having a vivifying and glorifying effect upon the whole of the created order (Romans 8; Revelation 21–2).

Revelation that is personal

Strangely, the broad sweep of God's promises, and its primary corporate nature, do not eradicate the intensely personal (but *not* individualistic) aspect of revelation. Revelation is not simply information about God's intentions for humanity and the world: it means a certain unveiling of God's being, a willing divine vulnerability, if you will, so that we can know and be known. In one sense, the first revelation to humanity begins with creation itself, and especially with the creation of humankind in the image of God, 'inbreathed' by his spirit. That the ones created in God's image are meant to know him is clear from the intimacy between the first couple and God in the Genesis narrative. Indeed, since revelation is initiated by a personal God, it should be understood as in the *first* place personal, that is, through persons, not simply as imparted knowledge. Truth is a person, made known in and by persons. ('God was pleased to reveal his Son *in* me' is the right translation of Galatians 1:16, though difficult to grasp in our cognitively oriented West.)

However, to say that Truth is a person does not mean that truth is always subjective, and that it can never be expressed propositionally. Truth is, in the first place, a Person who draws us in personally. In that sense, Truth in all his fullness seeks to know and be known by us: who he is and what he does, and how he loves and is just, and heals and challenges and comforts, is first of all expressed by him. Sometimes such self-disclosure comes in propositions; sometimes in visions; sometimes in (prophetically interpreted) actions, sometimes in silence. Carefully articulated propositions about God and the world are true in so far as they are vehicles by which we understand the One who is Truth itself.

Given what we have learned about God's ways through the covenants, we must expect to hear and understand within the context of the whole believing community, and not idiosyncratically.

Nevertheless, this does not preclude hearing and understanding personally. It is thus of note that perfect theology may come from the mouth of one who does not seem to match what he or she is saying. On the other hand, we may hear something already heard many times before which rings true because there is seemingly no gap between who that person is and what is being expressed. Truth does indeed pass in propositions, but only passes fully when the propositions come with integrity.

The Bible as the Word of God

Christians, as a community, have privileged the witness of those who have spoken with such integrity (John 1:24), because they not only speak about Christ but know him and show him in word and deed. We call the Bible the Word of God because it witnesses (authoritatively) to the One who is the Word: its character as Word is reflected, yet ultimately valuable. In the same way, the traditional symbols of the faith are significant and normative short forms for the narrative that belongs to the Christian family. To recognize that the story and the creeds come to us in human words does not mean that these words are makeshift or arbitrary. Rather, we see in Gospel, epistle, apocalypse and creed the glory of God's coming to be with us, for us and in us, so that we can indeed repeat this story with human lips.

Therefore, we can speak with some confidence, because, like Daniel, we have seen and know that there is a God in heaven who reveals mysteries (Daniel 2:28; 2:22). More particularly, we have seen and heard the 'mystery hidden for ages in God' (Ephesians 3:9 NRSV) – Jesus Christ. So, too, our present arguments, propositions and careful reasoning may well reflect truth: but they are true only in so far as they are, in some way, connected with the One from whom all truth springs, because he is Just and True.

Revelation occurs within the context of experience – especially, the common experience of the *ekklēsia*. One of the tools used in recognizing, understanding and passing on what (and/or who) has been revealed is the God-given faculty of reason.[3] The community is given to recognize the helpfulness of present words by weighing them together, with the help of the Holy Spirit, against the witnesses that we have already recognized and received.

The present limitation of revelation

Thus revelation comes in different ways, and in different kinds of words. Gospel narratives differ from one another, and from Paul's teaching on the resurrection. Both these genres differ from ethical injunctions, or from the Apocalypse's vision of the throne-room. Again, revelation can be seen to interpret the whole range of human history, past, present and future, showing that our times are connected with the One who is, was and is to come. Some truth translates better into human words, as Paul reminds us in 2 Corinthians 12, where he speaks of 'unutterable things'. Paul's words here, Old Testament diffidence about the divine Name, and curious passages such as Revelation 11:4 (spoken but uninterpreted thunder) remind us that revelation must (for now, at any rate) conceal while it reveals. Part of the reception of revelation is to recognize the mysterious character of what is being shown. Because this concerns the One who is True, and is beyond our present comprehension, there will always be a surplus of mystery that cannot yet be communicated, except in silence. (The Eastern Orthodox's equal stress upon mystery and creed may be helpful to us here, since in the West we tend to play off the mysterious and the propositional.) God still remains the *totaliter aliter*, alongside his intimacy with us in Christ and the Holy Spirit.[4] Along this line, it is presumptuous to leash the Word, assuming that we 'possess' him exclusively, and that revelation can occur only within our own arena. Yet the mystery of God enfleshed within the community of Israel, and the Spirit imparted through him to New Israel, suggest that the normal locus of revelation is in the community of Christ. The persistent biblical pattern of mysterious encounter, followed by faithful human witness, should be instructive here. God is not bound by us; yet he chooses to act through and in his community.

Within our talk and thinking about God, the *category* of revelation makes all the difference in the world, since it presupposes God's initiative. Revelation says that there is indeed someone there (and here) who speaks and acts and seeks to know us. Christians affirm that it is *the divine act of revelation* that makes our understanding possible, for God can only be known in that he shows himself. Interestingly, *that there is revelation* tells us something about God's nature: we know from the actions, words and silent communion of our Creator that he is in relationship. We also learn from revelation something about ourselves – that we are made for relationship. The disclosure of God's trinitarian nature is significant here, informing every part of our life and understanding. (But here I move far beyond a discussion of revelation to a discussion of its content.) Seen from this perspective, theology and prayer are a response to revelation, and a search for deeper connection (both personal and cognitive) with God's nature and his love. An ongoing worship of God, a respect for the whole community of God (past and present), an ongoing faithfulness to the witnesses we have already received, and a grateful but sober evaluation of our own place in the Body will protect us against subjectivism, which is the death of theology. The search to understand and know God is in itself life-giving. In knowing him, we come to understand ourselves. If we make self-knowledge the goal, we will never know anything.

The Challenge of Hearing Faithfully

Once we have recognized the all-important truth of God's desire to commune with us, we may fruitfully go on to consider the major witness that he has given to us, that is, the Scriptures. Only a little reflection leads us to see that the reading of Scripture is not only a gift, but, given the many voices that surround us, a responsibility for those who are in Christ. So we go on to ask, What constitutes a faithful reading of Scripture? Scripture is key to the thinking of the Christian church, and therefore of the Anglican communion. While we are first of all people of Christ, we are also people of the Book. It is most particularly in the Bible that the supreme glory of our Lord is shown so that the church can together know the One who is the Truth, and therefore worship together. As members of the Christian community, we are grateful for the many ways in which Christ as divine Word has spoken to us. We are also grateful for the manifold biblical narrative in which he speaks, through the Holy Spirit, to our human situation.

To read Scripture as it is meant to be read, we begin with an understanding of its character. It is not a static deposit of precepts to be mined, but a vibrant collection of books by which the church is taught, and by which she is identified. The story of Scripture has been helpfully understood in five great acts:[5] Act 1 tells us about a creator God; Act 2 speaks of a good creation gone askew by death, corruption and sin; Act 3 presents the call of the nation Israel to be a light to the world; Act 4 shows how that calling was fulfilled in a surprising and crucial way in the coming, life, death, resurrection and ascension of Jesus the Christ; Act 5, in which we find ourselves, describes the ongoing life and healing mission of the church through the Holy Spirit in this world. Though we are participants in this drama, as true actors in solidarity with the Messiah and God's people throughout the ages it is incumbent upon us to act with a view to the whole story, and to 'fit in' with the pattern of the story into which we have been placed. Our words and actions have a delightful element of spontaneity, and are inbreathed by God's Spirit, but this does not mean that there are no limits to what we say, think and do. The play has its own integrity, and our love for the playwright and main actor will mean that (to change metaphors) we will tune our music and shape our improvised leitmotifs to his purposes. In faithfulness and in truth we thus await the finale of this drama, but have been given wonderful intimations of God's purposes for his people and the entire cosmos in the body of the play so far.

Learning the story

This grand narrative is God's *poiēsis* (creation), as are we (Ephesians 2:10); yet the story has been told to us, by God's own choosing, in human words, particular to time and place. To recognize the human element of the Scriptures is not to suggest that they are arbitrary or without authority. Rather, we behold in the Bible's many forms –

narrative, law, Gospel, psalm, epistle, apocalypse – the wonder of God's coming to be with us, for us and in us. We learn this story intimately, so that we can indeed repeat it with human lips, and learn to play an authentic part in it. Particularly important to a faithful reading of Scripture is the recognition of this 'we' factor: the Scripture implies, and indeed states explicitly, that the Word is heard not privately, but by the whole community, past and present.

When we, as today's faith community, recognize, understand and pass on what (and Who) has been revealed, we are using the God-given faculty of reason. Our experience and reason are not actual 'authorities' as we understand Scripture or decide about present concerns. Instead, experience (especially the common experience of the church) is our context, the place where we receive God's love and wisdom; reason is a 'tool' or means of interpreting what we hear. Under the guidance of the Holy Spirit, we weigh our own thoughts and inclinations against the biblical and traditional witnesses that we have already recognized and received. In other words, we measure the helpfulness of current ideas against a long-established understanding of God, the world and humanity, to see if they stand up to the test.

The clarity of Scripture

There is a contemporary trend to appeal to 'mystery' when dealing with Scripture. Indeed, some matters are mysterious. As I said earlier, some truths translate better into human words than others. Paul reminds us of this in 2 Corinthians 12, where he speaks of 'unutterable things'. Indeed, to receive revelation is to recognize the mysterious character of what is being shown. Having said that, we must be careful not to appeal to 'mystery' and 'complexity' in those many cases where the Scriptures are straightforward, coherent with each other and clearly expressed. The recognition of 'mystery' and 'complexity' is appropriate where it encourages our capacity for wonder and reverence. We must not use 'mystery', however, in order to suggest that a clear but awkward passage is ambiguous, or hard to understand. Such a tendency is not moving in the direction of a faithful reading.

Humility in interpretation

As members and interpreters in the community of faith, we are thus actors in a divinely conceived drama; our role is not, however, to improvise with abandon. In reading the Scriptures together, and by honouring the 'actors' who have gone before us, we keep within our memories and hearts the central, major 'part' in the drama – God's. As those who have received the Spirit, we shall want to share in the mind of Christ, understanding the word personally, but not autonomously or individualistically. The church has, from the beginning, struggled over difficult matters. Her reflection and decisions about such matters subsequent to the time of the New Testament should not be relegated to the archives but, together with the New Testament, acknowledged as authoritative for us younger brothers and sisters in the same family. This is especially so of the decisions and creeds of the ecumenical councils of the church before the time of the Great Schism. Together with God's whole church, past and present, we are called to discern God's voice and will, in humility and in confidence that the Holy Spirit is active in our midst. This humility and confidence will mean that we do not lift our twentieth-century Western perspective above the perspective of other Christians in other times and places. What is more, we shall not consider the voice of the Scriptures to be simply another set of data among competing claims, between which we are then to arbitrate. It is true that the words of the Scriptures are interpreted words from God. However, in recognizing a limit to the canon, the church acknowledges that the 'interpretation' made by the Old and New Testament authors is authoritative.

The human authors of the Scriptures, then, wrote in particular historical contexts. This fact of itself says nothing about how the Bible is to be used in any particular controversy in the church today. The problem of moving from the context of the original writer to application today should not be used as a pretext for bypassing explicit teaching or perspectives we find difficult. Rather, in each case, we are to read all the pertinent texts carefully. Even where we see that a prescriptive passage is particular to a moment in the history of God's people (e.g.

prohibition of pork, or head coverings for women), we acknowledge and respect the underlying theological/ethical truths. Some prescriptions have an enduring claim (e.g. the command not to murder) because they are essentially linked to what has been revealed about the world, our nature and the nature of God in the salvation story.

A sensitive reading of the Scriptures will heed the cues given in each text concerning its historical and literary context, its genre and intent, and the way it is related to the divine drama. As Paul puts it, in concert with the perspective of Luke, Hebrews and 1 Peter, God acted definitively both 'at the right time' (Romans 5:6) and in 'the fullness of time' (Galatians 4:4 NRSV). To see a text as moored in historical space and time and at the same time transcending such particular moments calls for the most careful thinking. It does not call for us simply to relativize the detail and flow of human history, but to see each moment described in the text in relation to the greater story. In one sense the coming of Jesus renders pale the significance of every other time; in another sense, God's coming to us heals, dignifies and transfigures the whole of human life – and, in time, the life of the whole created order (Romans 8:18–26).

God works in a variety of ways, and in the Scriptures speaks a word that is at once challenging and confirming. The biblical record is unique in its authoritative witness to who God is in Christ. Yet that grace and light extend beyond the time upon which it centres, into the living tradition of God's people down to the present. God's entry point into humanity – the incarnation – questions, illuminates and transforms all that came before and all that comes after. A faithful reading of the Scriptures thus means that we seek to understand how the passages we are reading, and the questions we are asking, fit into this forgiving, healing and life-giving drama that has been initiated by God himself. While the meaning of the Scriptures is often obvious, all of us interpret the Bible from a particular time and place. We are sometimes influenced by *unacknowledged* sources. It is also true that we are sometimes confounded in our reading because of 'blinkers' that have been given to us by our formation or by the company we keep. This reminds us that there is no such thing as 'simply reading the Bible'. Thus there is a challenge for us to reflect seriously on the strengths and weaknesses of the traditions by which we have been formed and informed. The promise that the church would be led into all truth should strengthen our minds and imaginations as we struggle with what divides us.

The Bible and History

We have, then, before us this paradox: God speaks to us, intending us to understand; yet at every point God's Word is interpreted, handled by human hands. Even a divine 'Word' to God's people is an interpreted word. Yet the church has privileged the 'interpretation' of the New Testament writers in the process of canonization. In the creed that the church recites we hear about the life and death of Jesus 'under Pontius Pilate' – historical context, and historical questions, are bound up in this mystery of God showing himself and giving himself to us. Again, the very existence of *four* separate Gospels in the canon (over against a *Diatesseron* or Harmony of the Gospels), along with their common rhetorical impulse, which points away from themselves towards the One presented there, legitimates a modest historical quest. The Gospels (even the 'theological' Fourth Gospel) do not present themselves either as exhaustive portraits of Jesus, nor as wholly finished products of revelation. So, in John's two endings we read twice of the 'many other' things that Jesus did (John 20:30; John 21:26); and in the Synoptic Gospels the life of Jesus opens into the life of the church (a movement wholly programmatic in Luke-Acts). Moreover, the Gospels do not always obscure their interpretive moves, but leave tantalizing details about the hermeneutic that has informed their retelling(s) of the story of Jesus (e.g. Mark 7:19b; Mark 13:14, where the narrator intrudes into the episode, or into the words of Jesus himself). So, then, the Anglican emphasis upon what is 'reasonable' comes into play: the clues in the text suggest that it is *not* presumptuous for us to ask questions about places where the four Gospels sit uneasily side by side or where the texts themselves suggest a process of reception and transmission.

Thus the Scriptures themselves ask us to take seriously the complementary Pauline statements (clearly articulated by Paul, but intimated also in Luke, Matthew, Hebrews and 1 Peter) that God acted definitively *both* 'at the right time' (*kairos*; Romans 5:6 NRSV) *and* in 'the fullness of time' (*chronos*; Galatians 4:4 NRSV). A full-blooded understanding of the incarnation/crucifixion/resurrection and ascension will recognize and marvel at the particularity of God's Word. Yet that Word does not simply relativize the detail and flow of human history (though he does this), but also aims to dignify and transfigure the whole of human life – and, in fact, the life of the whole created order (Romans 8:18–26). Moreover, God's healing and energizing activity is seen as both coming from without ('*For God has done* what the law [Torah], weakened by the flesh, could not do: *by sending* his own Son'; Romans 8:3a NRSV; my emphasis) and as working from within ('to deal with sin, he condemned sin *in the flesh*'; Romans 8:3b NRSV; my emphasis); 'Likewise the Spirit' [working within us and within creation] 'groans' and 'intercedes with sighs too deep for words', Romans 8:22–6 NRSV).

So God works in a particular way and mode, and in so doing speaks a word that is at once iconoclastic and confirming. Nothing in our history or in the created order can fill the place of God's gift of himself; yet our history and God's entire world are utterly significant. By extension, the biblical record is unique in its authoritative witness to what and who God is, yet extends that 'grace' and light beyond the time upon which it centres, into the living tradition of God's people.

The unified witness of Scripture

As we reflect upon the 'unveiling' (revelation) of God's activity and God's speaking, we are called to speak in concert with the experience of the Christian family, taking our cue from the creeds, and turning deliberately to the Scriptures as a variegated but unified witness to God's work and word. We recognize that these Scriptures have been written within the flow of human history, and within the context of human culture, but that they speak about that particular One who both entered ('pierced'?) and took on ('assumed') our common humanity, thus disclosing a nature completely 'other' than ours but one that is able to engage, unite with, indwell, fulfil, and transfigure what we are. That engagement and proleptic transformation means that nature, as well as human nature, are disclosed as (at least potentially) 'good' and 'very good' – despite the many barriers to this fulfilment that have come about as the result of death and sin.

Our reading and understanding, then, has been shaped by the ongoing Christian tradition, and deliberately so, since the Scriptures themselves intimate that this is fitting. The centring of the events and words of Scripture upon the person of Jesus is a move that has been learned from the church herself, in creed, song and liturgy, but is an orientation that emerges naturally from a sympathetic hearing of the New Testament's interpretation of the Hebrew Bible. My understanding of God's purposes for humanity and for the whole cosmos are founded, I hope, upon the entire range of biblical writings. My words, however, have been consciously articulated by terms used in the patristic, Reformed, evangelical Wesleyan and Eastern Orthodox traditions (strange bedfellows, to be sure!). It is probable that my identity within the Anglican communion, a communion predisposed towards 'inclusivity', has enabled me to listen to voices that others might assume are mutually exclusive. Despite their differences, I hear them, at the most important point, singing in harmony. (I am conscious of the irony that it is the 'I' who is borrowing these ideas, while I am trying desperately to avoid a 'Protestant' stance. For those of us this side of the Enlightenment, living within the living tradition of the church, and avoiding 'private' opinion, will of necessity be a struggle.) Within the various expressions of the church, we see the wonder of a God who is concerned for both healing and recreation, for both the particular and the whole – and neither at the expense of the other. More incredibly, he calls us into his own life, indwelling us personally and together by his Spirit, and calling us to put on the mind of Christ. Living in this way enables us to see God's ongoing self-revelation in our midst, in the world, and in the rest of the 'natural order'. At times we are also afforded less mediated glimpses of a cosmos and a Person bigger and more inviting than we can ever think or imagine.

The Bible and Culture

Reflection upon the diverse cultures of God's church leads us to the question of human culture per se, and how the Bible directs us to think about it. Steve Martin's hilarious film *LA Story* was perhaps relatively unsuccessful because it was too subtly allusive for the average American viewer – playful references to *Hamlet, The Tempest,* popular hymns, and the Bible interweave its lines and inform its zany plot. At one point the two main characters, on the verge of love, enter a muse or courtyard garden between two city buildings. As they enter its gates, we go into slow-mo, and the two stone lions at the entrance pillars turn their heads to gaze on the couple. Around them the garden bursts into bloom, reminiscent of the luxurious growth of Eden. They continue walking together, hand in hand, and the camera pans down to their feet, where we notice, with a shock, that their adult shoes do not fit them anymore. The lovers walk out of them into bareness, and have become innocents in Paradise, leaving behind all the complexity of their urban, jaded, postmodern lives. This theme of a return to innocence is a controlling one for the film, and seems to reflect Martin's wistful longing for simplicity, as does the climactic musical moment, in which a lone bagpipe intones 'Amazing Grace'.

The return to Eden has been an insistent theme since 'modernity' made its mark on the West. Despite its charm, the theme is not nuanced enough for a fully biblical response to our ill-conceived complexities. The canonical shape of the biblical narrative should be sufficient to remind us that although the archetypal human couple begins in a garden, the final scene envisaged for humanity is that of an enfoliated and fruitful city, inhabited by (or identified with?) a multitude and built on a foundation of two twelves, prophets and apostles. Despite its condemnation of Babylon, the Apocalypse does not bring its seer or its reader back to an unretouched Eden. The full answer to godless or God-defying society is not a razing of that city, but a new city, the New Jerusalem, prepared in time (the temporary 'time, times and half a time') and in space (the desert) and also, mysteriously, in the heavenlies (whence she appears, 'from God'). The New Jerusalem incorporates not only the heritage of the tribes of

About the Contributors

Peter Ackroyd

Revd Dr Peter Ackroyd trained at Wycliffe Hall in Oxford. Following a curacy at St James, Carlisle, he worked for the Proclamation Trust and is now Vicar of St Mary the Virgin, Wootton, Bedford. His doctorate from Edinburgh University was awarded for research on the Italian Reformer, Peter Martyr.

Phil Baskerville

The Revd Phil Baskerville is Associate Minister in Barnston. He has worked in Kenya with the Africa Inland Church in Turkana as a volunteer with CMS, and has also worked as a Crosslinks mission partner as a tutor at Kapsabet Bible College and at St Paul's Theological College, Kapsabet, Kenya (1993–97).

Wallace Benn

The Rt Revd Wallace Benn is President of CEEC and of the Fellowship and Word and Spirit. After twenty-five years in parochial ministry, he was consecrated Bishop of Lewes in 1977. A well-known speaker, he has published books on Philippians and John 14–16 together with a variety of articles. A Dubliner by birth, he is a graduate of University College Dublin and London University and currently serves on the Working Party on Women Bishops.

Gerald Bray

Revd Prof. Gerald Bray (doctorate from the Sorbonne) is Anglican Professor of Divinity at Beeson Divinity School, Alabama. Until 1993 he was tutor in Christian Doctrine and Philosophy at Oak Hill College. His book *Biblical Interpretation: Past and Present* (Leicester: IVP) was voted as one of the top ten books every pastor should read. Other academic works include *The Anglican Canons* (1998) and *Tudor Church Reform* (2000). A master linguist, he lectures in theology in many countries and is editor of the journal *Churchman*.

Andrew Cornes

Revd Andrew Cornes is Vicar at All Saints, Crowborough, Sussex. He has worked on the staffs of St Michael-le-Belfry in York and All Souls, Langham Place in London, where he was also involved in theological training. He has written several books in the areas of marriage, divorce and remarriage.

Graham Cray

The Rt Revd Dr Graham Cray is Bishop for Mission in the Diocese of Canterbury. He is chairman of the Soul Survivor Trust. Previously he was Principal of Ridley Hall Theological College, Cambridge, and before that, Vicar of St Michael-le-Belfrey, York. His recent publications include *Postmodern Culture and Youth Discipleship* and *Youth Congregations and the Emerging Church*.

Tim Dakin

The Revd Canon Tim Dakin has been General Secretary of the Church Mission Society since April 2000. Prior to that, he was Principal of Carlisle College in Nairobi. He is a theologian and an honorary Canon Theological at Coventry Cathedral.

Dave Fenton

The Revd David Fenton has been Youth Co-ordinator for Spring Harvest-Word Alive week and for Keswick. Having started as a school teacher, he became head of Maths in a large comprehensive school in Sheffield. He moved to church ministry and served as the Youth and Children's co-ordinator for twelve years at Christ Church, Fullwood, Sheffield, where he had responsibility for over 1000 children. He is now Minister at Above Bar Church in Southampton.

Paul Gardner

The Ven. Dr Paul Gardner is Archdeacon of Exeter. He is Chairman of the Church of England Evangelical Council and of this NEAC. After receiving a Cambridge doctorate for work on 1 Corinthians (later published), he taught at Oak Hill Theological College (1983–90) then moved to parish ministry in Cheshire until 2003. He has published a number of books and articles, including commentaries on Revelation, and 2 Peter and Jude.

Ida Glasser

Ida Glaser is seconded from Crosslinks to work with the Edinburgh Centre for Muslim-Christian Studies. For Crosslinks, she first worked as leader of their Other Faiths Team, and then as director of the Faith to Faith consultancy, and as tutor at Crowther Hall. She has written *Partners or Prisoners? Christians thinking about women and Islam* with Napoleon John and *Sharing the Salt-making friends with Muslims, Hindus and Sikhs* with Shaylesh Raja.

Chris Green

Revd Chris Green is Vice Principal at Oak Hill Theological College, where he teaches Church Leadership, Mission and Preaching. He has written various Bible commentaries (including 2 Peter and Jude) and is currently working on Acts. Chris is chairman of the Anglican Evangelical Assembly and on the NEAC steering team.

Edith Humphrey

Prof. Dr Edith M. Humphrey is Associate Professor of New Testament at Pittsburgh Theological Seminary. Her PhD is from McGill University, and her writings include articles on the New Testament and contemporary theological issues, as well as two books, *Joseph and Aseneth* and *The Ladies and the Cities, Transformation and Apocalyptic Identity in Joseph and Aseneth, 4 Ezra, the Apocalypse and The Shepherd of Hermas.* She is a co-author in the Primate's Theological Commission (Anglican Church of Canada) of the multi-volume workbook *Wrestling with God.*

Simea Meldrum de Souza

Revd Simea Meldrum de Souza is vicar of the Anglican Church of Living Water in Recife, Brazil. She has been involved in a new form of church linked to the community of people who live on the city rubbish tip. She has pioneered forms of church and community involvement among some of the poorest people on our planet.

David Zac Niringiye

Dr David Zac Niringiye from Uganda is Regional Director for Africa of CMS. His doctorate in Theology and Mission History is from Edinburgh. After twelve years as National Director of FOCUS (Fellowship of Christian Unions) in Uganda, he became Regional Secretary for English- and Portuguese-speaking Africa for IFES (International Fellowship of Evangelical Students). A renowned international speaker, he has published widely on mission, including *The Christ of the Cross and the World Mission of the Church*.

Rico Tice

Revd Rico Tice is Church Evangelist and Associate Minister at All Souls, Langham Place, London. He has developed the *Christianity Explored* course and materials and written a book for non-Christians with the same title. His specialist areas of research and ministry are evangelism and apologetics.

Tim Ward

Revd Dr Timothy Ward is a curate in Crowborough, England. His doctorate from Edinburgh was published by Oxford University Press in 2002: *Word and Supplement: Speech Acts, Biblical Texts, and the Sufficiency of Scripture.* He has written a number of other articles mostly on subjects related to hermeneutics.

Chris Wright

Revd Dr Chris Wright is the International Ministries Director of the Langham Partnership International, a group of ministries founded by John Stott for equipping leaders in the churches of the Majority World. Previously Principal of All Nations Christian College, he has also taught Old Testament at Union Biblical Seminary, Pune, India, and is currently honorary President of Crosslinks. His books include *Living as the People of God* (on Old Testament ethics), *Knowing Jesus through the Old Testament* and *The Uniqueness of Jesus.*

Israel and the apostles of the Lamb, but also the 'glory' of the nations (Revelation 21:24). The city is characterized by boldness, as its gates lie perpetually open, and John repeats that 'they' are able to 'bring into it the glory and the honour of the nations' (21:26 NRSV). Yet there will be no night there, nor anything accursed, nor anything/anyone 'unclean'; rather, by the twelvefold fruits of the tree of life the nations shall be healed (22:2).

Here, then, is the wonder: God's creation will itself mirror, in its eschatological fullness, the unity and plurality of the One who made it. Just as God is revealed in the story of Israel and of Jesus to be Trinity and not a simple monad, so here the created order, and redeemed humanity within it, are seen in all fullness and fecundity as united in common worship (22:3). The overall narrative of the Bible, while not naive about human abominations that make desolate, affirms that human culture, alongside 'nature', is redeemable. Even more, we see that human culture is bound for transformation so as to share in the glory of God himself.

A Metanarrative for All

Our departure point for a discussion of 'the Bible and culture' goes beyond seeing in the Bible a multiplicity of stories, until we discern that particular and pesky 'metanarrative' that makes a claim upon our affections, our assessment of reality, our worldview and our hopes. This narrative, while it can employ the language of myth (as well as the language of epic, history, prophecy, prescription, wisdom, dialogue, proverb and poetry) refuses to be confined to a mythological netherland, or to an inner world of the human psyche. The story impinges upon our world, insisting that what it relates has touched our lives forever.

The story itself is told in human language, and uses especially (though not exclusively) the conventions and traditions of the Hebrews/Israelites/Jews and the Graeco-Roman world. It takes up these forms of thought and speech but also makes the audacious claim that its story is for everyone, not just for those who are comfortable with such cultural expressions. That is, the story is inculturated, but claims not to be so by default (Romans 5:16; Galatians 4:4; Hebrews 1:1); as such, it denies that it is culturally confined.

For these reasons, we may with confidence speak about the Bible and culture, and not simply (as some have done) about the gospel and culture, or about Christ and culture, both of which are important subsets of the question. We need not look to a human distillation of the gospel message in order to get a handle on God's concern for human culture, but see it in the very phenomenon of the Scriptures themselves.

It is against this backdrop that we must weigh some of the ecumenical voices within the Christian community who are struggling with the challenges of contemporary culture.[6] Some of these seem to see as a stumbling block what is better understood as the glory of the gospel – its incarnate quality. A lingering popular 'Platonism' is sometimes discernible in the drive to move through the layers of Scripture (many of which are now considered obsolete) to a pure and universal 'core' of truth. In this vein, we hear Netherlands professor Antonie Wessels, who is seemingly unaware of the integrity of the divine drama, declare that 'every age has the task of writing its own "fifth gospel"'.[7] Or, alternately, we note a syncretistic approach from two Canadian United Church clergy who admit the danger and impossibility of seeking an 'irreducible core' but plead for us to 'recognize *revelations of God – the face of Jesus –* in peoples and cultures that are different'.[8]

Neither approach, the search for a 'core' meaning within the Scriptures, or the relativization of God's Word so that it speaks equally in all cultures, does justice to the rich story we have been given. We are called to recognize the intricacies of human culture and also to remain faithful to the story of the One who has come into human history at a particular place and a particular time to call us, in all our peculiarities, to be fully human. There is one face of Jesus, seen only on the One who is the Image of God, although every human reflects the *imago dei*. God has come to us in a particular way; God's Spirit is never leashed, and is active where he wills. Our approach to Bible and culture must reflect upon both poles, particularity and universality, so as to compromise neither.

Notes

[1] The following meditations took place in the context of the first three years (1997–2000) of study and consultation of the Primate's Theological Commission (Anglican Church of Canada). I am grateful to my fellow commissioners for the discussions that led to these reflections, and also for their responses to my work. Some of the following, and inter-connected discussions, are reproduced in a much more concise form in the handbooks put out by the Commission, and painstakingly edited by Joanne McWilliams, specifically in vol. 1 of *Wrestling with God*, entitled *Longing for God: Anglicans Talk about Revelation, Nature, Culture and Authority*, Toronto, ABC, 2001.

[2] I am fully aware of the irritation that this masculine pronoun is likely to elicit among some. Because I take very seriously the Scriptures and the consistent tradition of the church as the arena for God's revelation, I am determined not to avoid the language that is used there for the One whom we worship in the Christian community. This is not a statement about the 'gender' of God, however, who is neither male nor female. It is an attempt, rather, to accept the language used by the Israelite and early Christian communities, and by Jesus himself, in recognition that we cannot be certain which parts of metaphor are expendable and which are essential. I reject impersonal and abstract language for God as sub-Christian, and am intensely uncomfortable with feminine language in that it emphasizes gender, imports a novelty into our Christian talk, and may well evoke eco-pan-theistic notions that detract from God as Creator.

[3] It will be apparent from the use made here of Scripture, tra-dition, reason and experience, that I consider the so-called Wesleyan quadrilateral (i.e. Scripture, tradition, reason and experience) to be somewhat skewed. Scripture and the creeds were articulated and are understood in the context of the ongoing living tradition of God's people. Experience and

reason are not properly sources of authority, but the locale of reception, and one of the tools for interpreting what has been received.

4   The distinction between God's energies and essence may be helpful here: the former may be known, but the latter remains mysterious.

5   For a more careful explanation of this bird's-eye view of the Book, see N. T. Wright, *The New Testament and the People of God*, Minneapolis, Fortress, 1992.

6   The following two references are short pamphlets that represent the views of World Council of Churches representatives who in 1996 reflected upon the issue of 'gospel and cultures'. Their reflections are reproduced in a series entitled 'Gospels and Cultures'.

7   Antonie Wessels, 'Secularized Europe: Who Will Carry Off Its Soul?' *Gospels and Cultures 6,* Geneva, WCC, 1996, p. 32.

8   My italics; Stan Mckay and Janet Silman, 'The First Nations', *Gospels and Cultures 2,* Geneva, WCC, 1996, pp. 50–51.

Chapter Six

The Bible and Confidence in Local Mission

Wallace Benn

Wallace Benn examines the phenomenon of church growth from two angles: one in which the Bible is central to the life of the congregation and the other, a postmodern perspective, which has cut itself adrift from absolutes. He asks whether our postmodern society, with its lack of clear moral boundaries, can be impacted by the Bible, and concludes that it can. Using examples from his own ministry of 30 years, first as a parish priest and later as a bishop, he argues that, like the early church, modern Christians must engage biblically in society. If the Bible is restored to centrality, the church will once again burst forth with new life and become a force for good in the world around us.

Introduction

In this chapter I want to look at the question of how churches grow in the Western world, and in particular whether churches that are Bible-centred, which uphold biblical convictions, are the kind of churches that grow. Over the years, many have argued that the most consistent growth has been seen in those churches where the centrality of Scripture to the church's teaching, preaching and life has been the clearest. Few recent writers have put it more strongly than David Eby who says that

> The ministry of the Word is the main weapon in the spiritual arsenal, the only seed for church planting, the primary tool for church building, and the principal strategy in God's plan to disciple the nations. No preaching, no church. No proclamation, no church growth.[1]

John Stott made a similar point when he wrote:

> In such a variegated situation, in which overall the Church is losing ground, is it possible to pinpoint a single cause of weakness? Many would say 'no'. And certainly the causes are many. Yet personally I do not hesitate to say that a (even the) major reason for the Church's decline in some areas and immaturity in others is what Amos called a 'famine of hearing the words of the Lord'. (Amos 8:11)[2]

Nowadays, though, many have come to doubt that growth will most likely be found in churches where the Bible and the preaching of the Word are central. Clearly all Christians would believe that there is the need for each church to present and live by some Christian 'core'. This, after all, is what makes a church recognizably Christian. There must be loyalty to and love for Jesus of Nazareth, the Son of God and Son of Man, the one the early Christians believed was the Saviour of the world (John 4:42). But some Christians then suggest that because the Bible was written a long time ago much emphasis on the biblical text and biblical convictions will be thought by many to be strange to modern ears.

Indeed the Bible sounds strange to postmodern ears as well! – for the Bible is all about a metanarrative. It is about the overarching story of the love of the Creator God, and his plan to redeem a people for himself through the death and resurrection of his Son, the Messiah or anointed King of his kingdom. This is not always acceptable to a postmodern mind, for it is about an account of God's revelation and of truth which, it is claimed, is universally applicable. It centres on the exclusive claims and ministry of Jesus Christ. Furthermore, it is surely true that the Gospel accounts reveal that Jesus himself would hardly have been acceptable today as he proclaimed his message! On the one hand, he went beyond barriers to reach people but, on the other, he was clear in his dealings with them! 'Neither do I condemn you,' he said to the adulterous woman (very postmodern – but more profoundly, grace without conditions), but he also said, 'Go now and leave your life of sin' (John 8:11). These boundaries set by Jesus in his moral teaching are surely largely unacceptable in today's world, and yet in the very places where our world often sets boundaries (between people, races and ethnic backgrounds, for example) Jesus set none. There were no boundaries in his quest to reach people in their need.

Others also speak against placing too clear an emphasis on the supernatural wonder of the Bible story. So will the moral boundaries of the Bible's teaching be too hard to swallow for today's generation bred on 'If it feels right, it's right' to quote Lionel Ritchie? Will an emphasis on the supernatural wonder of so much of what is recounted in Scripture turn people off? It might be thought so but, I am convinced, the evidence contradicts that conclusion.

I have been reading a book by the American sociologist Christian Smith.[3] Some of his conclusions provide fascinating food for thought:

1. 'Pluralistic modernity can promote the vitality of culturally well equipped traditional religions . . .'
2. 'Evangelicalism thrives in pluralistic modernity, we suggest, because it possesses and employs the cultural tools needed to create both clear distinction from and significant engagement and tension with other relevant groups, short of being counter-cultural . . .'
3. 'By contrast, the classical American fundamentalist strategy of isolationist separatism, and the theological liberal approach of radical accommodation appear to undermine those traditions' religious strength . . .'

4. 'Distinction with engagement appears to be the most effective strategy for maintaining religious vitality in the American culturally pluralistic environment.'

5. 'Embeddedness in relational networks of identity and obligation can help to hold the fabric of religious commitment and affiliation tight. Congruously, it is primarily relational disruptions that provoke religious disaffiliation and disenchantment when they do occur ...'

6. 'In the end, as an internal religious subculture, American evangelicalism thrives ...'

7. 'In America, strong religious subcultures like American evangelicalism will flourish into the foreseeable future ...'[4]

In other words, conviction Christianity, with a strong commitment to the authority of the Bible can and does thrive in the modern world when it engages with the world around it, and when it provides an attractive countercultural statement. 'Distinction' and 'engagement' are two seemingly contradictory ideas and yet both are at the heart of our evangelical gospel commitment. The distinctiveness of our commitment to Christ and to his Word in Scripture – our desire to live by, enjoy, and obey that Word – is clear to the world around us. Yet it is also from that very commitment to God and his revelation in Scripture that we find ourselves called by God to engage with our world. Though not 'of the world' (John 17:14), though constantly distinctive as 'aliens and strangers', we are also 'in the world' (1 Peter 2:11). Here we witness to our Lord and Saviour as people who have been called to be the 'light of the world' (Matthew 5:14), thus following in the footsteps of our Lord who 'desireth not the death of a sinner'[5] but rather that he may turn from sin to life.

We see an American sociologist arguing his case and we know what Scripture teaches on 'distinction' and 'engagement', yet we may still be tempted to question whether what is said to be true for America may also be true in postmodern Britain. We may accept the principle and yet question the practice. According to Christian Research, the only group growing in the English church is the group they refer to as 'mainstream evangelical'. They tell us this group has grown over the 1990s by 68 per cent![6] Furthermore, a recent survey carried out on behalf of Forward in Faith (a traditionalist Anglo-Catholic group in the Church of England), suggests that orthodox Christian and biblical belief is held most faithfully by definite evangelicals out of any grouping in the church! Surely, the evidence indicates that sound doctrine and growth are not necessarily enemies but friends! It is people who are credally and morally orthodox who are holding their own or gaining ground.

Engagement comes as this commitment to the truth of the Bible goes hand in hand with a passion to work out our faith in service in the world in which we live. We must work with people and for people as we live out the gospel that we preach and teach within our church communities but also within our social communities. Certainly, we must also build imaginative bridges to our neighbours and friends who are not yet believers, and who we hope and pray will come to faith. This engagement is 'daring' to us as we maintain our distinctive and clear commitment to the Lord Jesus Christ and yet work in our world among and with friends and neighbours who perhaps know nothing of Christ or have already rejected what little they may have heard of him.

None of this should really surprise us. For when we look at Scripture we see the difference that conviction makes to evangelistic enterprise. Acts 4 provides a clear example. The early Christians were in danger. Their leaders Peter and John were imprisoned; then threatened and released, having been warned not to speak anymore in the name of Jesus (Acts 4:17). They must have wondered whether they would end up being crucified like Jesus!

In this chapter, we have a fascinating insight into the life of the early church (4:24ff.). If it had been me, I would have prayed for personal safety or, at the very best, safety for other believers. But their prayer contains no such request. The nearest we get to that is in verse 29 – 'consider their threats'! There is no preoccupation with 'personal peace and affluency' (to use Francis Schaeffer's memorable phrase). Rather, their preoccupation is fashioned by the Easter event. Even their prayer is fashioned by the content of the message they were preaching and which had thrilled them – the resurrection of

Jesus (4:2, 33). Here then is what makes them 'distinctive' and drives them forward to 'engagement'.

Good Friday had looked to the disciples like a terrible tragedy, but Easter Sunday had showed them otherwise! The resurrection was the vindication of all that Jesus had said and done. God had raised him from the dead. And in the light of whom they now, very clearly, saw Jesus to be, there was nothing more important for them than to seek to obey their risen Lord who had so loved them. It is not surprising that their thoughts and prayers go back to his final command 'go and make disciples'. So their prayer in Acts 4 is dominated by their request to God to fulfil his promise to give them strength to carry out their Saviour's agenda, 'enable your servants to speak your word with great boldness' (4:29).

It is the disciples' conviction of who Jesus is and what he has done for them, and that he is the living, reigning Lord who has conquered death and opened heaven to them, that fires their preaching and their evangelistic zeal. They see with great clarity that 'Salvation is found in no-one else, for there is no other name under heaven given to men by which we must be saved' (4:12).

Their profound convictions motivated them. These fuelled their prayer life and their determination to tell a lost world the good and saving news of Jesus. In Acts 4 we see the church as it is meant to be. This same agenda is the Lord's agenda for the church of our own day.

It has been my observation over 25 years of parochial ministry and 5 years as a bishop that when passionate commitment to and belief in Scripture and in the biblical apostolic testimony to the life, death and resurrection of Jesus grows in people's hearts, then they have a new desire to engage with serious, creative and imaginative mission. As their confidence and joy in Christ grows, they cannot be silenced, for they live for him and speak for him among all those they meet.

As I look at the New Testament and at my own experience it is clear to me that evangelism never really works when only left to a few – it needs to be the vision caught by the whole people of God. It is when we are collectively praying, longing and working to see people won for Christ that things begin to happen. The fuel for that fire is a Holy Spirit-given, deepening conviction and confidence in the truth of the Bible and the gospel message about Jesus. Trust in and instruction from the Bible, modelled in the pulpit, causes Christians to grow and engage with the evangelistic task and the world around.

Currently, we are seeking to encourage each other to a deeper commitment to Scripture – a commitment that will build and help us clarify our 'distinctive' life as Christians under Christ's sovereign lordship. But this deeper commitment to Scripture will also encourage us to ever greater 'engagement' as we follow our Lord into this world. Some were afraid that stressing 'Bible' and 'cross' as major themes in this book was to fall into the trap of looking backwards and living in the past rather than the present and future, but such a view is entirely to miss the point: that true and profitable 'engagement' with today's world springs out of a commitment to the Word of God and the encouragement it provides. It springs out of the challenge the Word of God provides and the 'distinctiveness' of life and obedience it demands.

We are also seeking to encourage each other through a deeper commitment to 'the cross', that is, to the Christ who died in our place and who bore the penalty for our sin. The distinctiveness of this commitment reminds us that our salvation is entirely of grace. It also reminds us that we too are asked to follow the way of the cross. Yet this also draws us again to 'engagement', for the cross is the ultimate demonstration of God's engagement with his created people – that he should be prepared to come among us and die for us.

In this book we are also seeking to encourage each other to a deeper commitment to, and understanding of 'mission'. Of course, this cannot possibly be separated from 'Bible', or 'cross'. Indeed as we share the commitment of the disciples in Acts 4, we begin to understand more of that heart of God and his desire for people to experience his love and gracious forgiveness, and so we are encouraged and our confidence is built up to be distinctively biblical in our commitment to 'Christ crucified' and as fully 'engaged' with our world as the Christ who has gone before us.

In conclusion, let me share with you some personal experiences of how I have seen distinctive Christian biblical commitment lead to engagement, first of all in my own ministry.

In a large youth group in Cheadle, Staffordshire, it was a growing conviction about the truth in Jesus (revealed in Scripture) that enabled us to take our courage in our hands and reach out to 12 local schools in some daring evangelism, which was wonderfully blessed by God. It was a renewal in faith that fed the reaching of others with the gospel.

A little later, it was the growing conviction of the truth of the gospel and the change in people's lives that enabled us to pray and reach out to our community in Audley, Staffordshire, where I was the second evangelical vicar in 700 years!

For us, it was a deepening conviction not just to be evangelical in name, not just to be 'Bible believing' and 'cross centred', but to be so *in practice* that caused us to rejig our whole mission agenda at Harold Wood, London, where I served my next incumbency. Among other things, this caused us to engage far more seriously with youth work and a generation of unchurched young people. Our experience was truly extraordinary when we stepped out with just a little faith, determined to obey the Great Commission, for we were met with the goodness of God already at work opening doors for us. I would love to tell you how we obtained a community centre, due to be sold for a million pounds, for £1 per year for 20 years! It was only the courage brought about through renewed conviction in the relevance and power of the Word of God that motivated and compelled us.

In my work as a bishop I have seen the same. I think of a successful country village church, somewhat isolated, that has had biblical preaching and faithful pastoring. This church has grown significantly. Rural situations can be hard and discouraging but this church is a shining example of what can be done. The incumbent has now just retired, but people have said, 'Please get us a vicar that believes, teaches and practises the Bible. It is that that has caused us to grow!' It is that passion that has caused love and effective outreach to grow in the church.

I think of another church in my area of East Sussex that has built and financed a two-and-a-quarter-million-pound extension. What is the secret? People thrilled by the gospel of grace, the influence of excellent and effective Bible teaching, and the consequent release of vision, giving and outreach that has proved so effective.

We tend to forget that in the New Testament sound doctrine is literally 'healthy' doctrine. It relates to the health of the church. It is when the written Word is loved, listened to, respected and obeyed that people grow, empowered by the Holy Spirit, in love and obedience to the living Word, the Lord Jesus himself.

There is a deep attractiveness in those who believe their faith in the way the apostles believed it, and whose lives show the change that it brings about. It is when we have confidence in the Bible as trustworthy that we begin to have a deep conviction to motivate us to take seriously our Lord's commission to go into our bit of the world in his name and in his strength.

Notes

[1] David Eby, *Power Preaching for Church Growth. The Role of Preaching in Growing Churches,* Fearn, Mentor, 1998.

[2] John Stott, *I Believe in Preaching*, London, Hodder and Stoughton, 1982, p. 115.

[3] Christian Smith, *American Evangelicalism, Embattled and Thriving*, Chicago, University of Chicago Press, 1998.

[4] Ibid., pp. 218–20.

[5] Book of Common Prayer, 1662. From the Absolution at Morning Prayer.

[6] See *UK Christian Handbook, Religious Trends No. 2*, 2001–2002, London, Harper Collins, p. 12.3.

Cross

Part Two

Chapter Seven

The Cross, the Centre

Chris Green

In this chapter Chris Green opens the section on the cross by show-ing that evangelicals are defined by being Bible-bound, united by being cross-centred and inspired by being mission-minded. He then shows how, within the range of biblical material on God's relation-ship to sinful people, his holy attitude to sin, and his saving solution through the atonement, Jesus' bearing the penalty for our sin is the central belief that the Bible identifies as the key to all the others.

Introduction

Each of the themes in this book, the Bible, the Cross and Mission, can make a valid claim to being its heartbeat, and that is quite right. Any movement or organization can be explored in a number of comple-mentary ways, but these three are particularly vital to us, because God is truthful, just and loving, and the one who rightly rules our world. But perhaps examining them slightly distinctly might be useful for us. To see the Bible as our boundary, beyond which we shall not stray and up to which we must live; the cross as our centre, from which everything we believe and do flows; and mission as our task, to which we are all committed, explains why each one can rightly claim to be crucial to our identity as evangelicals, and why each is crucial in a different way.

Three Central Themes

First, we might identify the limits we place around ourselves. That is an unpopular thing to do in a culture that prefers fuzzy edges, and the evangelical Anglican identity problem, as J. I. Packer famously called it,[1] has been a pressing issue for us since the first National Evangelical Anglican Congress in 1967. There are still disagreements among us over whether we are primarily Anglicans who happen by conviction to be evangelicals, or evangelicals who happen by conviction to be Anglicans. But they are disagreements among those who are otherwise in considerable agreement. What is characteristic of evangelical thinking is the way we solve such issues, by appealing to the Bible as God's final and complete authority,[2] and we work on the assumption that his answers can be found there, clearly and consistently. The Bible is God's finished Word to his people.

So whether a debate is over the content of creeds ruling out certain positions as untenable for Christians, the Reformers laying out the theology of justification, a home group discussion of the work of the Holy Spirit or a contemporary evangelical contribution to a Deanery Synod, the careful and thoughtful appeal to the Bible is a final and adequate one. The reason why this is characteristic of evangelical theology is that the question of the relative authorities of tradition, reason, church hierarchy, church councils, personal experience and the Bible were hammered out at the Reformation. Those, such as the Church of England's first theologians, who appealed to the sole sovereignty of the Bible over all those other authorities, called themselves 'evangelical'. Although the word was new, the pattern of thinking was, they claimed, as old as mainstream Christianity itself, and can be observed in such pivotal theologians as Tertullian, Athanasius, Hilary and Augustine. People with other assumptions may quote the Bible, but it is dangerously possible to quote the Bible in a way that leaves the one quoting in charge. As Hilary noted, we can easily let our desires rule Scripture and not the other way round (*De Trinitate* 10.1). The Bible has in that case stopped being the voice of God and become a pet or token, or even worse, a pawn in a dangerous power game.

It is a defining characteristic of evangelicals, however, that we submit to the Bible in all matters and over all other authorities even – or perhaps especially – when we disagree with it, and that we are willing to make that commitment knowing that our understanding must constantly be corrected by God's Word. We make the commitment to submission in advance of knowing what the Bible may teach on a subject. And we happily restrict our thinking to what it says because it is characteristic of evangelical thinking that the Word of God, which shatters all human thought structures, replaces it with a coherent one of God's own making which must be explored and understood, and that this new framework is God's good provision for us. As Article 20 puts it, the Bible is 'God's Word written'. Evangelicals are *Bible-bound people.*[3]

Second, we might identify ourselves by our core beliefs. Any number of evangelical organizations has done that for themselves, with an impressive array of doctrinal bases and statements. They vary in length and detail, but I describe them as impressive because of the substantial agreement on one thing: however much they may disagree, say, over God's timings at the beginning of the world or its end, that Jesus' death is central to what we believe is non-negotiable.

Some may wonder whether this 'centre' is too narrow. After all, Paul said, 'if Christ has not been raised, your faith is futile; you are still in your sins' (1 Corinthians 15:17). Perhaps we should make the resurrection central. And Paul also said, 'if anyone does not have the Spirit of Christ, he does not belong to Christ' (Romans 8:9), so perhaps we should make the Holy Spirit central. But that is to mistake cause and effect: it was because Christ was crucified for our sins that he was raised from the dead, and it was because he was raised from the dead that he was able to give us the Holy Spirit. We cannot separate those three out (and we might want to add other items to the chain too), and they are all three essential to being a Christian, but the cross is the formal cause of the other two. Without the cross the other two would not have happened. So we are not downplaying the resurrection or disparaging the work of the Spirit, and we are in continuity with the early church when we say that evangelicals are *cross-centred people.*

Third, we might identify ourselves by our purpose. There are many caricatures of evangelicalism around: Archbishop Robert Runcie famously observed that 'the Church of England is like a swimming pool, and all the noise comes from the shallow end' – and he meant us. Archbishop Rowan Williams has recently said, 'Sometimes you just need to sing "Blessed Assurance" and hit a tambourine' – and he meant us.[4] We are widely thought to be simplistic, naive, overconfident and triumphalistic. I pray that this book will show – as our history would also show – that whatever our many sins and stupidities, *at its best* evangelicalism is about a profound, authentic meeting with the living God, on his terms.

But for all the caricatures, we are always correctly understood to be concerned with mission, because we want others to meet the living God as their Saviour too. From the duty we each feel to tell our neighbours, through to considering major national and even international initiatives, evangelism and evangelicalism are seen as twins, even to the point of being confused. True, some accuse us of being unconcerned with social or political issues (a charge that has always been easier to make than to substantiate) or of only being concerned with numbers rather than individuals (again, show me the church where that is the case). But if we are asked why we Christians are here on earth, biblically bound and cross-centred answers will always be *mission-minded.*

These three do not attempt to be a final definition of evangelicalism, and we certainly have not paid enough attention to evangelicalism's authenticity as central Anglicanism, except for the few notes above that our position makes best sense of the Articles. There is no one settled definition of evangelicalism, and that is perhaps inevitable. The historian David Bebbington has famously proposed the quadrilateral of '*conversionism,* the belief that lives need to be changed; *activism,* the expression of the gospel in effort; *biblicism,* a particular regard for the Bible; and what may be called *crucicentrism,* a stress on the sacrifice of Christ on the cross'.[5] This quadrilateral has started to function as if it were the universally accepted definition, but it is important to note that although there has been widespread support for it, senior evangelicals such as John

Stott and Don Carson have expressed serious reservations about its adequacy.[6] Both, for instance, make the correct point that these four give the impression of evangelicals being theologically eccentric, obsessed with obscure debates, and do not highlight that evangelicals are doctrinally mainstream and (at our best) deeply trinitarian. Our understanding of creation, the church, or the work of the Spirit flow from a standard, orthodox theological understanding.[7] But perhaps the three aspects I have isolated will allow us to explore why evangelicalism is *distinctive within* orthodox Christianity because of the clarity with which we resolve the issue of authority, and perhaps show why we make the claim that 'we do not see ourselves as offering a new Christianity, but as recalling the Church to original Christianity'.[8]

The Cross, the Centre

This section of this volume allows the spotlight to fall on the cross of Christ and our claim that it is central to a loving relationship with the living God in a way that nothing else can be. The chapters that follow look at four ways this is worked out: Peter Ackroyd explores the implications of this as Anglicans, Andrew Cornes explores the implications as disciples, Rico Tice explores our message to others, and Gerald Bray examines whether the cross is central for us in reality, rather than in theory, as evangelicals.

But first we need to remind ourselves of the centrality of the cross. We are a forgetful people, sometimes by accident and sometimes by design, and, as Peter said, we need constant reminding of what is central (2 Peter 1:12–15). I want to explore this by way of six claims about the Bible's message about the cross, and each of these claims comes in two parts. The first part of each claim looks at the breadth of some aspect of God's truth, and this is so that we don't become obsessive and focus on one aspect of God's truth as if it were the only one. This is particularly true when we come to the cross itself, for the Bible has a breadth and depth that we need to acknowledge. The second part of each claim, though, does focus on one aspect of the truth as what I shall call the 'defining centre', by which I mean that the Bible does not allow us to choose which of the many aspects we prefer, but puts them in order, with some being more central than others, and often with one being the central truth under which all the others are ordered. Once that central truth is identified all the other truths must be seen in the light of it, which is what I mean by its being the *defining* centre. For example, there are many names and titles that God has in the Bible, but quite clearly some are more central than others. 'Lord' is more central than 'Rock'. Although the title 'Rock' is true, when implications from it clash with 'Lord', it is 'Lord' that is in charge. So, although he is a 'Rock', God is not impersonal, silent, unemotional, inscrutable or rooted to one place, all of which could flow from that title. Instead, the title 'Lord', and all that it means in relation to Israel, clarifies that the Lord our Rock is a person who speaks, loves and is known by us wherever we are, *but* he is also a safe and secure refuge in a time of attack. 'Lord' has a much better claim to be the defining centre of God's character than 'Rock' (Psalm 18:2).[9] Inevitably, all we can do in each section is touch on some relevant Bible passages, and in any study it would be good to search other places where these issues are explored.

There are many ways to describe God's attitude to humankind ...

God is the universal creator, who made everything and everyone. Right from the start, then, we can see that we should never invite a non-Christian to 'come into a relationship with God', because he or she is already in one. Everyone and everything stands in a relationship of utter dependence on God for their existence, and for the continuing natural order that allows them to live. People are made in his image and even the most stubbornly atheist worldview cannot stop its adherents working, speaking, loving and separating right from wrong. As Paul said in Athens, in his benchmark apologetic and evangelistic critique of culture, God 'himself gives all men life and breath and everything else' (Acts 17:25). God calls this intimate relationship with him 'love'. He loves people.

It is not, of course, a love between equals, and no human relationship can do anything but reflect it in part. Perhaps we should tie together the themes of our utter dependence on him (which is not reciprocal) and yet his desire for our greatest good, by calling it 'Lordship Love'. That is why he can *command* us to *love,* and why our love for him is best expressed in obedience to his command. He is a God who shows 'love to a thousand [generations] of those who love me and keep my commandments' (Exodus 20:6). 'If you love me,' said Jesus 'you will obey what I command' (John 14:15).

God's love needs to be defined in God's way, because it would be easy to misread it as an indulgent affection or even as if God needed human love to satisfy some deep need in himself. Paul was quite clear in his Athenian speech that this God is 'the Lord of heaven and earth' (Acts 17:24), and far from being dependent on us, we are dependent on him. He does not need us to build homes for him, as even some Christians have claimed for their buildings, because he made the very home we live in. Nor does he need us to provide our gifts for him to do his work 'as if he needed anything' (Acts 17:25), for he gave us everything. So supreme is this lordship that Paul can speak in the capital city of a nation that had known nothing of biblical revelation, and had developed a philosophy, theology and political system that were completely at odds with it, and still say that God had made their nation and controlled their history and geography (Acts 17:26). In other words, Greece, the nation that is still the most widely acclaimed example of what humanity can achieve in wisdom, beauty and architecture, and which has consistently been held up for the last two thousand years as the best humane alternative to Christianity, is utterly dependent on the Lord Jesus for every one of its achievements.

Paul spoke in national terms here, but elsewhere the Bible affirms that God is intimately involved with every aspect of every person of every nation of the world, and he not only knows every individual's thoughts, actions, and destinies (Psalm 94, especially vv. 8–11) but plans the most minute and apparently random detail (Proverbs 16:33).

There are many ways to describe God's attitude to humankind, but judgement is the defining centre

Paul's next evangelistic move is as daring today as it was then, and it should not surprise us if we have paid close attention to what he has said. He casually summed up the wisdom of Aristotle and Plato, the mythological poetry of Homer, the architectural grace of the Parthenon, the Athenian sculptors, priests and poets as 'ignorance' (Acts 17:30). Not ignorance in the sense that we have nothing to learn from them, but wilful, culpable ignorance. They ought to have known better, as some of their own poets had remarked (Acts 17:28), but they had stumbled blindly on. Now, though, the situation has changed, because God's attitude towards them has moved on. No longer is God willing to 'overlook' such ignorance. He has changed the context of the world and the message is now one of imminent and very particular judgement. So, says Paul, 'Repent' (Acts 17:30).

Two factors make it possible to say that judgement is the defining centre of God's relation to the world. The first is that the massive backdrop to the whole history of humankind from God's perspective is our rebellion against him. He is our creator and Lord to whom we owe obedience, and yet our race has stood up against him. Furthermore, he is by his nature a Holy God, who views our rebellion as not only deeply affronting but deeply wrong. As a Holy God who is true and right, he must find our rebellion wrong. And that brings the language of the law court centre stage in our dealings with him. Amid the range of truths about us, the one that defines all the others, in the sense that it determines and gives proportion to all the others, is that we are guilty. Hurt, broken, fallible, loved, stumbling, seeking, yes – but none of those contradicts, mutes or subtracts from the word 'guilty'.

The second factor that makes it possible to say that judgement is the defining centre is that Paul ties this motif of judgement to the death and resurrection of Jesus. His enthronement as Lord and Saviour makes judgement of the guilty more, not less, likely, precisely because he is the one whom God has made the judge (Acts 17:31). We shall need to come back to this, but it does begin to explain the curious feature of evangelism in Acts that the message of Jesus is often met as bad news (Acts 2:37) before it is rejoiced in as good news (Acts 2:46–47).

So the first question we should ask ourselves is whether our evangelism sufficiently centres on judgement. It is not enough for it to be one motif among many, or for us to choose a more positive and affirming way into people's lives. This is the first thing God wants people to know about themselves, because they then know both his verdict on them, and that their own unaided thoughts cannot come to a true knowledge of him. As we have seen, God's Word shatters our human idolatrous thinking, and replaces it not with a silence or a question, but a glorious and life-giving truth.

There are many things God has done for humankind ...

God is, as the basis for Paul's argument shows, our intimate creator. Creator, because God 'made the world and everything in it' and 'made every nation of men'; intimate, because this was not a remote, long-gone creation by a blind watchmaker, but an ongoing sustaining of each individual by God, 'in whom we live and move and have our being' (Acts 17:24–8). Jesus reminds us that we are dependent on God for our food and warmth (Matthew 6:23–34), and that he extends this loving Fatherly care to every person he has made (Matthew 5:45).

So we should never think or act as if God were only interested in some small, religious element in our lives, or that having food and warmth is an irrelevance. On the basis of God's overarching and generous provision, Christians must be people who are concerned to feed the hungry and shelter the cold. As James writes:

> What good is it, my brothers, if a man claims to have faith but has no deeds? Can such faith save him? Suppose a brother or sister is without clothes and daily food. If one of you says to him, 'Go, I wish you well; keep warm and well fed,' but does nothing about his physical needs, what good is it? In the same way, faith by itself, if it is not accompanied by action, is dead. (James 2:14–17)

Sharing food with the hungry is important. Nevertheless, this all-embracing care should not be taken as a more pleasant alternative to what we have already seen of God as Judge. He has the right to judge us precisely because he is our intimate creator, because he can prove from every scrap of our DNA that we are 'without excuse' (Romans 1:20). Nor should we accept the idea that sharing food and sharing the gospel are *equally* important, let alone be confused. Sharing the message of Jesus' death and resurrection must be presented verbally for it to be heard, understood and believed.

There are many things God has done for humankind, but Jesus is the defining centre

The reason is that the Bible identifies Jesus as both the Lord of creation, who sustains us, and as our Judge. 'The Son is the radiance of God's glory and the exact representation of his being, sustaining all things by his powerful word. After he had provided purification for sins, he sat down at the right hand of the Majesty in heaven' (Hebrews 1:3). And although we could equally find passages that locate the Father and the Holy Spirit as creator and sustainer of the universe, only the Son reigns *because he died for us and rose again.*

So although there are many things that God does for us, each of them is only truly seen for what it is when we see it in the light of Jesus' reign and judgement. There is no broad category of things 'God' does (and the name of any god would do for that general, providential care) and a narrow category of things 'Jesus' does (which he only does for Christians). No, everything that God did before and after Easter must be seen in the light of it, and everything God does today must be seen in the light of it.

This is worth stressing because Christians have a history of separating things out that God intends to join together. So we might hear someone talk of a 'creation mandate', which gives us a theology of work and leisure from Genesis 1:28, alongside the 'Great Commission' from the Gospels, which tells us to make disciples. But there is no 'creation mandate' outside the gospel. Humankind was commanded to 'Be fruitful and increase in number; fill the earth and subdue it. Rule over the fish of the sea and the birds of the air and over every living creature that moves on the ground' (Genesis 1:28), and that was fulfilled in Jesus, when God 'raised him from the dead and seated him at his right hand in the heavenly realms, far above all rule and authority, power and dominion, and every title that can be given, not only in the present age but also in the one to come. And God placed all things under his feet and appointed him to be head over everything for the church, which is his body, the fullness of him who fills everything in every way' (Ephesians 1:20–3). The existence of the church, believers, is the fulfilment of that Genesis 1 trajectory, and the command to 'Fill the earth and subdue it' finds its New Testament echo in the Great Commission. Not two mandates, but one, because everything relates through the gospel of Jesus.

There are many things Jesus has done ...

So if we take the largest possible view, everything that God has done for any part of creation has been effected by the work of his Son, 'whom he appointed heir of all things, and through whom he made the universe ... sustaining all things by his powerful word' (Hebrews 1:2–3). And if we narrow that a little and enquire about the plan for salvation, again we find that the risen Jesus is the focus. As he explained to his followers after his resurrection, 'beginning with Moses and all the Prophets, he explained to them what was said in all the Scriptures concerning himself'. And later that same day, he said that 'Everything must be fulfilled that is written about me in the Law of Moses, the Prophets and the Psalms'(Luke 24:27, 44). So Jesus saw himself as the defining centre of the Old Testament.

That explains the extraordinary authority with which he handled the Old Testament, at one and the same moment lifting the laws that marked Israel out racially, and reinforcing the ones that marked her out morally (Mark 7:17–23). He could disregard the Sabbath laws to heal, or even feed, his people, but take people behind the laws to the groundwork of creation to underline the permanence of marriage (Mark 2:23–3:6; 10:1–12). It is important for us to notice as Anglicans that this way of handling the Law is not a mark of evangelical inconsistency but goes back to Jesus himself, as the Articles noted (Article 7).

Even given the selectivity that the Gospel writers impose on themselves, the ministry of Jesus is vast in its impact. Mark, for instance, notices that however many people came to hear John the Baptist, the areas from which people flooded to hear Jesus was much greater (Mark 1:5; 3:8). That impact has continued today, not merely in the growing numbers who continue to flood to him, but in the profound way his teaching enables us to address contemporary problems. Jesus does not mention child prostitution, mass terrorism, human cloning, homosexuality or biological warfare, but many millions of people rightly address those questions with his instructions in mind.

There are many things Jesus has done, but his death is the defining centre

Yet for all the breadth of his life, teaching and ministry, Jesus was clear that on their own they would not accomplish his central work. Even within that range of activity he operates with a priority, because, as he explained to Peter, 'Let us go somewhere else – to the nearby villages – so that I can preach there also. That is why I have come' (Mark 1:38). But within that range of teaching it is clear that one event takes priority, and Mark has structured his Gospel to show that. Mark notices that the three clear predictions of Jesus' death and resurrection are the central elements of Jesus' teaching (Mark 8:31; 9:31; 10:45),[10] and another comes as the pressure increases in the final days in Jerusalem (Mark 14:27–8). It is also notable that Mark opens his Gospel with Jesus described as the Son of God, which is clarified at both his baptism and his transfiguration, but reaches its climax in the recognition of that title by a Gentile centurion as Jesus hung on his cross (Mark 1:1, 11; 9:7; 15:39).

So when Jesus explained that the whole Old Testament pointed to him, he was quite specific, as those three predictions make clear. In each it is the 'Son of Man' who 'must' suffer, and both the title and the plan show deep Old Testament roots.[11] In the Luke passages we looked at above the prediction was that 'the Christ [would] have to suffer these things and then enter his glory' (Luke 24:26), and this became a main theme in the early church's preaching from Acts 2 onwards.

For us, as for the early Christians, it is difficult to learn this important lesson. Important as all the other things that Jesus said and did are, it is the death that explains everything else, and which therefore demands to be central. Both the creeds that we say most Sundays, and the third authorized creed, the Athanasian, leap from Jesus' birth to his death, not because they are denying that Jesus taught or did miracles, and certainly not because belief in them is optional,[12] but because without the Virgin birth, sin-bearing death, and resurrection they are empty. Once again, we meet a defining centre.

There are many ways to describe Jesus' relationship with sinful humankind ...

Of all the actions of Jesus that caused scandal, it was his actions as 'a glutton and a drunkard, a friend of tax collectors and "sinners"' (Luke 7:34) that lay at the root of the offence. He was both tolerant and blasphemous. Here was a man who claimed not only to be the great teacher, but to exercise God's authority on earth, and who chose to exercise it in letting people off the hook (Luke 5:24). It is a theme particularly important to Luke in his Gospel.

This is a very important starting point for those who wish to construct a 'moral' picture of Jesus, as a great and good man, and it cuts two ways. To those who want to use him to define themselves as 'good enough for Jesus' and others as 'too bad for Jesus', he reminds us that he does not operate with those categories. The only people he will meet and forgive are those who will describe themselves as needing his help. 'Jesus answered them, "It is not the healthy who need a doctor, but the sick. I have not come to call the righteous, but sinners to repentance"' (Luke 5:31–2).

By the same token, though, Jesus claims the right to describe us as we are, sick sinners. There are no people whom he accepts on their own terms, with a mild smile and a welcoming embrace. To say that

Jesus 'accepts us as we are' is a mistaken emphasis, because it implies that we are acceptable as we are, which we are not. We are acceptable only as those who recognize their sin and their need of forgiveness.

There are many ways to describe Jesus' relationship with sinful humankind, but penalty-bearing self-substitution is the defining centre

If that is the case, then the question emerges about how Jesus is able to forgive, and the answer comes in two parts. First, we need to understand, as we have seen, that among the whole range of things sin has done, its first and greatest impact was the destruction of a loving relationship with God and its replacement with one that has offended his loving holiness to its infinite heart. Again, the note of the defining centre should be sounded, because there are many other aspects of sin, and many other aspects of God's relationship with sinners, but the offence against God's holiness is the point from which all else derives. Sin is the attempt to murder God and replace him with an idol of our own making that will allow us to make our own moral laws and break them with impunity.

The second part of Jesus' authority to forgive lies in his death as bearing that penalty in our place. The lesson is as old and as long as the Bible story itself. Sacrifice after sacrifice taught the lesson that an individual sinner could transfer his or her sins on to an animal, laying hands on it, and it died in that person's place (e.g. Leviticus 4:14–15, as one example among many). When the remnants of the temple system collapsed in the great destruction of the captivity and exile in Babylon, Judah was taught that she, who thought of herself as God's servant, was bearing her own sins but that another sinless Servant would come who would bear her sins for her (Isaiah 52–3).[13]

Within Luke's Gospel it is the parable of the Pharisee and the tax collector that most clearly deals with sin and forgiveness (Luke 18:10–14), and that contains the approved attitude, 'But the tax collector stood at a distance. He would not even look up to heaven, but beat his breast and said, "God, have mercy on me, a sinner."' We should notice the basis for this forgiveness, which the NIV obscures. The Greek word it has translated 'have mercy' *(hilasthēti)* means more clearly 'be propitiated', and has all the overtones of God's wrath being turned aside that the word usually implies in the New Testament (e.g. Romans 3:25; Hebrews 2:17; 1 John 2:2; 4:10).

Of course it is illegitimate to pluck one parable out of its Gospel context and use it as the key to explain everything else, although that is often done with Jesus' parables, most notably the parable of the prodigal son. But we should notice that Jesus, in the precise context of his death, revealed himself as that Servant whom Isaiah prophesied (Luke 22:27). The Gospels describe a story with a plot, and the climax of each is the cross. Here in Luke each part of the story builds towards it until the crucifixion itself, where he makes it so clear it is unmissable. Who is the first beneficiary of Jesus' death? Barabbas, a man who should have been killed for his murder and insurrection (Luke 23:25).[14] And in case Luke's readers misunderstand him, the second beneficiary is also a criminal (Luke 23:40–3). Jesus has borne a condemned man's punishment, and because of that a guilty man can enter Paradise. That he did this willingly needs to be emphasized, because some parody the evangelical doctrine as if we were saying that Jesus changed the Father's mind, or that the Father was guilty of some cosmic child abuse in mounting the salvation plan. But the thrust of the Gospels is clear. This was a task that Jesus willingly took on himself and, whatever the price, carried through, and that the Father eternally approved. Hence the clumsy but necessary qualification '*self*-substitution'.

There are many ways to describe the result of Jesus' death ...

This way of talking about Jesus' death as our penalty-bearing substitute, or the Doctrine of Penal Substitution as it is technically known, is one of the touchstones of evangelicalism. It is this partly because it is central to the work of Christ, but also because it so goes against our common sense that it is one of the first doctrines that people leave when they wish to cease being evangelical. It is so profoundly offensive to be told that we are such radically condemned sinners that only God's loving self-substitution in the person of his Son can save us, that we want to find alternative ways of explaining things.

There are, of course, many ways of describing the death of Jesus, and it does not take long to come up with a list of concepts such as 'sacrifice', 'redemption', 'love', 'servanthood', 'example' or 'victory'. They are all true, and have at various times been reclaimed and brought to Christians' notice. The danger, though, is to imagine that each has an equal claim to be the defining centre.

Take, for instance 'redemption'. It is a strong biblical word with rich background elements. It is a financial word loaded with ideas of slavery and domineering ownership. Animals due to be sacrificed could be bought back for a redemption price. When Judah was in captivity in Babylon she understood herself to be in bondage and in need of a redeemer – one who would pay the price of her freedom to her captors and buy her freedom, which is what redeemers do.

Jesus is in that sense our Redeemer. We were enslaved captives and Jesus paid the price of our freedom (Galatians 3:13). But if we start to probe more we see that we are dealing here with a metaphor, a picture. As Peter wrote, 'For you know that it was not with perishable things such as silver or gold that you were redeemed from the empty way of life handed down to you from your forefathers, but with the precious blood of Christ, a lamb without blemish or defect' (1 Peter 1:18–19). To talk of Jesus' death as a 'price' or to compare it with gold or silver automatically shows both what is true in the picture (that Jesus' death was precious) and also where the picture breaks down.

Many descriptions of Jesus' death function like that, but others are not metaphors and they do not break down. The ones to do with God's wrath, for instance, are non-metaphorical, as are the ones to do with God's victory. But if, as we have seen, God's offended holiness is central to his attitude to my sin *because it is central to his character,* then language to do with guilt and the law, God's judgement and our salvation from that judgement are non-metaphorical too. They can claim to be the defining centre.[15]

There are many ways to describe the result of Jesus' death, but justification is the defining centre

The term that most clearly defines the legal impact of the work of the cross is 'justification'. When the Pharisee and the tax collector went back to their homes, Jesus noted that it was the tax collector who 'went home justified before God' (Luke 18:14). It means that a guilty person is treated as if he or she were innocent, and the language finds its origin in God's final courtroom on Judgement Day. Christians know that they live today as God's forgiven people because they know (on the basis of Jesus' death for them) what God's gracious verdict on them will be then, and they can dare to be confident. That is not presumptuous, because it is based on God's faithfulness to his own promise, not on our good efforts. If God is not faithful, there is no assurance, and in believing his promise of justification we believe that he will continue to act in line with his revealed character. In short, that God will be God. When someone is justified on the basis of the cross, God's wrath for his sin is placed on Jesus (like Barabbas's model) and Jesus' righteousness is placed on him (like the forgiven thief's model). This double imputation is the heart of the cross. As Paul says, God 'did this to demonstrate his justice, because in his forbearance he had left the sins committed beforehand unpunished – he did it to demonstrate his justice at the present time, so as to be just and the one who justifies those who have faith in Jesus' (Romans 3:25–6).

There is a high price to be paid, then, when we are tempted to say that justification is merely one model of the cross among many, or that its legal language is unusable today, or that other models are preferable. Neutral terms such as 'atonement' or 'peace-making' can deny the reality of God's hatred of sin. Even the little phrase 'God hates sin but loves the sinner' does not adequately penetrate to the core of the problem, which is that God hates sinners even while he loves them:

> The Lord examines the righteous,
>> but the wicked and those who love violence
>> his soul hates. (Psalm 11:5)

There are many things believers are to do ...

We have simply two duties – to love God and to love our neighbours – but from those two spring a limitless range of ways to praise God by obeying him. The Bible is not moralistic, so we are never told to do things without a gospel reason, but equally it is never theoretical, and the gospel always has gospel consequences. This is most transparent with some of the letters where, for instance, Ephesians knits Paul's theology of marriage and his theology of the church together, and shows how they are both derived from the death of Jesus. When a parochial church council considers their agenda against the action list of Hebrews 13 or compares their relationships with those in 1 John, they know that they can never reach the point of having successfully completed one area of discipleship, but that they are exploring the impact of the gospel.

If we lift our eyes from the personal or the congregational to national or international affairs, not only is the necessity of implementing the commands for justice and care evident, so is the bewilderingly complex response from Christians. If there ever was a Christian who said that all we should ever do is evangelize, that person has manifestly lost the argument.

There are many things believers are to do, but proclaiming the penalty-bearing, substitutionary, justifying death of the Lord Jesus is the defining centre

Once again, though, we are faced with the biblical material that forces us to prioritize and not merely to balance out these tasks. This will not allow us to excuse ourselves from some duty or other, but it will help us see some biblical logic and order so we can think clearly. So far we have sketched in material from Mark and Luke, and here we can add something distinctive from Matthew and John. Matthew 28:18–20 gives us his famous Great Commission, and the pattern of what Jesus intends is crystal clear:

> All authority in heaven and on earth has been given to me.
> Therefore go and make disciples of all nations, baptizing them

in the name of the Father and of the Son and of the Holy Spirit, and teaching them to obey everything I have commanded you. And surely I am with you always, to the very end of the age.

Everything in that Commission that we are to do depends on Jesus' ultimate authority, and he exercises that authority in the first place by commanding us to make more disciples for him. That can be done only by making clear who he is and what he has done, and by people being converted. Evangelism is therefore the defining centre. In consequence of their conversion, disciples do not merely learn but *obey everything* that Jesus has commanded, which includes all the duties to God and neighbour that Matthew has presented. So the Great Commission is not a narrow command to make shallow converts but a broad and deep command to make wholehearted disciples on the pattern of Jesus' own disciple-making.

John's understanding of the task today is similarly logical. After Jesus' resurrection he said, '"Peace be with you! As the Father has sent me, I am sending you." And with that he breathed on them and said, "Receive the Holy Spirit. If you forgive anyone his sins, they are forgiven; if you do not forgive them, they are not forgiven"' (John 20:21–3). 'Sending' in John is a technical term which means that the Father commanded and the Son obeyed. Just as in Matthew, then, Jesus uses his risen authority to commission his disciples to go. The *basis* of their message is his resurrection (notice how he shows them his hands and sides to reinforce both halves of the message), the *content* of the message is 'Peace' (stated twice), and the *consequence* of the message is forgiveness and the gift of the Holy Spirit. John's Great Commission is gospel focused. How that is lived out, of course, is in terms of the servanthood that Jesus has patterned throughout the Gospels, but verbal proclamation is the defining centre of the task of those 'sent'.

Conclusion

This chapter has made six assertions: (1) there are many ways to describe God's attitude to humankind, but judgement is the defining centre; (2) there are many things that God has done for humankind, but Jesus is the defining centre; (3) there are many things that Jesus has done, but his death is the defining centre; (4) there are many ways to describe Jesus' relationship with sinful humankind, but penalty-bearing self-substitution is the defining centre; (5) there are many ways to describe Jesus' death, but justification is the defining centre; and (6) there are many things that believers are to do, but proclaiming the penalty-bearing, self-substitutionary, justifying death of the Lord Jesus is the defining centre. I pray these truths may excite and convict us once again.

Notes

[1] J. I. Packer, *The Evangelical Anglican Identity Problem: An Analysis*, Oxford, Latimer House, 1978.
[2] Both sides would agree that such an understanding is fundamental to being an Anglican. Cf. Articles 6, 21.
[3] This is, legally, the view of the Church of England. See Articles 6 and 20, and Canon A5.
[4] Rowan Williams made this comment in an interview reported in *The Melbourne Anglican* (June 2002) *www.media.anglican.com.au/tma/2002/2002_06/williams2.html*.
[5] D. W. Bebbington, *Evangelicalism in Modern Britain: A History from the 1930s to the 1980s*, London, Unwin Hyman, 1989, p. 3.
[6] John Stott, *Evangelical Truth*, Leicester, Inter-Varsity Press, 1999, pp. 27–28; D. A. Carson, *The Gagging of God*, Leicester, Apollos, 1996, pp. 449–50. Bebbington's historical analysis is being questioned too, see Garry J. Williams, 'Was Evangelicalism Created by the Enlightenment?' *Tyndale Bulletin* 53.2 (2002), pp. 283–312.
[7] That is, a Western, Catholic, Reformed, Protestant reading of orthodoxy, of course, but as the Reformers endeavoured to show, that is the true patristic heritage of the church on which the Reformed churches, such as the Church of England, were building.

8 John Stott, writing in David L. Edwards and John Stott, *Essentials: A Liberal–Evangelical Dialogue*, London, Hodder and Stoughton, 1988, p. 39.

9 The same case should be put against the title 'Mother', because mother-like characteristics are only occasionally attributed to God, and he is never addressed in those terms.

10 Each is followed by a section on being a disciple.

11 Daniel 7:13 is the most obvious starting point, but the title itself would imply a root back to Adam.

12 Hence the weakness of identifying what is *doctrinally* orthodox with what is *credally* orthodox. The creeds define orthodoxy against certain errors, but were powerless to resolve debate at the Reformation because both sides agreed on them. It is a weak argument to say that because an issue is not mentioned by the creeds it is a secondary issue.

13 Israel could not be this perfect servant because she was sinful herself.

14 The word 'released' has been a key to Jesus' ministry, Luke 4:18–19.

15 For an extended treatment of this subject see Chris Green, 'Incarnation and Mission', in *The Word Made Flesh: The 2002 Oak Hill School of Theology*, ed. D. Peterson, Carlisle, Paternoster, 2003.

Chapter Eight

Anglican Evangelicals and the Cross: From Reformation to Revival

Peter Ackroyd

Evangelicals are often portrayed as a new, and rather brash phenomenon, wedded to contemporary styles and a shallow modernity. Peter Ackroyd's chapter shows how the profound understanding of the cross called 'penal substitution' is as old as the Church of England itself, and is the centrepiece of its founding theology. When this theology has been understood clearly, it has always broken out in powerful revival and evangelism.

Alone in his room, a 19-year old student sat in despair. For the first time in his life, his spiritual bankruptcy had dawned on him, unarguable and without remedy. He felt wretched. Later, he would describe how this 'distress of mind continued for about three months, and well might have continued for years, since my sins were more in number than the hairs of my head'. He knew that before a holy God, he stood condemned, utterly unfit to enter his presence. He knew there was nothing he could do to repair the breach. Friends and books seemed to offer no help. Then, in his desperation, God found him:

> But in Easter week, as I was reading Bishop Wilson on the Lord's Supper, I met with an expression to this effect: 'That the Jews knew what they did when they transferred their sin to the head of their offering'. The thought rushed into my mind, What! may I transfer all my guilt to another? Has God provided an offering for me, that I may lay my sins on his head? then, God willing, I will not bear them on my own soul one moment longer. Accordingly I sought to lay my sins upon the sacred head of Jesus; and on the Wednesday began to have a hope of mercy; on the Thursday that hope increased; on the Friday and Saturday it became more strong; and on the Sunday morning (Easter-day, April 4) I awoke early with these words on my heart and lips, 'Jesus Christ is risen today; Hallelujah! Hallelujah!' From that hour peace flowed in rich abundance into my soul; and at the Lord's table in our chapel I had the sweetest access to God through my blessed Saviour.[1]

The year was 1779, and the student's name Charles Simeon. He never forgot how he realized that the cross reveals the holy God to be a God of mercy and love. He never lost the joy and amazement of forgiveness through Christ's death in his place. And his delight in the grace of God in the cross fuelled a remarkable ministry. Before completing his studies, Simeon was vicar of Holy Trinity church, Cambridge. For 54 years, he proclaimed the gospel of Christ crucified among its people, from the pulpit, in midweek meetings, and with individuals. More, he also transformed the Church of England, deliberately inspiring and encouraging hundreds of students into cross-centred Christian service, modelling a ministry built around warm-hearted and searching expository preaching, and ensuring that the right of appointing the incumbent in dozens of parishes remained in evangelical hands.

Half-forgotten today, Charles Simeon nevertheless remains relevant to us. In his day, many evangelicals were tempted to lose confidence in the Church of England. The new streams of spiritual life generated by the preaching of John Wesley, George Whitefield and others, were flowing away from the spiritually moribund established church, which had often, shamefully, obstructed their ministry. The future of biblical, living Christianity seemed to lie in nonconformity. As Simeon soon found, some evangelicals remained within the Church of England. But more than any other, his ministry marked the turn of the tide. He recognized that the message of the crucified Saviour which had saved him was no novelty, but lay at the heart of the Church of England's doctrine and liturgy. And so he laboured, by forceful example and dynamic instruction, to encourage evangelicals to reclaim the established church for this gospel.

Simeon's account of his conversion shows that the cross was at the heart of his faith. Indeed, the description indicates that he held to the traditional understanding of the cross as the place where Christ willingly bore our punishment – penal substitution. 'The lost state of man by nature and his recovery through the blood of Christ are the two principal doctrines of our religion,' he wrote. And for Simeon, penal substitution was not one model among many, but the central doctrine: 'As all the iniquities of all the children of Israel were transferred to the scape-goat under the law, that he might bear them away into the land of oblivion, so were all the sins of the whole human race transferred to Christ, that, having borne the curse for them, he might take them away from us for ever.'[2] The cross is the costly, loving act of both Father and Son, in which the punishment due to us from the Father's hand is borne by the Son. As such, it was for Simeon the central theme of the Bible, sufficient for a lifetime of meditation, nourishment, and ministry.

Though unfamiliar to many of his contemporaries, and unwelcome to many – his own church wardens prevented people from occupying the church pews to hear him! – the penal substitutionary doctrine of the cross was not new. Simeon saw himself as upholding the plain message of Scripture, not as an innovator. He was confident that his belief coincided with the biblical position, and was the doctrine of the Church of England, as established and upheld by Anglican evangelicals for hundreds of years. Other chapters in this volume examine the biblical basis of the doctrine; in this chapter we track the commitment of Simeon and his evangelical Anglican forebears to its message.

A Reformation Invention?

Though this understanding of the atonement received its fullest expression in the sixteenth century, its roots stretch back much further. Recent research has shown that almost all the theologians of the church's first six centuries taught that on the cross, Christ bore the punishment for sin in our place – penal substitution.[3] So while the doctrine received particular attention during the Reformation, it was not the invention of the Reformers. Like Simeon, they aimed to recover and teach no more than the message of Scripture, and found that their discoveries corresponded to the teaching of the early church.

The contribution of the Reformation was to identify and describe penal substitution from the Bible more thoroughly than ever before. The reason is not difficult to understand. The definition of doctrine can be compared with learning to ride a bicycle: experience precedes full understanding. Just as a child experiences riding a bicycle before she can explain the mechanical process, so the church through its deep acquaintance with Scripture knows the core of its beliefs long before its theologians scrutinize, explore and expound them in detail. In other words, the church, like the individual believer, is always playing theological 'catch-up'. Over time, it develops integrated explanations for what it sees and experiences through the Scriptures, clearing up misunderstandings, and spotlighting unbiblical – and therefore dangerous – beliefs. It is very often controversy that generates this doctrinal definition. In the fourth century, for example, the Arian heresy drove the church to clarify its beliefs about the person of Christ – his divine and human natures. So it was with the doctrine of penal substitution in the sixteenth century. It was the arguments of the Reformation era – notably over justification – that drove the Reformers to spell out with pungent clarity what the church had always known from the Bible about the death of its Saviour and Lord.

In the English context, we can identify a twofold reason – biblical and historical – why since the age of Henry VIII, Anne Boleyn and Thomas Cranmer the cross has been firmly at the heart of Anglican belief and practice.

First, the Church of England shared in the Reformation recovery of the good news about Jesus Christ: that humanity's greatest need, the full forgiveness of sin that reconciles us with God, is given not earned. In theological language, we are justified by faith alone. And this is the case because salvation is entirely God's work, not ours: Jesus secured our rescue on the cross, bearing the penalty for sin that we should have paid. It is because of the cross that there is nothing to add, nothing to do. Christian faith, as often said, is an empty hand, joyfully held out to receive a free gift.

Second, the Church of England in the sixteenth century embedded this good news in its foundation documents, most significantly the Book of Common Prayer and the Thirty-Nine Articles. Justification by faith has been at the core of its corporate worship and doctrinal identity ever since, and so its theological foundation in the death of Christ for us has remained central to authentic Anglican spirituality.

Martin Luther and Thomas Cranmer

The Church of England claims that its faith is the faith of the Scriptures, no more, no less. When Thomas Cranmer and others affirmed its doctrinal basis in the sixteenth century, they aimed to restore the priority of the Bible in the church's life. In this, they deliberately followed in the footsteps of the continental Reformers.

It was the German monk Martin Luther, a professor in the university at Wittenberg, who realized that the Bible teaches justification by faith alone. This breakthrough, probably made in 1515, was electrifying for him. It was as though he had been peering through the viewfinder of a camera, seeing only blurred shapes and confused colours, and then discovered the focus button. The outlines and shape of God's plan of salvation suddenly leapt into focus, sharp, distinct and revolutionary. How sinners could be reconciled with God, until now a baffling blur owing to the doctrinal confusion of the late medieval church, was now clear.

One result was that the central place of the life and death of Jesus Christ in God's plan was revealed with a new sharpness. There was in principle little official disagreement over the person and work of

Jesus between the Reformers and their Catholic opponents. Everyone agreed that Jesus Christ was fully man and fully God, and that his death was the turning point of salvation. The great debate in the Reformation concerned not how salvation was achieved by God but how its benefits are received by men and women: by faith alone, or through the priestly sacramental system of the late medieval church.

But confusion over how we receive salvation had obscured the central place of the cross. Dependence on the sacraments, on the priesthood, on the church's penitential system, had replaced dependence on Christ and his work. The sufficiency and finality of Jesus' sacrifice was in practice downplayed.

Justification by faith alone restored the cross to centre stage. Luther himself highlighted the role of Christ's death in satisfying God's righteous wrath, taking on himself punishment for sin: 'But if he was to be priest and reconcile us with God through his priestly office, he had to satisfy God's righteousness for us. But no other satisfaction was possible than that he offered himself and died and in his own person conquered sin together with death.'[4]

Here we see how Luther recovered the traditional, 'catholic' (i.e. universally orthodox) understanding of Christ's death as the substitutionary bearing of God's wrath. He frequently quoted Galatians 3:13: 'Christ redeemed us from the curse of the law by becoming a curse for us – for it is written "Cursed is everyone who is hanged on a tree."' Christ's death was therefore a 'fortunate exchange'. Commenting on the letter to the Romans, Luther testifies of Christ, 'He is the one who has made satisfaction, he is the one who is righteous, he is my defence, he is the one who died for me.'[5] Though this does not exhaust Luther's understanding of the cross – he also endorsed Christ's sacrifice as his victory over death and the devil, and as an example of obedience and service – it represents the heart of it.

The Book of Common Prayer and the Thirty-Nine Articles, originating with Thomas Cranmer, aligned the Church of England unambiguously with this reassertion of cross-centred Christianity. Writing in 1550, Cranmer distinguished the unrepeatable uniqueness of Christ's sacrifice from the sacrifices of praise and thanksgiving offered by his people:

One kind of sacrifice there is, which is called a propitiatory or merciful sacrifice, that is to say, such a sacrifice as pacifies God's wrath and indignation, and obtains mercy and forgiveness for all our sins, and is the ransom for our redemption from everlasting damnation. And although in the Old Testament there were certain sacrifices called by that name, yet in very deed there is but one sacrifice whereby our sins be pardoned, and God's mercy and favour obtained, which is the death of the Son of God our Lord Jesus Christ.[6]

This is the background to England's replacement of the Mass with the commemoration of the Lord's Supper. It placed the cross, as the one sacrifice sufficient to propitiate God's righteous anger with sin, at the heart of Anglican worship and doctrine. As a result, the prayer at the centre of the Prayer Book's order for the Lord's Supper begins with the following very significant words: 'Almighty God, our heavenly Father, who of thy tender mercy didst give thy only Son Jesus Christ to suffer death upon the Cross for our redemption; who made there (by his one oblation of himself once offered) a full, perfect and sufficient sacrifice, oblation and satisfaction for the sins of the whole world . . .'

Here, following both the continental Reformers and the early church, the means of redemption is explicitly identified as Christ's death. The cross is very carefully described. First, it is a unique and willing offering. Jesus offered himself, once. The eucharist is therefore neither a representation of Christ's offering, nor a joining of human offerings to his, but has at its heart the commemoration of an unrepeatable historical event. Next, Jesus' death is described as a 'sacrifice, oblation, and satisfaction'. In other words, it had God as its object. In the words of the General Confession, sin's most serious effect is to provoke the righteous anger of God: 'We acknowledge and bewail our manifold sins and wickedness, which we from time to time most grievously have committed, by thought, word and deed, against thy divine majesty, provoking most justly thy wrath and indignation against us.'

It is therefore the 'Maker of all things, and Judge of all men' who is offended, and who must be propitiated. Christ's offering of himself is made to his heavenly Father: no one but God needs to be offered satisfaction for the sins of the world. The satisfaction Christ made was of this divine 'wrath and indignation', paying its penalty in his own body and so securing our freedom and redemption. Hence, Christ's sacrifice is described as 'full, perfect and sufficient'. No further offering is required since no sin is beyond the reach of the forgiveness secured on the cross. Its satisfaction is therefore redemptive: it fully met the demands of God's justice and accomplished a full reconciliation.

This understanding of the cross pervaded the English Reformation. In 1547, shortly after Edward VI came to the throne, a book of official sermons – the 'Homilies' – was published. The third sermon, on justification, outlines three steps needed for this reconciliation to come about:

> Upon God's part, his great mercy and grace; upon Christ's part, justice; that is, the satisfaction of God's justice, or the price of our redemption, by the offering of his body, and shedding of his blood, with the fulfilling of the Law perfectly and thoroughly; and upon our part true and lively faith in the merits of Jesus Christ; which yet is not ours, but by God's working in us.[7]

Thus the love of God in Christ perfectly supplies believers with what they lack: the obedient life and sin-bearing death of Jesus provide their righteousness with God.

This portrayal of the cross as the payment of a ransom price, satisfying divine justice and discharging our debt, was confirmed in the Elizabethan settlement. Cranmer had been burnt for his Protestant beliefs under Mary, but after her death his liturgical and doctrinal reforms were restored with only minor adjustments. In 1563, further homilies were issued, including two on Christ's passion. The introduction to the first concludes, 'And yet, I say, did Christ put himself between God's wrath and our sin, and rent that obligation, wherein we were in danger to God, and paid our debt.'[8]

The homily explicitly sees this as penal substitution, in fulfilment of prophecy: 'For himself he was not punished, for he was pure and undefiled of all manner of sin. He was wounded, saith Isaiah, for our wickedness, and striped for our sins; he suffered the penalty of them himself, to deliver us from danger.'[9]

The second homily summarizes the human plight and the divine remedy:

> When all hope of righteousness was past on our part, when we had nothing in ourselves, whereby we might quench his burning wrath, and work the salvation of our souls, and rise out of the miserable estate wherein we lay: then, even then, did Christ the Son of God, by the appointment of his Father, come down from heaven, to be wounded for our sakes, to be reputed with the wicked, to be condemned unto death, to take upon him the reward for our sins, and to give his body to be broken on the cross for our offences.[10]

Finally, the restoration of evangelical Protestantism under Elizabeth I saw the adoption of the Thirty-Nine Articles as the church's doctrinal standard. Article 31, mostly drafted under Cranmer, spells out its doctrine of the atonement:

> The Offering of Christ once made is that perfect redemption, propitiation, and satisfaction, for all the sins of the whole world, both original and actual; and there is none other satisfaction for sin, but that alone. Wherefore the sacrifices of Masses, in which it was commonly said, that the priest did offer Christ for the quick and the dead, to have remission of pain and guilt, were blasphemous fables, and dangerous deceits.[11]

Interestingly, the article reveals that the debate in the sixteenth century was not *whether* God needed to be propitiated: God's righteous anger against human sin was common ground between the Reformers and their Catholic opponents. Rather, the confusion was over whether it was necessary to continue to offer Christ, in the Mass, or whether the cross itself was complete satisfaction. The decisive Anglican conclusion was that Christ's sacrifice was sufficient for all people, for all time. As Article 2 describes, it is therefore also the means by which we know God's favour again, since Jesus is the one 'who truly suffered, was crucified, died and buried, to reconcile his Father to us, and to be a sacrifice, not only for original guilt, but also for all actual sins of men'.

The Seventeenth Century

Unlike some other doctrines, the Thirty-Nine Articles' view of Christ's sacrifice attracted little controversy in later years. When towards the end of Elizabeth's reign, the theologian Richard Hooker outlined how Protestants differed from Roman Catholics over the vital question of justification, he pointed out that both sides formally accepted that Christ's death was a sufficient sacrifice for sin:

> For are not these our arguments against them? 'Christ alone hath satisfied and appeased his Father's wrath: Christ hath merited salvation alone.' We should do fondly to use such disputes, neither could we think to prevail by them, if that whereupon we ground, were a thing which we know they do not hold, which we are assured they will not grant.[12]

Hooker's argument is that Christ's substitutionary sacrifice *was* common ground. Roman Catholic writers acknowledged of Christ that 'he is the propitiation for our sins'.[13] Hooker's doctrine of justification by faith *alone* came from the Reformers and depended on the cross being a substitutionary sacrifice, but the point of disagreement with Rome was not the latter.[14]

So it is not surprising that despite the religious turbulence of the Stuart era, few questioned the traditional doctrine of the atonement. Theological debate centred on predestination, church government, the liturgical revolution attempted under Charles I, and the consequences of James II's Catholicism for nation and monarchy. The nature of Christ's sacrifice attracted little controversy. The Socinian criticism of the penal doctrine as biblically mistaken and immoral, had only a limited following in England, and on the continent it received a full riposte from Hugo Grotius, who defended the traditional doctrine more comprehensively than had ever before been attempted.[15]

Hence, penal substitution was controversial neither during the era's attempts to augment England's doctrinal standards nor in the long-running debate over whether Christ died for all sinners or for the elect alone ('limited atonement'). The first half of the century saw several attempts to modify or supplant the Elizabethan settlement, but none proposed change to the traditional understanding of the cross as the place where God's wrath and justice were satisfied and reconciliation achieved.[16] Hence, when the Thirty-Nine Articles were reaffirmed, unaltered, after the restoration of the monarchy under Charles II, their theology continued to reflect the Protestant consensus. Similarly, when the Book of Common Prayer attained its final form in 1662, there were no modifications to its doctrine of the atonement.

Such debate as there was over the atonement revolved around the extent of its achievement, rather than over its substitutionary character. Richard Baxter and John Owen, for example, agreed that the death of Jesus satisfied God's wrath and justice, but differed over whether he died for all sinners, or only for the elect. It is arguable that both resorted to philosophical or political arguments to sustain their case. Yet both were committed to a penal, substitutionary view of the atonement, though they came to differ over precisely how Christ's sacrifice met the demands of God's holy character.[17]

This debate was not resolved, but the religious turmoil of the century effectively came to an end with the affirmation of England's allegiance to Protestantism in the Act of Settlement of 1700. The doctrinal legacy of the Prayer Book and Thirty-Nine Articles, with their affirmation of justification by faith and the penal doctrine of the atonement which underlies it, had survived. Indeed, although for many the century's crises had bred a weariness with doctrinal controversy, it was not long before the preaching of the cross was once more back at the heart of life-changing Christianity in England.

Revival and Renewal

If evangelicals today can confidently look back to the Reformers for our doctrinal foundations, we can look back to the eighteenth century for evangelistic enterprise. John Wesley, George Whitefield, John Newton and many other figures, culminating in Charles Simeon, roused England from the spiritual torpor into which it had sunk. Accounting for their zeal, and dominating their preaching, was the message of the cross.

Though Whitefield was certainly his peer in preaching, Wesley was the most influential of the leaders of the revival in mid-century, establishing an organization which eventually evolved into the Methodist church. Yet Wesley was a Church of England minister rather than a dissenter. His passion was for men and women to hear and respond to the gospel of Jesus Christ, in a nation where Christianity was increasingly seen as little more than a moral code. Central to his evangelistic enterprise was the atoning death of Christ. Shortly after his famous experience of conversion in London, Wesley preached on salvation by faith at St Mary's Oxford, the University Church:

> This then is the salvation which is through faith, even in the present world: a salvation from sin, and the consequences of sin, both often expressed in the word justification; which, taken in the largest sense, implies a deliverance from guilt and punishment, by the atonement of Christ actually applied to the soul of the sinner now believing on Him, and a deliverance from the whole body of sin, through Christ formed in his heart.[18]

Wesley's notion that it was possible for the Christian to be free from the presence of sin was novel. But his insistence that freedom from the guilt and punishment of sin comes through faith in the cross was a powerful reassertion of orthodox doctrine. Indeed, the atonement has been called the 'burning focus of faith' for Wesley.[19] His understanding of the cross was dominated by the doctrine of penal substitution. Commenting on Romans 3:25, he observed that the cross was a propitiatory sacrifice 'to appease an offended God. But if . . . God was never offended, there was no need of this propitiation'.[20] Together with Galatians 3:13, with its description of Christ 'becoming a curse for us', this verse establishes that the atonement is not only objective, but also to be understood in retributive, judicial terms.[21] 'The central point of the penal substitutionary theory was of great importance for Wesley. Christ is the satisfier of our sin and guilt, the one who died as the sacrifice to satisfy the divine wrath and to provide for our forgiveness by the infinite value of his sacrifice in satisfaction of God's justice.'[22] This satisfaction of justice was, for Wesley, the supreme demonstration of God's love for humanity.

As a consequence of the revival pioneered by Wesley and White-field, in the second half of the eighteenth century, evangelical ministry began to flourish again in the Church of England. Perhaps the best known of its exponents was John Newton, the converted slave trader and author of 'Amazing Grace', an incumbent first in Olney, Northamptonshire, and then at St Mary Woolnoth in the city of London. In his preaching and hymn-writing, the death of Christ for sinners was central, as a sermon from 1785 clearly shows:

> As the Lamb of God, Christ superseded the sacrificial system, dying as the one voluntary substitute for death-deserving sinners. This way of redemption satisfied the rights of God's justice, the demands of his law, and the honour of his government, and provided an atonement which was fully efficacious to deliver a believer from the guilt and penalty of sin. Sin removed, the soul is open to Christ whose grace is richly imparted for a life of continuing obedience.[23]

For both Wesley and Newton and many contemporaries, the centrality of the cross as the place of reconciliation was more important than the seventeenth-century debate on the extent of the atonement. While on this and other points Wesley disagreed with the more Calvinist Whitefield, they recognized their unity on core doctrines, including the atonement. All held tenaciously to the objective character of Christ's death: the cross assuaged God's righteous wrath and achieved a complete reconciliation with God. Further they resisted strongly the contention that Christ's death was no more than exemplary, as Socinian thought held.[24]

The penal doctrine found vivid, colourful expression not only in evangelical preaching, but also in the hymns of the era. John Wesley endorsed many of the hymns composed by his brother Charles as summaries of Christian doctrine. In those which deal with the cross, it is portrayed as the highest expression of God's love:

> Amazing mystery of love!
> While posting to eternal pain,
> God saw His rebels from above,
> And stoop'd into a mortal man.

His mercy cast a pitying look;
By love, unbounded love inclined,
Our guilt and punishment He took,
And died a Victim for mankind.

His blood procured our life and peace,
And quenched the wrath of hostile Heaven,
Justice gave way to our release,
And God hath all my sins forgiven.

As this suggests, God's love in these hymns is epitomized by the sin-bearing death of his Son. Normally, this is described in penal terms, as in 'All ye that pass by':

For what you have done
His blood must atone:
The Father has punish'd for you His dear Son.
The Lord in the day
Of His anger did lay
Your sins on the Lamb, and He bore them away.

He dies to atone
For sins not his own
Your debt He hath paid, and your work He hath done.
Ye all may receive
The peace He did leave
Who made intercession, 'My Father, forgive!'[25]

Accordingly, the evangelical revival and the new life that flowed from it had the cross at their centre. Despite opposition from many within the established church, the preaching of the cross by its leaders transformed England, as even George III recognized in conversation with Charles Wesley junior: 'It is my judgment, Mr Wesley, that your uncle and your father, and George Whitefield and Lady Huntingdon, have done more to promote true religion in the country than all the dignified clergy put together, who are so apt to despise their labours.'[26]

As Charles Simeon's ministry began, John Wesley's was drawing to its close. Methodism was on its way to independence, but Simeon's work, built on the same doctrinal foundation, more than any other marked the renewal of evangelical strength within the Church of England. The core of their message was the same. In the hands of Wesley and Whitefield, the evangelical doctrine of the atonement had transformed England. Through Simeon's work, as in that of Cranmer, it would once again be restored to the heart of the nation's established church.

Conclusion: A Thrilling Heritage

It is no coincidence that every era of church growth has been an age of recovery of confidence in the Bible. As Paul told Timothy, 'it is the Scriptures which are able to make you wise for salvation through faith in Christ Jesus' (2 Timothy 3:15 ESV). When the Bible's message is heard, men and women are turned to Jesus Christ in repentance and faith.

In the sixteenth century, the rediscovery that the heart of the Bible's message is the sin-bearing death of Jesus Christ transformed the doctrine, liturgy and life of the Church of England. It was a costly revolution: much that was familiar, even comforting, had to be jettisoned; and, tragically, many paid with their lives. But the outcome of such courage was that men and women were free to hear in their own language, week by week, that Christ had suffered in their place, and that through simple faith in him they could have peace with God.

Two centuries later, the preaching of Christ crucified swept the nation, breathing new life into the church and bringing the news of God's 'amazing grace' to thousands. It was a costly movement: Wesley's message was opposed tooth and nail by many churchmen, while Simeon endured for years the hostility of many of his congregation. But the outcome of their perseverance was an upsurge of evangelical ministry in cities, towns and villages, in the Church of England and beyond, and authentic new life in thousands of men and women.

It is no coincidence that the penal substitutionary doctrine of the cross, preached with passion and compassion, was at the heart of these two quite distinct revivals of biblical Christianity. For as other chapters in this volume show, without it there is no salvation 'through faith in Christ Jesus'. Our evangelical forebears in the Church of

England were not ashamed of it. Nor were they afraid to pay the price of preaching and believing it.

Notes

1. W. Carus, *Memoirs of the Life of the Rev. Charles Simeon*, 1847, pp. 6–9, cited in *Charles Simeon (1759–1836): Essays Written in Commemoration of his Bi-Centenary*, eds A. Pollard and M. Hennell, London, SPCK, 1959, pp. 24–25.
2. Sermons 968, 969, cited in D. Webster, 'Simeon's Pastoral Theology', in *Charles Simeon,* Pollard and Hennell, p. 87.
3. G. J. Williams, 'A Critical Exposition of Hugo Grotius' Doctrine of the Atonement in *De satisfactione Christi*', DPhil thesis, Oxford University, 1999, pp. 68–90.
4. *Luther's Works*, eds J. Pelikan and H. T. Lehmann et al., Saint Louis, Concordia; Philadelphia, Fortress, vol. 52, 1958–, pp. 280–81.
5. J. Pelikan, *The Christian Tradition*, vol. 4, *The Reformation of Church and Dogma (1300–1700)*, Chicago, University of Chicago Press, p. 161; *D. Martin Luther's Werke: Kritische Gesamtausgabe*, vol. 56, Weimar, Böhlau, 1883–, p. 204.
6. Thomas Cranmer, *A Defence of the True and Catholic Doctrine of the Sacrament of the Body and Blood of Our Saviour Christ*, 1551, 1907 ed.; repr. Lewes, Christian Focus Christian Ministries Trust, 1987, p. 235 (spellings modernized).
7. *Sermons or Homilies Appointed to Be Read in Churches*, London, Prayer Book and Homily Society, 1833; repr. Lewes, Christian Focus Ministries Trust, 1986, p. 14.
8. Ibid., p. 285.
9. Ibid., p. 287.
10. Ibid., p. 293.
11. Summary statements of the achievement of the cross are also found in Articles 2 and 15.
12. R. Hooker, 'A Learned Discourse of Justification, Works and how the Foundation of Faith Is Overthrown', printed in

R. Hooker, *Of The Laws of Ecclesiastical Polity*, vol. 1, London, Dent, 1907, p. 64.

13 Ibid., p. 65.

14 W. J. Torrance Kirby, 'Richard Hooker as an Apologist of the Magisterial Reformation', in *Richard Hooker and the Construction of Christian Community*, ed. A. S. McGrade, Tempe, Ariz., 1997, p. 225.

15 Grotius' work *De satisfactione Christi* was written in response to an attack on the penal doctrine by Socinus in his 1594 work *De incarnatione Christi*. It is a measure of the historic doctrinal consensus on the atonement that Grotius' was the first major attempt in the history of the church to isolate the penal doctrine and devote a whole treatise to it. Though the terms in which he defended the doctrine in themselves gave rise to further Protestant debate, it is therefore hardly surprising that Grotius saw himself not as articulating a new doctrine but rather as defending the Catholic doctrine of the atonement from a radical, unbiblical assault. On this, see Williams, 'Critical Exposition', pp. 56–64, 102–48.

16 See notably the Canons of the Synod of Dort, 1619, attended by an official English delegation and nearly adopted in 1625; and the Westminster Confession of Faith, 1647, drawn up as the basis for a single, British church. *Documents of the English Reformation*, ed. G. Bray, Cambridge, James Clark, 1994, pp. 453–78, 486–520.

17 On this, see A. C. Clifford, *Atonement and Justification: English Evangelical Theology 1640–1790*, Oxford, Clarendon, 1990, pp. 125–32.

18 J. Wesley, sermon on justification by faith, 11 June 1738, printed in *Religion and Society in England and Wales, 1689–1800*, ed. W. Gibson, London, Leicester University Press, 1988, p. 112.

19 C. Williams, *John Wesley's Theology Today*, London, Epworth, 1960, p. 75, citing G. C. Cell, *The Rediscovery of Wesley*, New York, Henry Holt, 1935, p. 297.

20 J. Wesley, *Explanatory Notes on the New Testament* (1755), Romans 3:25. The full text reads (of Christ), 'whom God put forward as a propitiation by his blood, to be received by faith. This was to show God's righteousness, because in his divine forbearance he had passed over former sins' (English Standard Version).

21 Clifford, *Atonement and Justification*, p. 132.

22 Williams, *Wesley's Theology*, p. 83.

23 D. B. Hindmarsh, *John Newton and the English Evangelical Tradition*, Oxford, Clarendon, 1996, pp. 162–63.

24 Thus Henry Venn, who saw revival in Huddersfield under his ministry, devoted much of *The Deity of Christ* to refuting the Socinianism and rationalism he saw in the Church of England. G. M. Ditchfield, *The Evangelical Revival*, London, UCL Press, 1998, pp. 33–34.

25 J. E. Rattenbury, *The Evangelical Doctrines of Charles Wesley's Hymns*, London, Epworth, 1941, pp. 192–93.

26 Clifford, *Atonement and Justification*, p. 57.

Chapter Nine

The Revolution and Reconciliation of the Cross

Andrew Cornes

Our understanding of the cross can never remain a matter of ideas but must always flow into our lives, individually and together. Andrew Cornes shows how the cross should be central to our meetings, our relationships, and the price God may call us to pay as we follow a crucified Christ on the way to the cross before our glory with him. This is a strange and uncomfortable message for today's Christians, but Andrew challenges us to rethink whether we have a truly biblical view of what it means to suffer with Christ.

Introduction

The cross changed everything for those who came to understand and love it. For example, the cross changed their attitude to God. It changed their whole idea of what it means to say that God is powerful and that God is wise. Paul could say, 'we preach Christ crucified: a stumbling block to Jews and foolishness to Gentiles, but to those whom God has called, both Jews and Greeks, Christ the power of God and the wisdom of God' (1 Corinthians 1:23–4).

Before their conversion, Jews had taken offence at the cross of Jesus of Nazareth. It was power and miracles that demonstrated the presence of God (v. 22); how could God be present in such weakness? And the Greeks had scoffed at this religion founded on the criminal execution of a wandering Jew. How could there be any philosophy (v. 22) in such an abrupt and meaningless death?

But once the cross had been properly understood, it was revealed as the supreme demonstration of God's wisdom: providing the perfect, comprehensive and only solution to the problem of human sin and death; and it was shown to be the ultimate concentration of God's power: defeating the forces of evil and setting human beings free.

And the cross changed their attitude to humanity. It meant that the early Christians saw themselves in a totally new light. Paul memorably captured this: 'I have been crucified with Christ and I no longer live, but Christ lives in me. The life I live in the body, I live by faith in the Son of God, who loved me and gave himself for me' (Galatians 2:20). Christ's death meant the end of the Christian's old self; and specifically – in context – of the old way of trying to get right with God by constantly whipping ourselves to live up to his standards (v. 9). But it also meant the start of a new way of life: living by trust in the Son who has unequivocally demonstrated his love for us. And the cross changed not only the early Christians' attitude to themselves but to the world around them: 'May I never boast except in the cross of our Lord Jesus Christ, through which the world has been crucified to me, and I to the world' (Galatians 6:14).

The cross still has this power to revolutionize our thinking and our actions:

> The community of Christ is the community of the cross. Having been brought into being by the cross, it continues to live by and under the cross. Our perspective and our behaviour are now governed by the cross. All our relationships have been radically transformed by it. The cross is not just a badge to identify us, and the banner under which we march; it is also the compass which gives us our bearings in a disorientated world.[1]

In this chapter I want to point out three areas in which the cross was, is and must be specially revolutionary: worship, human relationships, and suffering.

Worship

From a very early stage, the heart of Christian worship has been the remembering and proclaiming of Christ's death. This was *Christ's own intention*. First Corinthians 11:23–6 represents the earliest New Testament account of the Last Supper. Paul says, 'I received from the Lord what I also passed on to you' (v. 23), by which 'he probably does not mean that Jesus gave these words to him personally and directly ... but ... that Jesus himself is the ultimate source of the tradition'.[2]

Christ broke and distributed bread, and said, 'do this in remembrance of me'. He passed round the cup and said, 'do this, whenever you drink it, in remembrance of me'. So Christ intended his death to be constantly remembered by means of bread and wine consumed in the company of other Christians. And Paul adds, 'whenever you eat this bread and drink this cup, you proclaim the Lord's death until he comes' (vv. 24–6).

This was also *the earliest church's practice*. Luke has no sooner described the Day of Pentecost and the remarkable response to Peter's sermon than he adds one of his summary paragraphs to describe the life of the church in its earliest days (Acts 2:42–7). It includes the statement 'They devoted themselves to ... the breaking of bread' (v. 42); and 'They broke bread in their homes and ate together with glad and sincere hearts' (v. 46; cf. Acts 20:7; 1 Corinthians 10:16). F. F. Bruce quotes R. Otto, who says that to call the Lord's Supper the 'breaking of bread' makes this act, despite being 'wholly trivial in itself' into 'the significant element of the celebration ... But it could only be significant when it was a signum, viz. of Christ's being broken in death'.[3]

Moreover, the celebration of Christ's saving death is also *at the heart of heaven's worship*. Revelation 4 and 5 picture the worship of heaven as centring round the Father and the Son: the Father as the everlasting, enthroned Creator and the Son as the slaughtered and triumphant Lamb. The four living creatures and the twenty-four elders sing (5:9–10):

> You are worthy to take the scroll and to open its seals, because
>   you were slain,
>   and with your blood you purchased men for God
>   from every tribe and language and people and nation.
> You have made them to be a kingdom and priests to serve
>   our God,
>   and they will reign on the earth.

Countless numbers of angels take up the same theme: 'Worthy is the Lamb, who was slain' (5:11; cf. 5:13; 7:9–10).

It seems ironic, then, and misguided that we evangelicals often have the least cross-centred worship. We pride ourselves that the unique, saving and glorious death of Christ is at the centre of our theology. We decry the fact that it is far less central in other theologies, particularly those more formed around the incarnation rather than the crucifixion. And yet it would be hard to discern our proclaimed emphasis in the liturgies we choose.

In *Guidelines,* the book written for the first National Evangelical Anglican Congress at Keele in 1967, Michael Green wrote,

> To Anglo-Catholics and Plymouth Brethren alike, the Lord's Supper is the main and central service on the Lord's day. This is so manifestly the New Testament emphasis that many have doubted whether the early Christians had any other service of worship than the Eucharist. How often is Holy Communion the main emphasis, the central service, of an evangelical church? How much do evangelical congregations seek to know of the grateful recollection of the Cross, the joyous feeding in the risen Lord, the exultant foretastes of heaven, which the Bible associates with the Eucharist? We too must be biblical.[4]

Some evangelical churches have moved towards more eucharistic worship since these words were written, but since around the mid-1980s there has also been a move in the opposite direction, particularly with the introduction of more Family Services or All-Age Worship. These services often operate on the mistaken assumption that a service with children present should never be a celebration of the Lord's Supper. Two main objections are raised by evangelicals against the frequent use of Communion Services.

The first is that it leads to *a shortening of the sermon*. There is no doubt that the Parish Communion movement has had a disastrous effect on preaching. The sermon has often been reduced to a brief 'homily', not worth much preparation time by the minister or much attention by the congregation. Sometimes it has even been dropped altogether. However, this need not be an inevitable result of regular Communion Services. Many churches shorten the rest of the liturgy in order to ensure that the preaching of the Word of God is given due time and weight. Some churches have a freely structured and changing liturgy at the start of the main Sunday service and only join the specifically Communion rite at the Peace or the Eucharistic Prayer. It may also be necessary to multiply places in the church for the administration of bread and wine in order to free more time for preaching. What is certain is that with careful planning and judicious pruning it is perfectly possible to have a regular celebration of the Lord's Supper and a meaty and satisfying exposition of Scripture. At Troas, the 'breaking of bread' certainly did not mean a short sermon (Acts 20:7–12)!

A second objection is *the presence of non-Christians*. It is argued that in a post-Christian era, when the Church of England in particular must constantly be in mission mode, the regular use of Communion Services excludes the non-Christian and makes him or her uncomfortable. It is true that this can be the effect on some, though it is hard to argue that this is experienced by many, in view of the enormous popularity of 'Midnight' Christmas Communion to which those who are not regular churchgoers flock, despite the fact that a number of them will not receive Communion.

Yet, it is equally arguable that the Communion Service is an excellent means of presenting the gospel. John Wesley called it a 'converting ordinance'. In it, we 'proclaim the Lord's death' (1 Corinthians 11:26); and Paul uses the same word *(katangellein)* which was earlier used for 'preaching the gospel' and for 'proclaiming the testimony about [or 'mystery of'] God' (1 Corinthians 9:14; 2:1).

In fact, this service clearly proclaims *the centrality of the cross*, because its main focus is on the saving death of Christ, *the grace of the cross*. Here the worshipper kneels or stands with open, empty palms ('nothing in my hand I bring; simply to thy cross I cling') acknowledging *the demand of the cross,* especially if the minister regularly and gently comments that the bread and the wine are for those who can say 'Christ is my Saviour and my Lord.'

Two examples may help illustrate how Communion can be this 'proclamation'. First, at a teenagers' Christian camp the bread was being passed along the rows. A teenage boy knew he had not yet given his life to Christ and understood that the bread and wine was only for those who belong to Christ. As the bread drew nearer his mind vacillated: 'Will I? Won't I?' Quietly he gave his life to Christ and as a newborn Christian for the first time received the bread and the wine. Secondly, a school teacher filled in a questionnaire at the end of an Alpha course. 'Has your Christian commitment changed in any way?' He wrote, 'For the first time I have felt able to take Communion.' Every Communion Service he had been to had reminded him he had a choice to make; now he had made that choice.

Human Relationships

The cross broke down the greatest divisions in human society and brought together on an equal footing those who were suspicious of each other.

Ephesians 2: breaking down barriers

The classic passage on this subject is Ephesians 2:11–19:

> Therefore, remember that formerly you who are Gentiles by birth and called 'uncircumcised' by those who call themselves 'the circumcision' (that done in the body by the hands of men) – remember that at that time you were separate from Christ, excluded from citizenship in Israel and foreigners to the covenants of the promise, without hope and without God in the

world. But now in Christ Jesus you who once were far away have been brought near through the blood of Christ. For he himself is our peace, who has made the two one and has destroyed the barrier, the dividing wall of hostility, by abolishing in his flesh the law with its commandments and regulations. His purpose was to create in himself one new man out of the two, thus making peace, and in this one body to reconcile both of them to God through the cross, by which he put to death their hostility. He came and preached peace to you who were far away and peace to those who were near. For through him we both have access to the Father by one Spirit.

Consequently, you are no longer foreigners and aliens, but fellow-citizens with God's people and members of God's household . . .

There were various divisions in first-century Jewish and Graeco-Roman society. Galatians 3:28 lists some of them: Jew and Greek, slave and free, male and female. Christ did not obliterate these but rendered them all insignificant in the light of the far more important fact that all Christians, whatever their background, social status or gender, are 'in Christ Jesus'.

Ephesians 2:11–22 develops this point. It takes the most difficult division in the New Testament Church – that between Jew and Gentile – and says that it has now become at most a peripheral issue. These Ephesian verses emphasize that this change has been brought about by the cross of Christ: 'through the blood of Christ' (v. 13), 'in his flesh' (v. 15), 'through the cross' (v. 16).

The division between Jew and Gentile was both racial and religious. The Jews looked down on the Gentiles as 'uncircumcised'. In fact, it was by this name that they often described the Gentiles (v. 11). Gentiles were godless (v. 12). They were 'excluded from citizenship in Israel' (v. 12) and to be kept excluded. For this reason Gentiles were only allowed into one courtyard of the temple. A barrier kept them from going further into the temple and at the 13 entrances to the Jewish area tablets were placed, written in Greek and Latin. One of these was found in 1871. It reads, 'No foreigner is to enter within the forecourt and balustrade around the sanctuary. Whoever is caught will have himself to blame for his subsequent death.' It is probably this barrier which is referred to as 'the dividing wall' (v. 14).

The contempt and hostility (vv. 14, 16) of Jew towards Gentile affected all the relations between these races. As just one example, a Jew was forbidden to help a Gentile woman in labour, because his help might bring another hated Gentile into the world. The Jew was also convinced of his superiority over the Gentile, based on God's 'covenants of the promise' (v. 12) which Israel enjoyed and from which Gentiles were excluded, and on the Jews' possession of 'the law with its commandments and regulations' (v. 15; cf. Romans 9:4).

The Greeks for their part had a contemptuous name for all those who did not speak their language: barbarians (Colossians 3:11). Plato called all non-Greeks 'our enemies by nature'. They thought that the Jewish law was at best irrelevant and at worst both ridiculous and divisive. Gallio dismissed the charges brought against Paul: 'If you Jews were making a complaint about some misdemeanour or serious crime, it would be reasonable for me to listen to you. But since it involves questions about words and names and your own law – settle the matter yourselves' (Acts 18:14–15). For the early Christian Church this was the fundamental fissure to be overcome: Jew and Gentile hated and despised each other. The cross of Jesus Christ healed the rift.

The cross brought *closeness instead of distance* between Christians. Gentiles had been 'excluded from citizenship in Israel' (Ephesians 2:12). As far as the Jews were concerned, Gentiles had been 'foreigners and aliens' (v. 19). 'But now in Christ Jesus you who once were far away have been brought near through the blood of Christ' (v. 13). In this passage (vv. 11–22), reconciliation *both* between sinful human beings and God *and* between Jew and Gentile are constantly in mind. It was Christ's death that made them no longer 'far away' from God but 'near' to him. It was equally Christ's death that made Jew and Gentile no longer miles apart ('far away') but close to each other ('near') because both Jew and Gentile were saved by the same death.

The cross brought *peace instead of hostility* between Christians: 'For he himself is our peace, who has made the two [Jew and Gentile] one and has destroyed the barrier, the dividing wall of hostility, by abolishing in his flesh the law with its commandments and regulations' (vv. 14–15). The law had got in the way. It had caused Jews to keep away from Gentiles and Gentiles to look down on Jews. It was symbolized by that barrier in the temple, brusquely announcing a division that was itself mandated by the law. But Christ 'destroyed' and 'abolished' all that. How? Verse 15 answers: 'in his flesh'. A similar passage in Colossians has the longer phrase 'But now he has reconciled [you] in the body of his flesh through death' (Colossians 1:22). It is Christ's death that breaks down all barriers between Jew and Gentile – whether caused by the law (v. 15) or by human action (cf. v. 11) – and makes peace between them, because that death has also made peace for both of them with God (vv. 16–17).

The cross brought *unity instead of division* between Christians. Paul has just written of what Christ did 'in his flesh', which here means, as we have seen: in his body given up to death on the cross. Paul immediately adds, 'His purpose was to create in himself one new man out of the two, thus making peace' (v. 15). This statement reminds us of the Christian doctrine of marriage: 'the two will become one flesh' (Ephesians 5:31, quoting Genesis 2:24). Jesus' comment on it was: 'So they [husband and wife] are no longer two, but one' (Mark 10:8; Matthew 19:6); no longer divided but, in marriage, made one. Jew and Gentile had been divided (Ephesians 2:14), Gentiles had been 'excluded' (v. 12), but now the cross has made them into a single entity: 'one new man out of the two' (v. 15). Just as the most important thing about husband and wife is no longer their individuality but their oneness, so the most important thing about the members of Christ's family is no longer their Jewishness or their Greek heritage but that they are 'in Christ' (v. 13) by the grace of Christ's death for them.

The cross brought *equal standing instead of discrimination* among Christians. Before, the Jews had discriminated against the Gentiles treating them as 'foreigners and aliens' (v. 19). And the same treatment was returned. While Jews were allowed certain concessions in the Roman Empire, they felt they were discriminated against in their whole way of life and in their religion. But God treated Jew and Gentile in exactly the same way, with no privileges for either group. In fact, all the richest of God's privileges were now provided for both groups equally: 'For through him [Christ] we both have access to the Father by one Spirit' (v. 18) . This sentence is one of several (probably) unconscious references to the Trinity in the New Testament. 'Through him' (v. 18) means through Christ's death, 'through the cross' (v. 16). It is once again Christ's death that gives Jew and Gentile this equal standing before God, because both come to him in exactly the same way. Because of the cross, they both belong to the people of God ('fellow-citizens with God's people' – a political image) and the family of God ('members of God's house-hold' – a domestic image) (v. 19).

2 Corinthians 5: re-evaluating people in the light of the cross

Ephesians 2 speaks of how the cross breaks down barriers between Christians. Second Corinthians 5:16 shows how the cross also makes Christians re-evaluate everyone, including those who are not yet Christians. Paul has just written about the cross, 'Christ's love compels us, because we are convinced that one died for all, and therefore all died. And he died for all, that those who live should no longer live for themselves but for him who died for them and was raised again' (2 Corinthians 5:14–15). Then he draws a conclusion from these facts: 'So from now on we regard no one from a worldly point of view' (v. 16).

The Corinthians were very aware of different 'human standards' by which people could be judged. 'Human standards' in 1 Corinthians 1:26 translates *kata sarka,* exactly the same phrase translated 'worldly point of view' in 2 Corinthians 5:16. In 1 Corinthians 1 Paul points out that these Corinthian Christians came from very different backgrounds. Some were 'influential', some 'weak', some 'of noble birth' or 'lowly' or 'despised'. Some were 'wise' and some 'foolish' (1 Corinthians 1:26–9). But all this counted for nothing 'from now on' – that is, since Paul and his companions had grasped what Christ's death meant for them. To add force to the point, Paul adds, 'Though we once regarded Christ in this way [*kata sarka* again], we do so no longer' (2 Corinthians 5:16).

Commenting on this, Furnish asks what is the opposite of *kata sarka* (literally, 'according to the flesh'). We might expect the answer to be *kata pneuma* ('according to the Spirit'), but Paul does not mention the Spirit in the surrounding context. Rather, the context is dominated by Christ's reconciling death. 'For Paul, the opposite of knowing Christ "according to the flesh" is knowing Christ "according to the cross" *(kata stauron).*'[5] This would mean that all human beings should now be seen not according to human distinctions but in the light of the cross (v. 16a).

The early church found it extraordinarily difficult to integrate Jews and Gentiles. Yet Christ's achievement on the cross demanded that these barriers be overcome and that unity be fought for and maintained, principally within the church (Ephesians 2) but also in the way Christians thought of, and related to, non-Christians (2 Corinthians 5).

Racial and religious divides are some of the greatest challenges facing Britain and the world. In the summer of 2001 race riots broke out in Oldham, Bradford and Burnley. There is continuing tension over asylum seekers, who are regarded with suspicion ('economic migrants') and hostility by many in the population and are held in detention centres or dispersed by the authorities to parts of England where they have no relatives or contacts. It is not long since the destruction of the Twin Towers in New York and of part of the Pentagon in the name of Arab nationalism, of the Palestinian struggle and of Islam. We have had war in Afghanistan and the Allies are taking the war against terrorism to other countries.

Tensions between Jew and Gentile continue to be alarming and extremely dangerous. Since the start of the *intifada* in 2000, sparked by the visit of a Jewish leader to an Arab (Gentile) holy site, the Israeli Minister for Tourism has been assassinated and Jewish voices have been calling for the same response to Palestinian terrorism shown by the Americans to the Taliban: a politically impossible ultimatum leading to all-out war.

Amid these challenges at home and overseas, how are the churches responding in the light of the cross? One scandal has been to accept the solution of racially divided churches. I remember visiting an Anglican Church in the state of Mississippi. It had been a racially integrated church, with a large congregation of blacks and whites. The rector could point to the exact day when that changed and the black congregation left en masse to found their own church. Today, the congregation which I visited is entirely white. In Britain too, black immigrants have sought to be part of existing churches, have felt that they were in some cases not welcomed and in many more not valued, and have founded their own 'black churches' instead.

These divisions – and other churches based mainly around uniformity of age ('youth churches'), class or wealth – have been justified on grounds of evangelism. The 'homogeneous unit principle' argues that people who are not yet Christians will feel more at home with those from similar socio-economic backgrounds who share many of the same tastes. But people who argue this way have forgotten the cross: 'Here there is no Greek or Jew, circumcised or uncircumcised, barbarian, Scythian, slave or free, but Christ is all, and is in all' (Colossians 3:11).

If Christians are to show partiality to anyone, it should be to the poor (James 2:17). If we are to go out of our way to care for any more than others, it should be for older widows (1 Timothy 5:3–16). If we are to show special practical love to any, it should be to those who differ from us by race and religion (Luke 10:25–37). When people of other races come into our churches we will want to welcome them warmly without smothering them, to listen to them without treating them as if they had come from another planet, to understand them, their insights and their needs, to value them and their contribution, and increasingly not to think of 'us' and 'them' at all but of all together as fellow members of Christ, redeemed by Christ's death.

This concern to break down barriers of race, and unnecessary barriers of religious misunderstanding, must also characterize our churches in our relations with the community around us. Churches cannot stick to their own Christian ghettos, ministering only to those who are at least nominal Christians. In the light of the cross, we no longer judge people *kata sarka*: by the colour of their skin, or the language they speak in their family or the food they eat. We no longer keep away from the Samaritan whose religion the Jew had been taught to despise. Churches can offer help in the name of Christ not only to the hospitals and schools of Muslim Indonesia, via short-term and long-term missionaries, but also to the community centre down the road, largely attended by Muslims, via our personal involvement and the offer of practical help. We can send water engineers to Hindu villages in India, and also those who will help in campaigns for better housing conditions in the areas of our own town where the local Indian population is concentrated.

The breaking down of divisions between human groups has always been a result of the cross of Christ.

Suffering

The Jews looked for escape from suffering through a triumphant leader. In the light of the cross, Christians learned to face suffering in company with their suffering Lord. They didn't like it at first. At Caesarea Philippi, Peter came to that great turning point when he stated unequivocally, 'You are the Christ, the Son of the living God' and received Christ's warm response, 'Blessed are you, Simon son of Jonah, for this was not revealed to you by man, but by my Father in heaven' (Matthew 16:16–17). But as soon as 'Jesus began to explain to his disciples that he must go to Jerusalem and suffer many things at the hands of the elders, chief priests and teachers of the law, and that he must be killed', Peter would have none of it. He 'took [Jesus] aside and began to rebuke him. "Never, Lord!" he said. "This shall never happen to you!"' (vv. 21–2). Suffering was not for the Messiah.

The cross changed all that. First, Christians realized that the Messiah did suffer, that his suffering had always been predicted (Isaiah 53) and that his suffering was central to God's purposes (e.g. 1 Peter 3:18, where the most likely text is 'Christ also *suffered* for sins once for all' NRSV). Then they realized that they too would need to suffer (John 15:18–21). And then they grasped something more profound still: that in suffering, they were not just suffering *for* Christ but *with* Christ. They were suffering with him in his sufferings, and he was suffering with them in theirs.

First Peter has a great deal to say about Christ's suffering and Christians suffering. In many places it brings the two together. To my mind, the most striking is 1 Peter 4:12–13: 'Dear friends, do not be surprised at the painful trial you are suffering, as though something strange were happening to you. But rejoice that you participate in the sufferings of Christ, so that you may be overjoyed when his glory is revealed.' It is not just that we are to grit our teeth and put up with suffering, because we simply have to go through it in order to share in Christ's future glory. It is that our suffering can draw us closer to Christ, that our sufferings can unite us to Christ in his sufferings, and that this can transform our experience of 'the painful trial' and cause us to rejoice.

For this same reason Paul positively *wants* to suffer, not out of some perverted masochism but in order to go deeper into Christ: 'I want to know Christ and the power of his resurrection and the fellowship of sharing in his sufferings, becoming like him in his death, and so, somehow, to attain to the resurrection from the dead' (Philippians 3:10–11). Suffering for its own sake holds no interest for Paul. But he recognizes it as an essential way to 'know Christ', because the only true Christ is not only someone invested with resurrection power but a man of suffering, and therefore it is impossible to know him fully or deeply without experiencing suffering. This suffering will not, however, just be in imitation of Christ. It will be a 'sharing in' Christ and his sufferings. It will not lead merely to knowing more about Christ, but to knowing Christ.

Indeed, we have no part in Christ's glory unless we first share in his sufferings: 'if we are children, then we are heirs – heirs of God and co-heirs with Christ, if indeed we share in his sufferings in order that we may also share in his glory' (Romans 8:17). Paul here, as with Peter, is not saying simply that if we want to be glorified with Christ we will have to put up with some suffering first. He is saying that just as we will one day be glorified with Christ (*syndoxasthmen*), so now we suffer with Christ (*sympaschomen*). We are not left to suffer alone. Rather, suffering draws us closer to our brother, our co-heir in God's family, the Christ who suffered.

Contemporary Christian attitudes to suffering

We today, by contrast, seek to avoid suffering at all costs, for ourselves and for our churches. While designing a new church in Crowborough, we decided to put up a stone inscription in the apse, the focal point of the new building. It was a shortened form of Philippians 3:10 and read, I WANT TO KNOW CHRIST, HIS POWER AND HIS SUFFERINGS. Several Christians suggested that we should omit the phrase 'and his sufferings', on the grounds that it was a rather gloomy message or that it would put off those visitors who were not yet Christians. On the same grounds we would have to take away all visual or verbal reference to the cross, because at the heart of the Christian faith is the Lord who not only suffers himself but calls us to share in his sufferings.

Yet this is still a message that we resist. We will give money as long as it does not significantly lower our living standards but never 'as much as we are able, and even beyond our ability' (2 Corinthians 8:3). We will live a little more simply than our neighbours but draw the line at moving into a poorer neighbourhood for the sake of the gospel. We will be known as a Christian at work but will not rock the boat by calling into question some of the workplace practices.

The same is also true of our church life. We are proud if the vicar is asked to be the Mayor's Chaplain but feel it's better if he stays out of local politics. We want a baptism policy that will not ruffle feathers in the community. We may refuse remarriage in church but will offer a service of blessing because, in a difficult pastoral situation, that solution will cause least offence. We will lay on an Alpha course and invite people to come, but we will not visit door to door. It doesn't achieve much and it's painful to be rejected. The result is that we cut very little ice in the community around us. We are harmless; we can safely be ignored.

Moreover, we are bewildered when suffering does come to us. We weren't expecting it! We thought God would protect us from any kind of serious difficulty or pain. So when we suffer, it calls our whole faith into question. This shouldn't be happening to us. Perhaps God isn't there, or doesn't care, after all.

New Testament attitudes to suffering

The early Christians, whose understanding and imagination had been fired by the cross of Christ, saw suffering very differently. And it will be equally life-changing for us if we can see our suffering, in the light of Christ's death, as a way of sharing with Christ in his suffering.

We can then *rejoice in our suffering:* 'Dear friends, do not be surprised at the painful trial you are suffering . . . but rejoice that you participate in the sufferings of Christ' (1 Peter 4:12–13). Suffering gets us down when it seems pointless: merely painful without any positive outcome. That is why in bereavement people often look for the good that has come from the otherwise unbearable pain of the death. But Peter here tells us that no Christian suffering is pointless. On the contrary, it helps us to share more deeply with Christ and his suffering. And anything that draws us closer to Christ is a cause of rejoicing.

We can even *boast of our suffering.* Paul was suffering from what he called 'a thorn in my flesh, a messenger of Satan'. On three occasions he pleaded with Christ to take it away from him. But he received the reply 'My grace is sufficient for you, for my power is made perfect in weakness.' It was a hard message to hear, but when he had fully assimilated it, he was able to say, 'Therefore I will boast all the more gladly about my weaknesses, so that Christ's power may rest on me. That is why, for Christ's sake, I delight in weaknesses, in insults, in hardships, in persecutions, in difficulties. For when I am weak, then I am strong' (2 Corinthians 12:7–10).

Is it possible to feel that a cancer is a feather in our cap? That the collapse of our business is something to be grateful for? That the break-up of our marriage is something that gives us pleasure? That the persecution we suffer at work warms our heart? At one level, this is ridiculous. Cancer, bankruptcy, marriage breakdown and persecution are all evils; they are enemies of Christ and of us. Paul knows this full well. His thorn in the flesh never stops being 'a messenger of Satan' (v. 7). But it is also a way of knowing Christ's power that would simply not be open to him without this intense and multiple (he gives a long list in v. 10) suffering. Personally, I have certainly known people who have been grateful for all the kinds of suffering I have mentioned – cancer, business failure, marital collapse and persecution – because in these sufferings Christ has led them far closer to himself, in ways they had hardly even imagined before they suffered.

The most radical proposal that the New Testament makes is that we *should ask for suffering*. As we have seen, Paul says, 'I want to know Christ and the power of his resurrection and the fellowship of sharing in his sufferings, becoming like him in his death' (Philippians 3:10). In Dave Bryant's song 'Jesus, take me as I am' we sing, 'Take me deeper into you [Christ]'. In singing that, we are asking to be taken into suffering. Paul knew well that the only genuine Christ was not only endued with resurrection power but immersed in crucified suffering. To ask to experience only Christ's power is to want to know only half of Christ. If we would know the whole Christ, we must want also to experience his sufferings.

I was recently reading through the letter to the Hebrews and was struck again by what the writer said to a suffering church: 'In bringing many sons to glory, it was fitting that God . . . should make the author of their salvation perfect through suffering. Both the one who makes men holy and those who are made holy are of the same family. So Jesus is not ashamed to call them brothers' (Hebrews 2:10–11). I thought about this for a long time and then very hesitantly and rather fearfully asked God to send me suffering, if that were his means of making me holy. It is not that I enjoy suffering for its own sake at all; I am a natural coward. But suffering was needed in order to make Christ 'perfect', and if I want to share in that same perfecting work of God then I must also be willing to – even want to – suffer with him.

Conclusion

The areas discussed in this chapter – worship, human relationships and suffering – are only examples of the way that the cross changes our entire outlook on life and the choices we make, our attitude to God, to fellow Christians, to those who are not yet Christians and to ourselves.

Paul's whole understanding was dominated by the cross. He knew it and he wanted it that way. 'I resolved to know nothing while I was with you except Jesus Christ and him crucified' (1 Corinthians 2:2). He saw this as the secret not only of his own spiritual growth but of his effectiveness as an evangelist: 'My message and my preaching were not with wise and persuasive words, but with a demonstration of the Spirit's power' (v. 4).

The church that allows itself to be revolutionized by the cross and to know its reconciling power will be able to bring the cross in all its fullness to our world.

Notes

[1] J. R. W. Stott, *The Cross of Christ*, Leicester, Inter-Varsity Press, 1986, p. 256.
[2] G. D. Fee, *The First Epistle to the Corinthians*, Grand Rapids, Eerdmans, 1987, p. 548.
[3] R. Otto, *The Kingdom of God and the Son of Man*, pp. 312ff., cited in F. F. Bruce, *The Acts of the Apostles*, London, Tyndale, 1952, p. 100.
[4] E. M. B. Green, in *Guidelines*, ed. J. I. Packer, London, Falcon, 1967, p. 114.
[5] V. P. Furnish, *II Corinthians*, New York, Doubleday, 1984, p. 331.

Chapter Ten

The Cross and the Logic of the Gospel

Rico Tice with Andrew Carter

R ico Tice is a passionate evangelist, and this chapter shows why. Clearly and boldly he outlines the true nature of humanity's deepest problem, our dangerous plight without Christ, and our wonderful hope in him. Rico wants us to have a clearer, more biblical, view of the gospel, and therefore a clearer, more biblical view, of evangelism.

Introduction

In 1 Corinthians, Paul wrote that 'the message of the cross is foolishness to those who are perishing, but to us who are being saved it is the power of God' (1 Corinthians 1:18). In our contemporary world there are two responses to that message. Mostly it is regarded as unrelated to the twenty-first century. Our society by and large carries on without any interest. But then our world denies that it is guilty because it doesn't know God, or – more correctly – refuses the true knowledge of God. And because its theology is wrong, its anthropology will also be terribly wrong, and the cross will be an illogical irrelevance.

Paul, however, took the other view. His theology began with the holy and righteous character of God. Accordingly, he knew that every human being is desperately guilty on account of his or her sin in God's created world. Paul saw the cross as the only logical solution to this predicament, and his passion to proclaim the message of the cross was born out of a knowledge that that message is our race's only hope in the light of our guilt before our Maker.

Knowing God

Whenever the Christian church down through the ages has recaptured the central truth of the death and resurrection of Jesus Christ, lives, churches and nations have been turned upside down. As we enter the twenty-first century the church in the United Kingdom needs to recover the message of the cross for today. Our age is surprisingly similar to the cultural climate in which Paul was writing. Corinth was a city of plurality where the idea of Truth would have been scorned and ridiculed. The people of the city were wedded to their polytheistic worldview. It was a city of immorality, prostitution and homosexuality. Yet out of this city a Christian church came into being, a new community of God's people who came to know forgiveness and cleansing from their sin. They were changed by an extraordinary event: the death of a man on a cross. If the church today is to see revival again and alter the course of this nation it will be because we recapture and proclaim with all our might the offensive message of the man Christ Jesus who died in agony upon a cross and then rose again. It is a simple message, and yet the most profound one we will ever hear.

Many Christians today, including evangelical church leaders and theologians, are confused and unclear in their proclamation of the gospel. One school of thought says that we can know little about God because we have insufficient information about him, while another says that God is so far removed from us in his transcendence that he is unknowable. Both scenarios give us permission to create our own version of the gospel. But as Christians faithful to the Scripture, we affirm the words of the Church Father, Hilary of Poitiers, 'For he whom we can only know through his own utterances is the fitting witness concerning himself.'[1] In other words, God is a faithful witness to himself and can be known through his revealed Word.

Another reason for our inadequate gospel is that so often we are ashamed to proclaim the message that Paul preached: it just doesn't go down well in our self-centred age. The result is that sometimes our teaching and evangelism can seem to owe more to the ideas of the postmodern age than to the clarity of biblical thought. It is the aim of this chapter to clarify the central message Bible-believing Christians should live by and preach, for our society faces a plight comparable to the voyage of the *Titanic*. It is critical that we focus on how the cross of Christ must be seen as our only hope in the face of God's holy character.

The God-Centred Gospel

In our post-Enlightenment, humanistic age the main reason for our faulty view of the gospel is that we too often begin our analysis with ourselves rather than God. The result is a human-centred rather than a God-centred gospel. Instead of the Almighty God he is now 'all matey'. To a large extent, we have abandoned our high view of God as the mighty creator, sustainer and judge of the world. We are no longer like the prophet Isaiah, who was 'undone' in the presence of the Almighty God whose holiness, righteousness and hatred of sin defines his being and nature (Isaiah 6:1–13). We hear plenty today about a loving God understood as one who forgives all and embraces us on whatever terms are acceptable to us because he is so desperate to be in relationship with us. Such a view of God is unknown to the Bible; it was unknown to the Reformers and is totally unworthy of the God they worshipped.

Inevitably, such an erroneous 'God' as this, one that we have constructed to fit in with our self-centred and comfortable lifestyles, has resulted in an erroneous gospel. Of course God is love, but he is holy even before he is love. The great theologian of the cross P. T. Forsyth correctly pointed out that the statement '"God is Love" is not the whole gospel. Love is not evangelical till it has dealt with holy law.'[2] Forsyth refused to speak of God's love on its own. Instead he always spoke of 'holy love'. Any gospel that does not begin with the holiness of God will be inadequate. Certainly, its understanding of the cross will be incomplete and defective. Such a compromised message will never meet people's deepest need, and will never be an answer for their hardest questions. Men and women are not good people going to heaven – we are sinners going to hell. The fact of God's holiness and eternal righteousness is the most significant reality that every human being faces every day of his or her life. It is *the* factor that determines and shapes so much of our behaviour, ideas and priorities in life. Ultimately it is the first reason why Christ had to die. In order to understand this, we have to go right back to the creation of this world and construct a simple worldview.

Humanity Created

God's intention for Adam and Eve in the beginning was that they should be the image and glory of himself. Being in his image, Adam was to reflect God as his son (Luke 3:38). He was to reflect God's purity, love, peace, kindness and so on. He was to fill the earth and subdue it, but under God's direction and plan. One problem with trying to understand humanity in its original condition is that none of us has ever seen a 'normal' (i.e. as God intended) human being. Since Adam and Eve, and with the exception of Jesus Christ, every human being who has ever been born has been born in sin and is therefore 'abnormal' – less than God's intention. But if we can imagine Adam as he was in the beginning, we shall realize that he was to be a glorious being. He was the pinnacle of a wonderful creation over which he was to rule (Genesis 1:26). God breathed his own glory into Adam and Eve, and they could look forward to an eternal destiny in harmony with God and each other. So life was (and still is) about relationships, both vertically (with God) and horizontally (with other people). Adam and Eve could only be in right relationship with each other as they existed in right relationship with God, and, for them to exist in the way they were designed to, they had to be dependent upon God for everything. Adam was to be the creature of a Creator, the son of a Father and the subject of a King. Outside these roles, he would no longer be truly human.[3]

The Fall and Its Results

The beautiful creation God had made was spoiled by the fall. Genesis 3 tells us that Adam was not content to be *like* God; rather he wanted to be *as* God. In other words, instead of learning good and evil by close dependence upon God, he listened to the voice of Satan, disobeyed God's command and in so doing drank of the 'poison' Satan himself had imbibed: rebellion and autonomy. Adam had committed high treason against his King and Creator by wanting to be as God and be the one who determined such knowledge himself. When Adam and Eve fell, they rejected the very principle of true existence: they broke their relationship with God and sought to find meaning themselves. The Bible calls this death: they (and we) didn't die physically, but the relationship with God died, and this was so serious that death is the only possible description. Ultimately the result is eternal death. For a human, being out of a loving relationship with God is an impossibility, as we are in one sense no longer properly human, and the ingredient essential to our existence ended. For Adam and Eve, life as God intended it ended. Instead of existing as the creatures of a Creator, the children of a Father and the subjects of a King, they opted to go their own way and were dislocated from all relationships. It would not be an exaggeration to say that all of humanity's problems throughout its troubled history are the result of this decision to break relationship with God.

The consequences are terrifying. To many they may seem hard to accept. However, God's love and our liberation, as revealed and outworked in the cross of Jesus Christ, will never be fully understood unless we look God's wrath and our condition full in the face. Here we examine three of those consequences.

Our suppression of the truth

Romans 1:18 makes it clear that 'The wrath of God is being revealed from heaven against all the godlessness and wickedness of men who suppress the truth by their wickedness'. Moreover, they know the truth of God, but exchanged it for a lie (Romans 1:25). Once Adam and Eve sinned, they became aware of their nakedness in the presence of God and hid themselves, and the history of their children down to the present day is testimony to that continuing attempt to hide from God and continue the quest to pursue autonomy from him. 'God is light; in him there is no darkness at all', John wrote in his first epistle (1 John 1:5). People cannot stand the moral shock of facing up to the implications of God's holiness and purity, and therefore they seek to suppress the truth. That is, they deliberately seek to organize themselves and their society to exclude God from his creation as far as they are able. Romans 1:18 makes it clear that they know that there is a Creator, but they refuse to submit to him.

Hence, humanity constructs its own new view of God (theology), itself (anthropology) and the world (cosmology). These new constructions are 'the lie' that Paul speaks of in Romans 1, and they either rationalize God out of the picture or they rationalize him into more convenient and less confronting forms such as are seen in liberal Christianity or man-made religions, which allow people to pursue their own autonomous existence. As the playwright Tom Stoppard rightly pointed out, 'atheism is the crutch for all those who cannot bear the reality of God'.[4] It is time Christians made clear that there are reasons for atheism which are spiritually rooted, and began to turn the tables on their opponents who point to psychological reasons for believing in God. Atheism functions as an obvious crutch or wish-fulfilment for many.

Such suppression of the truth gives rebellious people some rest from the demands of God upon them. They seek to convince themselves that the true order of the universe is not really as it is, but is in line with their wished-for reconstruction of it. Two obvious examples today are the attempts to persuade our society that homosexual relationships are as normal as heterosexual relationships, and placing unmarried cohabiting couples on a par with marriage. Both are examples of our society reversing God's true order for the creation and proclaiming that its new view of the world is the true one. In taking this stance, people replace the biblical view of sexuality with their own 'brand', and advocate the violation of the holy covenant relationship of heterosexual marriage which ultimately expresses the love of Christ for his church.

In taking these actions, sinful people are not passively unaware of God, but reconfirming the original decision of their ancestor Adam to rebel from God, seek autonomy and be like God himself. Humankind's individual and collective mutiny from God is reconfirmed in millions of decisions every day, and in the construction of prostitution gods (idolatry), which make no moral demands that we are unwilling to keep. As P. T. Forsyth said, 'God never finds us as silly straying sheep but as enemies with weapons in our hands.'[5]

The point that must be clearly understood here is that sinful people have to justify this new view of humanity, God and the world because to accept the truth would mean that we would have to face up to the moral demands of the Creator and submit to him. Furthermore, fallen consciences constantly remind us of our sin and failure in a world that is ultimately moral. We have an awareness that the wages of sin is judgement and death (Romans 6:23). Hence, the worldview we construct not only excludes our Creator but we also use it to shut out any awareness of judgement and death that would constantly spoil our attempts to enjoy life.

God's holiness, and his wrath against sin

What was God's reaction to this suppression of the truth? The answer lies in Genesis 3, but more importantly for us in Romans 1. Sin is personal with God. All sin is ultimately against him, his Kingship and his rule. In other words, it is an attempt to dethrone God, and once Adam and Eve had sinned God's anger and wrath was kindled. Adam was to struggle to make a living from the land, and Eve was to feel pain in childbirth. This was their punishment for sin, and was to be a reminder of their falleness and need for grace. From this time forward the history of the human race has demonstrated the continuation of that rejection of God. As we have seen from Romans 1:18, it is *because of our attempts to suppress God's truth* that God's wrath is being revealed against us.

Now we must be clear here. Paul is not talking about a wrath to come at the end of the age. There is a wrath to come as Paul himself discusses in his first letter to the Thessalonians, but this is not his point in Romans 1:18. Here the sense in the Greek is that God's wrath is being revealed *continuously*. God's wrath is being revealed from heaven every second of every day upon all the ungodliness and unrighteousness of those who suppress the truth by their wickedness.

This is the main point of this chapter: God's holiness is the most significant reality facing every human being in this world. This is because in his holiness he is angry with sin, and his wrath is directed against humankind.

Many Christians find the wrath of God a difficult teaching. Surely, they say, God is love, and they are right. But the apostle John, in 1 John 5:10, makes it clear that because God loves us, he dealt with his own wrath by sending Christ to be a propitiation for us (propitiation is the averting or appeasing of wrath). So, if God's love is demonstrated by his dealing with his own wrath, then we had better understand his wrath.

Why is God angry with the sinner every day? Why is his wrath being revealed from heaven? God's wrath is not the capricious and uncontrolled anger that fallen human beings display. It is his settled and controlled opposition to and hatred of all evil and rebellion. He made us in his image to reflect himself. We were to reflect God's goodness, truth, righteousness and love. We were to be a love child: like father like son. But when we fell and sought to suppress God's truth by acts of unrighteousness, we sought to suppress goodness by evil, truth by lies, righteousness by unrighteousness, and love by hate. Instead of God being reflected correctly by his creatures, his true character is now grossly distorted and defiled. In other words, his children contradict his character. In the light of this, shouldn't he be angry? What kind of a God would he be if he weren't angry? He is angry that his people who were made by him and for him have rejected him. On a day to day level we know that, despite all the attempts to undermine discipline in the family today, one hallmark of loving parents is that they discipline their children. If that is true for us, how much more of God, the perfect Father. Discipline and wrath is an aspect of his love; it is not separate from his love.

The early theologian Athanasius explained that intrinsic to God's wrath is a determination to be a faithful creator,[6] and this involves judging and ultimately destroying all sin and evil in his moral universe in order that he can once again restore it to its original intention. As Bingham says, 'perhaps in rejecting the wrath of God, we have rejected the deepest strata in the heart of God'.[7] God is angry with sin and the sinner because he is holy.

Paul tells us that the wrath of God is being *revealed*. This means that you can see it. He tells us three times in Romans 1 that God 'gave them [sinful people] over' to their *sinful desires* (v. 24), to their *shameful lusts* (v. 26), and to a *depraved mind* (v. 28). In other words, God gave them over into their sin and its consequences. He removed his restraint and allowed the consequences of sin to have their full outworking. He gives us up to our idols, fornication and homosexuality, to use a few of Paul's examples, all activities where we violate what we truly are. Contained within each sin is its own judgement, because sin goes against the way we were made and we are left with an accusing conscience that will never let us rest or find serenity. The wrath of God is found in the actions and dynamics of sin and guilt. They fasten on to us and destroy our serenity and joy. God personally immerses fallen people into the terrible perversion of sin: its distortion, its addictiveness, its slavery, its compulsion, its bondage. As Isaiah wrote:

> But the wicked are like the tossing sea,
>   which cannot rest,
>   whose waves cast up mire and mud,
> 'There is no peace,' says my God, 'for the wicked.'
>   (Isaiah 57:20–1)

How do human beings experience the wrath of God? It is experienced predominately in pain, fear, loneliness, terrors, insomnia, restlessness, and a sense of loss, failure and unfulfilment. Even such a partial list is a measure of how far we have fallen from the Garden of Eden when Adam and Eve had perfect peace and joy. It should come as no surprise that the two categories of drugs prescribed today for psychological problems are sedatives and stimulants. Sedatives are to replace the lost peace and stimulants are to replace the lost joy. The most deluded sinners of all are those who are so seduced by society's rebellious 'constructions' of reality that they rarely experience God's warnings in their consciences: warnings designed to point us to the truth of our predicament. This puts an enormous responsibility on church leaders who must warn their flocks of the consequences of sin. As evangelical Anglicans we must first watch ourselves to see that we do this, and then seek to speak out where we see others in our denomination failing to take this seriously.

Many, if not most, Christians in our age do not like to think of God like this. The problem is that so often we have constructed an idol that we call 'god', and which conforms to our whims and fancies. It is a god that will not challenge us, nor judge our sins, but a god that will allow us to continue with our own self-centred lives. Such a god is not the living God of the Bible. It is dangerous to think we have better ideas about God and his gospel than he has about himself. If we change the message of the revealed gospel, the truth will perish, and so will we.

Humanity and its guilt

One of the most neglected teachings about humanity concerns the guilt that follows rebellion from God. As we have already seen, being in God's creation, people cannot escape God's judgement and the wrath that acts in their conscience. What is more, they encounter God's holiness every second of every day as it presses up against them in wrathful and righteous anger. In our sinful state, we have never really recovered from the moral shock that this induces. Not only this, but we have fallen short of what it means to be truly human. Both of these factors result in our being deeply guilty. Here we are not talking about *feelings* of guilt. These may come and go. Instead we are concerned with the fact that we are *existentially* guilty, deep down in our being, and in our behaviour we demonstrate a continual and never-ending testimony to this fact. This guilt manifests itself in our having a deep sense of insecurity and failure, and results in our constantly trying to justify ourselves.

Moreover, this guilt is really God's amber warning light, which constantly reminds us of the eternal consequences of sin and calls us to repentance before it is too late. Unless we understand this guilt in the human heart, any attempt to assess human behaviour will be an exercise in futility. The church in our generation needs to recover this understanding of guilt and self-justification, instead of looking for psychological and humanistic explanations for the human condition. Only then will the doctrine of justification by faith come to life once more. Apart from God, guilt is the most powerful force in the entire universe. Perhaps all of our problems, especially in terms of our relationships at all levels, spring from our guilty state. There is a need to stress again the importance of the conviction of guilt and sin in God's economy.

As a consequence of individual guilt, everyone has a constant sense of personal failure, both as a human being and before God. Furthermore, a new identity has been established as an attempt to legitimize this new view of God, humanity and the world around. This deep sense of failure means that we cannot afford for our 'world' to be challenged, because our whole identity would disintegrate and our quest for autonomy would be threatened.

Accordingly, we have to justify ourselves constantly. This means that we must spend all our time and energies proving to ourselves and others that we are not really guilty, nor a failure. In other words, we are seeking to justify our existence without God as legitimate. This explains why we find it so hard to face up to being wrong, and are constantly defending and promoting ourselves while accusing other people.

In presenting this part of the gospel message, great sensitivity is needed on the part of the Christian because the gospel shatters a person's worldview, and with it his or her false identity. As human beings we spend time, money and energy building structures, relationships and systems where we feel secure and are able to protect ourselves from being threatened by others. This is all the result of our deep guilt before God and one another. It is so important to apply this analysis to our contemporary world and see why marriages fail, wars occur, churches split and so on. Our self-justifying existence results in little else. The late American writer R. J. Rushdoony put it perfectly:

The fact of guilt is one of the major realities of man's existence. Both personally and socially it is a vast drain on human energies and a mainspring of human action. Any attempt at assessing either political action or religious faith apart from the fact of guilt is thus an exercise in futility ... The human race, with a prostitution god is deeply involved in a rebellious claim to autonomy and the guilt that follows that claim. As a result of this omnipresent sense of guilt, there is an omnipresent demand for justification. The expression 'he is trying to justify himself' points to this demand by man for justification; an insistence on physical and spiritual wholeness. *A sense of guilt leaves a man feeling like a leaking sinking ship. All energies must be resolved to the repair of that breach.*[8]

This brief outline gives an indication of the dilemma facing the human race. We have fallen from God and have dashed our relationship with him. Although still in the image of God, we are a shadow of what we should be. We have broken God's holy law, and are under the judgement of the One who will never tolerate treason against his authority. In other words, part of the gospel message is to demonstrate that we must be saved from God's present and future wrath.

The Cross and the Logic of the Gospel

God's holy and righteous character demands justice for the sin that has been committed against him. People often say, 'Why can't God just forgive all sin?'; or 'Why does it take all the pain of the cross just for God to forgive sin?' Statements such as these demonstrate our inadequate understanding of the seriousness of sin described above.

The Bible tells us that God is love. Many people know that God forgives sin: they expect him to because he loves. It was probably the German philosopher Heinrich Heine who said on his deathbed, 'God will forgive me; that's his job.'[9] Such sentiments as these are expressed by people who have no understanding whatsoever of God's nature and holiness. Campbell Morgan, expressed this well:

You say to me, of course God can forgive sins, because He loves. I say yes, but then in God's name remember what love is.

Love is not sentimental softness that overlooks the poison in the blood. Love is not an anaemic weakness that weeps over cancer and refuses to cut it out. There is nothing we are suffering from today more than this weakened conception of the meaning of love. We begin to understand love only when we understand that at its heart, at its centre are purity and eternal righteousness.[10]

If God were gratuitously to forgive one sin, he would be obliged to forgive all sins. Sin is a serious matter. Sin and its accompanying guilt have caused untold grief to God, and both grief and harm to his creation. To sweep it under the carpet would mean that sin would go unpunished and the creation would cease to function according to justice, which is unthinkable if we give it thought. Ultimately, justice means to uphold righteousness, and without it unrighteousness would be upheld and the creation would never be rid of the curse of sin. Sin and its perpetrators would ultimately reign. The harm that would follow would be incalculable. Whenever people get away with crimes in a country, the law becomes a mockery and the whole system of justice breaks down. In these situations it is always the weak and vulnerable who suffer most. It would be even worse on a cosmic scale. Can we imagine a world where God dismissed the great genocides of history or the sins of our own hearts? Somewhere deep down inside of each of us is the knowledge that we will never be at rest unless we know that the scales of justice have been balanced. God has to deal with the full horror of sin, but only on the basis of a justice that must never be violated. Only if justice is upheld can there be a bright tomorrow with all wrongs put right.

Our analysis would suggest that there is no way out for fallen humanity. Fortunately, God did something when we were utterly helpless to help ourselves. The good news of the gospel is that we don't have to spend an eternity under the wrath of God paying for our sins where 'their worm[11] does not die, and the fire is not quenched' (Mark 9:44). Clearly, humanity had to bear its own punishment: it was under God's curse.

The logic of the gospel is that God became a man and bore that punishment. The second person of the Godhead was born into this world in the incarnation. God the Father sent him into the world to die because of his love for the world (John 3:16). Jesus lived as the perfect man. He kept God's law perfectly even though he was tempted as all other humans are. But the reason for his coming was to die (Matthew 20:28) because the punishment for sin is death (Romans 6:23).

The key to God's solution is in Romans 3:20–6. Paul begins by explaining that no one can be righteous before God by observing the law (v. 20). This means that the only way to earn right standing before God is no longer open. In other words, doing God's will and God's work will be of no avail. Then Paul says in verse 21–2 that 'a righteousness from God apart from law, has been made known … This righteousness from God comes through faith in Jesus Christ to all who believe.' This means that there is a righteousness that we can receive by faith. How is this possible? In verse 25 Paul says that 'God presented him [Christ] as a sacrifice of atonement', or more literally, a propitiation. Propitiation has to do with the averting or the turning away of wrath. In other words, God had his Son die in our place to bear his wrath upon sin. Jesus Christ died as a man to bear the punishment of each sinner in order that we should never have to bear the just wrath of God. Christ bore it in our place. Jesus Christ died because God's holy nature demanded it, so that we should be restored to God through forgiveness. As Luther once said, 'Christ died for God before He died for man.'[12] Sin can be forgiven but only on the basis of the cross of Jesus Christ and never ever on any other basis. If God forgave on any other basis he would be shown to be an unholy God.

Thus God's eternal righteousness and justice have been upheld because Christ became sin, and so retribution has been made for sin. P. T. Forsyth once said, 'nothing will satisfy the conscience of man that has not first satisfied the conscience of God'.[13] God is satisfied with the sacrifice he made for sin, and only because of this can we be too.

What are the implications for us as the human race? The anger and wrath of God has been borne. When we believe that when Christ died we died, then we become participators in his death and resurrection. Another has borne the wrath of God, the power of guilt and penalty for sin. This means that we don't ever have to bear them. In place of these things God gives us Christ's righteousness. This doesn't mean that we literally possess the righteousness Christ had, but it does mean that our standing before God is *as if* we were Christ, *as if* we'd never sinned. We are talking about justification by faith, of course.

Justified by Faith

Justification means a restored relationship with God and the prospect of being fully restored to God's original intention for humanity. It means that we never have to justify ourselves anymore. It means being declared 'not guilty' before God our Maker and Judge. We can know a new secure identity: it derives from our being liberated by God and being secure in God's acceptance and love. We no longer have to justify ourselves. The 'problem' of God's holiness has been dealt with. That God is love has been fully demonstrated. The cross is the power of God.

So we can return to those two views of humanity and God. If humanity is not guilty before God then there is no need for the cross. We can justify ourselves. But if we are guilty before God then the cross is essential for our justification. As evangelical Christians at the start of the new millennium, we must preach the truth of justification with all of our hearts, and the reality of the cross must become so part of us that our lives give testimony to God's justifying power. We have to stop protecting and justifying ourselves and find our identity in the grace of God. As we preach we will not be alone, for the Holy Spirit has come to 'convict the world of guilt in regard to sin' (John 16:8). The Holy Spirit works in those who hear this gospel and he goes on to empower all who repent to live changed lives, lives full of love and gospel concern for those around. Only God's Word, sharper than a two-edged sword, will penetrate the deceptions, idols and constructions of our age and culture. Let us reclaim the truth of the liberating, justifying power of the crucified Christ.

Notes

[1] Hilary of Poitiers, *On the Trinity* 1.18.

[2] P. T. Forsyth, *God the Holy Father*, repr. Adelaide, New Creation, 1987, p. 5.

[3] G. Bingham, *The Meaning and Making of Man*, Adelaide, New Creation, 1990, p. 16.

[4] Cited by Dick Keyes in a lecture 'The Dynamic of Idolatry', L'Abri Fellowship Audio/Video Library, tape X1241.

[5] Cited by G. Bingham on a cassette 'The Cross and Justification', Adelaide, New Creation Ministries, 1985.

[6] Athanasius, *On the Incarnation* 6, 7.

[7] Bingham, 'Cross and Justification'.

[8] R. J. Rushdoony, *Politics of Guilt and Pity*, Tyler, Texas, Thoburn, 1978, p. 2; italics added.

[9] *Dieu* [or possibly, *le bon dieu*] *me pardonnera. Cíest son métier*; cited *inter alia* by J. R. W. Stott in *The Cross of Christ*, Leicester, Inter-Varsity Press, 1986, p. 87.

[10] G. Campbell Morgan *The Westminster Pulpit*, vol. 3, London, Marshall, Morgan and Scott, p. 162.

[11] Ralph Venning, *The Sinfulness of Sin*, repr. Edinburgh, Banner of Truth, 1997, p. 87, was typical of the Puritans who saw the worm that never dies as the accusations of the conscience will be an eternal torment to those in hell.

[12] Cited by Bingham, 'Cross and Justification'.

[13] Ibid.

Chapter Eleven

The Cross in Contemporary Evangelical Worship

Gerald Bray

O ne way of studying what today's evangelicals really believe,
rather than what we say we believe, is to look at the way we
relate to God in our music and songs. As we pour out our hearts to
God, we expose what our hearts tell us about our standing with God.
In this chapter, Gerald Bray studies evangelical hymn- and song-
writing, looking back and looking around today, as a way into a critique of our contemporary spiritual health.

Introduction

Sitting on one of my bookshelves is a fading red volume of hymns,
The Anglican Hymn Book.[1] First produced in 1965, it was reprinted
three times before a second edition, with additional hymns, came out
in 1978. During those years, as British popular music was being revolutionized by the Beatles and their myriad imitators and the Church
of England was slowly working its way towards comprehensive

liturgical reform, *The Anglican Hymn Book* achieved fairly wide acceptance among evangelicals, as representing the best in classical hymnody suitable for congregational worship. It did its best to be 'modern' but nobody could have foreseen the musical revolution (largely inspired by the world of pop) that would soon make it seem hopelessly out of date. It is by no means a bad collection of hymns; on the contrary, many churches still use it, at least occasionally, and I discovered when I looked through it that there are remarkably few entries which I have never sung in church – a test, if any were required, of its general appeal and durability. There is certainly no reason why it should not serve as a benchmark for evangelical musical spirituality in the 1970s, and it is highly instructive in that regard. Hymnody is central to evangelicalism, and in its modern form can almost be said to have been invented during the eighteenth-century evangelical revivals, when the Wesleys and others used it as a way of communicating their gospel message to a largely semi-literate population. Hymnody transcends the insights and idiosyncrasies of individual preachers and acts as a unifying force for a movement that can so easily be divided by theological, ecclesiological or even psychological issues of greater or lesser importance. Its impact may be subtle and indirect but it is no less potent for that, and it probably gives a fairer picture of the state of evangelical belief than anything else.

As I looked through *The Anglican Hymn Book* for hymns dealing specifically with the cross and/or atoning work of Christ, I came up with 62, or slightly less than 10 per cent of the total, grouped in three different parts of the collection. The first of these parts, which is both the most obvious and the shortest, is the one devoted to Good Friday – a total of seven hymns, ranging in date from 1784 to 1904. The second group can be found in the section headed 'God the Son', which contains a total of 34 hymns, of which 18, or just over half, mention the cross/atonement. The dates here are more widely spread, ranging from 1709 to 1948, but only 3 of the 18 were written later than 1870 (all in the early twentieth century). Finally, there is a long section called 'The Christian life', which is subdivided into several different themes, and of its 179 hymns 34 are linked in some way to the cross/atonement theme. Once again, the dates range from 1709 to

1874, with 25 (or just over two-thirds) coming from the nineteenth century. Finally, it should be noted that the supplementary section, added in 1978, contains 29 hymns, of which nine are cross-related, and most of these were written after 1945. This is a rough and ready calculation, of course, but it strongly suggests that an atonement-centred evangelical spirituality flourished up until about 1875 and then declined until there was a partial revival in the years after the Second World War. That there was indeed a revival of evangelicalism after 1945 is now generally admitted, though it comes as something of a surprise to discover that the decline can be traced so far back.

But perhaps this is something of an illusion. After having been a fairly radical spiritual movement for the first century or so of its existence, revivalist evangelicalism was beginning to settle down by the mid-Victorian years, before lapsing into the rigid conservatism that sustained it until the 1960s and even later. Generations of churchgoers continued to be nourished on the 'old' hymns, and few people saw any need to add to the existing repertoire. Energies were directed elsewhere, and it may be a mistake to judge the period in question by its apparent lack of creativity in this sphere. It is certainly true that the cross-centredness of the modern (1960–75) hymns included in the supplement stands up well when compared with the hymns in the main body of *The Anglican Hymn Book*; so it seems clear that the authors of these hymns were inspired by the same gospel message as that which had animated the earlier verses. To that extent at least, evangelicals in 1975 could feel secure in the belief that the message of the cross was still at the heart of their worship and spirituality, and probably few would have questioned it at that time.

The first sign that all was not well in the evangelical vineyard comes from the preface to John Stott's book *The Cross of Christ*, which appeared in 1986. In this he says, 'My second surprise, in view of the centrality of the cross of Christ, is that no book on this topic has been written by an Evangelical author for thoughtful readers (until two or three years ago) for nearly half a century.' After paying a warm (and much deserved) tribute to Leon Morris, whose books *The Apostolic Preaching of the Cross* (1955), *The Cross in the New Testament* (1965) and *The Atonement* (1983) he recognizes as outstanding exceptions to this rule (though mainly geared to a scholarly audience), Stott goes on: 'Until the recent publication, however, of Ronald Wallace's *The Atoning Death of Christ* (1981) and Michael Green's *The Empty Cross of Jesus* (1984), I do not know of an Evangelical book for the readership I have in mind since H. E. Guillebaud's *Why the Cross?* (1937), which was one of the very first books published by IVF.'[2]

At a time when popular book publishing was expanding in previously undreamt-of ways, the matter at the heart of the Christian gospel seemed to be decidedly under-represented. Was it simply that everybody was so satisfied with Guillebaud's treatment that nobody saw any need to add to it? Or had evangelical spirituality subtly moved off in a different direction, leaving the cross of Christ to stand – empty and alone – on a green hill far away? John Stott did not ask (or answer) that sort of question directly, but the fact that he went on to produce a 350-page book covering virtually every aspect of the classical doctrine of penal substitutionary atonement, shows as clearly as anything can what his answer would have been. In his view, evangelicals quite clearly did need to be reminded of their theological roots, and the fact that his book remains a classic, which has been neither equalled nor successfully imitated in the years since then, shows just how right his intuition was.

How does this apparent lack of interest in the cross of Christ play out in the composition and general reception of modern hymns? No one today would seriously question the fact that there has been an explosion of hymn-writing since the 1970s, which has been accompanied by a musical revolution in the church. Even at official events like ordinations in a cathedral it is now possible (even probable) that the choir and congregation will be singing modern hymns and choruses at some point, and the use of guitars and percussion instruments, if not widespread, is not unheard of either. Though this is not a domain exclusive to evangelicals, there can be no doubt that its main inspiration has come from them, and future generations may well come to regard it as the chief evangelical contribution to liturgical renewal in the late twentieth and early twenty-first centuries. Much modern hymnody circulates widely in different forms of 'oral tradition' long before it gets written down, and several items quickly disappear from the repertoire, so it is hard to find a book truly representative of it. Probably only a fraction of what we now sing will survive into the middle years of this century, and it is impossible to predict what time's eventual selection will be. Nevertheless, an attempt can be made to examine a reasonably representative modern collection and to compare it with what is now the classical (or old-fashioned) choice of *The Anglican Hymn Book*.

For this purpose I shall take the widely used *Songs of Fellowship*,[3] which was first produced in 1991 and has gone through several subsequent printings. Strictly speaking, it is not a collection of modern hymns, because it contains a number of old favourites which have been accepted into the modern repertoire, but that is itself part of the current renewal of hymnody. Not many people realize it, but John Newton's famous 'Amazing Grace' was hardly sung at all by evangelicals (or anyone else) until it got to the top of the pop music charts in the 1970s; even *The Anglican Hymn Book* only includes it in its 1978 supplement, side by side with hymns more than 200 years its junior! Using the same criteria as above, *Songs of Fellowship* turns out to have at least 49 hymns that deal with the cross/atonement, of which 21 are 'oldies'. That leaves 28 which can be claimed as representative of contemporary hymn-writing. This is less than 5 per cent of the total (closer to 8 per cent if the 'oldies' are included), which is less than what we found in *The Anglican Hymn Book*. But if numbers are down somewhat, it can also be said that in most cases the amount of space given to the death of Christ within each hymn is substantially greater. Consider for example, some of the words of 'The price is paid', written by Graham Kendrick in 1983:

> The price is paid,
> Come let us enter in
> To all that Jesus died
> To make our own.
> For every sin
> More than enough He gave,
> And bought our freedom
> From each guilty stain.

> The price is paid,
> See Satan flee away;
> For Jesus crucified
> Destroys his power.
> No more to pay,
> Let accusation cease,
> In Christ there is
> No condemnation now.[4]

It would be hard to better that from the classical repertoire; indeed perhaps only William Cowper's 'There is a fountain filled with blood' (written about 1770) approaches it in both graphic depiction and theological power:

> There is a fountain filled with blood
> Drawn from Emmanuel's veins
> And sinners plunged beneath that flood
> Lose all their guilty stains.
>
> The dying thief rejoiced to see
> That fountain in his day
> And there may I though vile as he
> Wash all my sins away.

Interestingly enough, both hymns reflect the same medieval under-standing of sin as a stain that needs to be wiped away, but perhaps we can pardon this theological lapse as an instance of the 'poetic license' that versifiers claim for their art. At least it can be said that both hymns are extremely clear statements of the 'full, perfect and sufficient sac-rifice, oblation and satisfaction' of which the Prayer Book speaks and there has been no appreciable weakening of the evangelical doctrine of the cross in Kendrick's hymn – if anything, the reverse!

Examination of the other cross-related hymns in *Songs of Fellowship* will reveal a similar tendency towards graphic depiction of the sufferings of Christ, even if the theology is sometimes much less evident. But this can also be said of many classical hymns, and we should not judge modern productions too harshly on that score.

More recent evidence suggests that hymns continue to be writ-ten that are powerful in their descriptions of Christ's death and some indeed present a profound theological understanding of Christ's work on the cross. Some older hymns are also seeing the new light of day as excellent and moving modern tunes are written for this generation. For examples of both, one has to think only of hymns such as

> Before the throne of God above,
> I have a strong, a perfect plea;
> A great High Priest, whose name is Love,
> who ever lives and pleads for me . . .
>
> Because the sinless Saviour died,
> My sinful soul is counted free;
> For God, the Just, is satisfied
> To look on Him and pardon me . . .
>
> Behold Him there! the risen Lamb!
> My perfect, spotless, Righteousness,
> The great unchangeable I AM,
> The King of glory and of grace!
>
> One with Himself, I cannot die;
> My soul is purchased by His blood;
> My life is hid with Christ on high,
> With Christ, my Saviour and my God.[5]

Or think of the song 'Jesus Christ, I think upon your sacrifice',[6] or the hymn

> He gave His life in selfless love,
> For sinful man He came;
> He had no stain of sin Himself
> But bore our guilt and shame:
> He took the cup of pain and death,
> His blood was freely shed . . .
> He did not come to call the good
> But sinners to repent;
> It was the lame, the deaf, the blind
> For whom His life was spent:
> To heal the sick, to find the lost –
> It was for such He came . . .[7]

Another remarkable hymn is

> In Christ alone my hope is found,
> He is my strength, my light, my song;
> This corner stone, this solid ground,
> Firm through the fiercest drought and storm.
> What heights of love, what depths of peace,
> When fears are stilled, when strivings cease! ...
> In Christ alone! – who took on flesh,
> Fullness of God in helpless babe!
> This gift of love and righteousness,
> Scorned by the ones He came to save.
> Till on that cross, as Glory died,
> The wrath of God was satisfied,
> for every sin on Him was laid –
> Here in the death of Christ I live.[8]

Judging from the above evidence, it would appear that all is well in the evangelical world, that a cross-centred spirituality is as alive and well today as it was two centuries and more ago, in spite of the relative dearth of serious theological writing on the subject. But is that really true? If hymns like the above were all that we had to go on, we might well concur that indeed it is. Evangelicals speak about the cross today in much the same terms that they have always used, and in that respect there has been virtually no doctrinal 'slippage'. But the question we have to ask ourselves is rather different from that. It is not *what* evangelicals say about the cross that matters in this context so much as *how often* they say it. Granted that cross-centred hymns today are as robust as (or more so than) they have ever been, how much do they or the message they contain figure at the centre of contemporary evangelical worship and spirituality?

It is here that the doubts begin to surface. A modern evangelical may repeat the classical atonement doctrine when he gets around to it, but how often is that? We cannot rely on the hymn books for evidence concerning this, and have to use other criteria for deciding how to answer this question. John Stott's observations ring uncomfortably true – not many books on the shelves deal with the cross/atonement in a popular way, and they certainly cannot stand comparison (at least in quantity) with the seemingly endless tomes on 'spiritual experience', spiritual growth and counselling in its various forms. It is hard to believe, but the average Christian bookshop probably stocks more books dealing with homosexuality or divorce than with the atonement! Quantity is not everything of course, and few of these books would rise to the standard of John Stott's *The Cross of Christ*, but even so the discrepancy is startling. Fifty years ago, there would not have been a single Christian book devoted to homosexuality (and probably none specifically about divorce either), but while these subjects now fill the shelves, more traditional – and more central – theological themes take a back seat. As the book trade is governed by demand as much as anything else, we can only conclude that these are the books people want to read, and that something on the cross is likely to sell less well. That in turn can only mean that interest in the atonement is slight, and that for many people it is hardly a central aspect of what they perceive as the Christian life.

Surveys of this kind are inevitably subjective to a large extent, and backing them up by anecdotal evidence merely increases the element of uncertainty. So much depends on who you know and where you go – one church or conference may be full of cross-centred preaching, whereas another has hardly any. What this means for the church as a whole is almost impossible to assess, because individual samples are virtually useless when it comes to detecting overall trends. Perhaps the fairest thing which can be said from the above is that where the cross is preached, there has been little if any drift away from traditional evangelical teaching, but it is far from certain that such preaching is widespread, or characteristic of contemporary evangelical spirituality. Most observers of the evangelical scene today would probably find it difficult to recall when they last heard a sermon on the subject, and as we have already noticed, it is fairly certain that they would not have read anything substantial about it for a long time.

Influences Diminishing the Centrality of the Cross

It is difficult to account for this, but some of the factors that have influenced contemporary evangelical thinking may help us to understand why this may be so. It is possible that the great quest for spiritual 'experience' and spiritual 'power' and ecstasy have led to a greater emphasis on resurrection power and on the power of the Spirit in our lives. Perhaps, in turn, this has led to a people less inclined to be overwhelmed by a conviction of sin that can be unburdened only at the foot of the cross.

It seems fair to say that what we think of as contemporary style in worship is strong on proclamation and weak on confession – resurrection triumphalism as opposed to the crucifixion penitence more characteristic of 'traditional' worship.

Another factor at work may be the influence of theologians like Jürgen Moltmann, whose ideas have attracted a number of evangelicals in recent years. Moltmann is certainly a theologian of the cross, and no one could accuse him of downplaying the importance of suffering in the Christian life. His theology is about as far away from the triumphalist as it is possible to get within the bounds of traditional Christian orthodoxy. Yet it is noticeable that Moltmann tends to exalt suffering for its own sake, and to see the cross as an end in itself. This overemphasis on Christ's passion may be a useful and necessary corrective to the above, but it is another extreme, from which evangelicals understandably recoil. The New Testament doctrine of salvation does not begin and end at Calvary; the cross is one element – central though it is – in a drama of redemption that stretches back to the incarnation (and beyond) and forward to the resurrection and ascension. The atonement cannot be understood outside that context, though it must be admitted that there has long been a tendency to misapply the words of Jesus on the cross ('It is finished') to the atonement, which has allowed that error to flourish. Traditionally, and especially in debates with Roman Catholics, evangelicals have been quick to insist that the cross is empty, because the Christ who hung and died there has risen again from the tomb. Ours has always been a resurrection faith, and an emphasis on the crucifixion that tends to make suffering redemptive in its own right will have less attraction for evangelical believers than such 'cross-centredness' might at first sight suggest.

Another factor that may be playing a role in the current equation is the steep decline in standards of public, but especially of private, morality in recent years. Evangelicals feel under siege from a culture that has rejected traditional Christian values in favour of a hedonistic amorality that would make ancient Babylon envious. In a society where nearly 40 per cent of live births now occur outside matrimony there is clearly a crisis of the family, and evangelicals would not be true to themselves if they did not try to tackle this head-on. Unfortunately, it is possible to get so involved in good works that the theological rationale for them tends to get submerged. One reason may be that there are plenty of other people who are equally concerned about the moral dilemmas of our time, and making common cause with them, while it may be politically necessary if our voice is to be heard, means that the gospel message cannot be brought to bear on the situation in an overt way. A few years ago I was asked to contribute to a school textbook, and was amazed to discover that my piece had to be edited in a way which removed anything that could be interpreted as evidence of a Christian 'bias'. The reason I was so surprised is that the book was about Christianity, and intended for religious education classes in schools. If a supposedly Christian 'bias' has to be edited out of a book like that in order to make it more acceptable, imagine what must be going on in areas where there is no a priori reason for mentioning the Christian faith at all!

The impact of modern counselling and therapy is perhaps less obvious in evangelical circles, but its effect needs to be considered carefully. Most Christians reject Freudian psychology and all that has come out of it, but our entire culture has been influenced by it to some degree, and we have to be very much on our guard here. If we allow guilt, for example, to be regarded as a complex (which indeed it is in some cases) and accept that it is best treated by some form of therapy, we have already sold the pass to an anti-Christian way of thinking. To us, guilt is as much a sign of a healthy conscience as pain is a sign of a healthy body. It has to be dealt with, not by wishing it away but by getting at its root causes, which in this case will be sin in one form or another. The cross of Christ is the Christian remedy for sin and guilt, because on the cross Christ took our burden on himself and paid the price God's justice demanded. This is not a reinterpretation of guilt feelings that explains them away as something else, but a recognition of just how important they are as signs of the seriousness of sin. Any compromise on this score, and the gospel is gone for ever!

Yet another factor at work is one characteristic of the so-called church growth movement. This is a complex phenomenon, but one persistent theme which runs through it is the notion that churches ought to be growing ever bigger in numbers, and that the way to do this is to cater to the 'needs' (i.e. 'desires') of potential members. A church should offer a wide variety of activities for different types of people, so as to provide a social centre as much as a worshipping community. There is a lot to be said for this in many ways, and probably churches in Britain should be doing more to create the kind of social atmosphere taken for granted in other countries, especially in North America. But as always, the danger with this is that the focus tends to get lost. We live in a world that does its best to avoid talking about such unpleasant things as death, but what else is the cross about? Churches only really grow when men and women die to sin by being 'washed in the blood of the Lamb', but talk of this kind is off-putting. Therefore, church growth specialists tend to bypass it and concentrate on more appealing things like 'fellowship' and 'community'. People seem to forget that these things only work when the cross is kept firmly at the centre of our preaching and teaching ministry. Other things are fine in their place, but if the atonement is displaced from its proper position the balance is lost and these things become hindrances rather than helps to the preaching of the gospel – and the growth of the church.

Focused on Christ's work of salvation

Perhaps this last observation is valid for all the above situations. The real problem today seems not so much to be a change of theological thinking about the cross and atonement as a subtle relegation of these things to second place (or even lower). The main focus of interest seems to be elsewhere, and it is usually to be found in something perfectly valid and commendable in itself. This is the subtlety of the modern imbalance. The best heresies are always those that are true – up to a point. What they affirm may be perfectly valid in itself, but will somehow either miss the point or distort another aspect of the truth. Arius, for example, was quite right to stress the view that Jesus was a real human being who suffered and died an authentic human death for our salvation. The snag is that in saying this, he managed to relegate Christ's divinity to a secondary level, because the full affirmation of his Godhead seemed to him to get in the way of the message he was trying to proclaim. Modern preaching is different from this in many ways, but it does sometimes feel as if preachers want to make some other point, whether it is the need to receive spiritual gifts, to resist immorality or even to empathize with the suffering peoples of the world, and stressing the uniqueness of Christ's death and resurrection somehow gets in the way of this or seems to be irrelevant to it. None of this is intended to be a criticism of the issues with which these preachers (and writers) are concerned. Rather, we must constantly ask ourselves whether our main preoccupation should really be more clearly focused on Christ himself and on his saving work on our behalf.

Reintegration of the cross into church life

What we desperately need in the evangelical world today is not so much a *reaffirmation* of the classical doctrine of the cross of Christ, but a *reintegration* of that doctrine into the mainstream of church life. Reaffirmation is fair enough as far as it goes, but it is unlikely to achieve much on its own. The reasons for this are fairly clear. First of all, very few evangelicals dissent from the classical doctrine, and therefore it does not appear to be under attack from anyone. They will probably quite willingly 'reaffirm' it, just as they would reaffirm the supreme authority of Holy Scripture, and probably they would be happy to do so in the most traditional language as well. The trouble is that they are unlikely to see that such a reaffirmation has any practical application. We all believe it, so why bother to go any further? All one has to do is look at *past* 'reaffirmations' of basic Christian doctrines to see that they make little practical difference. What we need is not another statement of what most people think is obvious, but a serious attempt to demonstrate how and why the cross is not just relevant but *essential* to an authentically Christian spiritual life.

The cross as transforming teaching

The chief battleground here is most likely to be with the therapists and their like. Much of what calls itself pastoral care nowadays is basically a popular version of some kind of therapy, provided by the church more or less free of charge. Liberal Christianity of all kinds has virtually succumbed to this completely, and a surprisingly large number of evangelicals have followed suit – a little more discreetly perhaps, but no less effectively. The shift away from the regular teaching of and preaching of Scripture to the couch (or armchair) has certainly been going on in evangelical circles almost as much as anywhere else, and I know this from the experience of preaching in churches other than my own. I usually try to find something of pastoral relevance to challenge people with, and almost invariably the reaction shows that the congregation is not used to that kind of thing, even if they are fed on a steady diet of sound doctrine. Indeed, such a diet may be one of the problems we have to face. It is not that there is anything wrong with sound doctrine, of course – we would be nowhere without it – but if it is presented in what amounts to a lecture format, people are liable to absorb the facts without feeling challenged to do anything about them.

In our age of information explosion this is dangerous, since we are constantly bombarded with interesting and useful details, but which cannot possibly have a direct application to our everyday lives. Yet the message of the cross is not just interesting information, nor does it merely have an impact on the way we think. The message of the cross is a transforming teaching, which radically alters the very being of those who hear and who submit to it. It is this need for submission that I am talking about here. The blood of Jesus must *cleanse* my soul, not merely find a niche somewhere in my mind as a potentially useful bit of knowledge. Effective gospel preaching is never less than teaching, but it is also more – it is a challenge to make that teaching live and relevant. Sound teaching which does not have that extra dimension will not do its work effectively; and if that happens, the door is left open for other remedies, sacred (charismatic) or secular (therapeutic), to take its place. The recovery of what used to be called *anointed* preaching ought to be our priority if we want the message of the cross to be effective in the church today.

For this to happen of course, what is needed is a large supply of *anointed* preachers, and here too we face a difficulty. The modern minister is often an administrator-cum-counsellor, with little time left for the serious study and meditation required if preaching is to be effective. By 'study' I do not mean merely academic exegesis and systematic theology, important as those things undoubtedly are. Once again, it is not just a question of learning facts, but of absorbing them, of making them a part of oneself. People who listen to sermons seldom pick up much of the message in intellectual terms, but they can almost always tell whether the preacher knows what he is talking about or not – whether, in other words, he is speaking from the heart, or merely repeating the observations of some commentary or other. For a preacher to do this effectively, he must have lived the message himself, and that requires a period of meditation and absorption, which few ministers seem to have time for these days. The effects are obvious to any listener – sermon material is presented in a half-baked form, without any real conviction, and most people switch off after a few minutes, waiting for the next hymn to start.

This may seem to be a long way from the subject of the cross, but in fact it is central to the effective communication of that life-changing doctrine. The New Testament *shows* us (it does not merely *tell* us) that the cross is a message to be preached. Other forms of communication may be possible and I do not want to suggest that they are never effective, but preaching is *the* way appointed by God to get his message across, and for that reason it must always remain at the heart of the church's worship. The absence of the cross from today's spirituality is directly linked to the loss of powerful preaching, and only when that is remedied will the problem be put right again. We must be thankful for the other resources on which we can draw, not least on the cross-centred hymns that have reappeared in our generation, but it is only when those great statements of faith are turned into effective convictions that the cross will once again stand where it belongs – at the heart of our spiritual life and experience.

Notes

1. Oxford, Oxford University Press, 1965.
2. J. R. W. Stott, *The Cross of Christ*, Leicester, Inter-Varsity Press, 1986, p. 11.
3. Eastbourne, Kingsway Music, 1991.
4. Extract taken from the song 'The Price is Paid' by Graham Kendrick. Copyright © 1983 Thankyou Music.
5. The hymn was written in the late 1800s by Charitie L. Bancroft and the tune that has made it so popular is © 1997 by People of Destiny International.
6. Hymn written by Matt Redman and © 1995 Kingsway's Thankyou Music.
7. Words © 1982 Christopher Porteous / Jubilate Hymns. Used by permission.
8. Extract taken from the song 'In Christ Alone' by Stuart Townend and Keith Getty. Copyright © 2001 Thankyou Music.

Mission

Part Three

Chapter Twelve

Truth with a Mission: Reading Scripture Missiologically

Chris Wright

Although commitment to mission is one of the defining marks of evangelicals, there are many whose biblical understanding of mission begins only with the so-called Great Commission at the end of Matthew's Gospel. But where did Jesus get his understanding of mission from (both his own and the mission he entrusted to his disciples)? Luke's version of the missionary mandate starts with 'This is what is written' (Luke 24:46), showing that Jesus read his Scriptures (our Old Testament) as a textbook of mission as well as the source of his messianic identity. So what happens if we read the whole Bible from a missional perspective? What are its major themes that undergird our mission theology and practice? This chapter helps us integrate our evangelical commitment to the Bible with our belief that mission is in the heart of God and of the essence of the church.

What Is the Bible All About?

I remember them so vividly from my childhood – the great banner texts around the walls of the missionary conventions in Northern

Ireland where I would help my father at the stall of the Unevangelized Fields Mission, of which he was Irish Secretary after 20 years in Brazil. 'Go ye into all the world and preach the Gospel to every creature', they urged me, along with other similar imperatives in glowing gothic calligraphy. By the age of 12, I could have quoted you all the key ones – 'Go ye therefore and make disciples'; 'How shall they hear ...?'; 'You shall be my witnesses ... to the ends of the earth'; 'Whom shall we send?... Here am I, send me.' I knew my missionary Bible verses. I had responded to many a rousing sermon on most of them.

By the age of 21 I had a degree in theology from Cambridge, in which the same texts had been curiously lacking. At least, it is curious to me now. At the time there seemed to be little connection at all between theology and mission in the mind of the lecturers, or of myself, or, for all I knew, in the mind of God either. 'Theology' was all about God – what he was like, what he'd said and what he'd done and what mostly dead people had speculated on all three. 'Mission' was about us, the living, and what we've been doing since Carey (who of course was the first missionary, we so erroneously thought), or, more precisely, mission is what we evangelicals do since we're the ones who know that the Bible has told us (or some of us at least) to go and be missionaries.

'Mission is what we do.' That was the assumption, supported of course by clear biblical commands. 'Jesus sends me, this I know, for the Bible tells me so.' Many years later, including years when I was teaching theology myself as a missionary in India (another curious thought: I could have done precisely the same job in a college in England, but that would not have been considered 'mission'), I found myself teaching a module called 'The Biblical Basis of Mission' at All Nations Christian College – an international mission training institution. The module title itself embodies the same assumption. Mission is the noun, the given reality. It is something we do and we basically know what it is. And the reason why we know we should be doing it, the basis, foundation or grounds on which we justify it, must be found in the Bible. As good evangelicals we need a biblical basis for everything we do. What, then, is the biblical basis for mission? Roll out the texts. Add some that nobody else has thought of. Do some joined up theology. Add some motivational fervour. And the class is heartwarmingly appreciative. Now they have even more biblical support for what they already believed anyway, for these are All Nations students after all. They only came because they are committed to doing mission.

This mild caricature is not in the least derogatory in intent. I believe passionately that mission is what we should be doing, and I believe the Bible endorses and mandates it. However, the more I taught that course, the more I used to introduce it by telling the students that I would like to rename it: from 'The Biblical Basis of Mission', to 'The Missional Basis of the Bible'. I wanted them to see, not just that the Bible contains a number of texts that happen to provide a rationale for missionary endeavour, but that *the whole Bible is itself a 'missional' phenomenon*. The writings that now comprise our Bible are themselves the product of, and witness to, the ultimate mission of God. The Bible renders to us the story of God's mission through God's people in their engagement with God's world for the sake of the whole of God's creation. The Bible is the drama of a God of purpose engaged in the mission of achieving that purpose universally, embracing past, present and future, Israel and the nations, 'life, the universe and everything'. Mission is not just one of a list of things that the Bible happens to talk about, only a bit more urgently than some. Mission is, in that much-abused phrase, 'what it's all about'.

Now this is a bold claim. I would not expect to be able to turn any phrase that began 'The Biblical Basis of' around the other way. There is, for example, a biblical basis for marriage, but there is not, I presume, 'a marital basis for the Bible'. There is a biblical basis for work, but work is not 'what the Bible is all about'. However, I take some encouragement for my claim from an impeccable authority: it seems to me that Jesus came very close to saying 'This is what the Bible is all about' when he gave his disciples their final lecture in Old Testament hermeneutics. 'This is what is written,' he said. 'The Christ will suffer and rise from the dead on the third day, and repentance and forgiveness of sins will be preached in his name to all nations, beginning at Jerusalem' (Luke 24:46–7).

Now Jesus is not quoting a specific text here, though we would love to have been able to ask which Scriptures he particularly had in mind (doubtless the two from Emmaus could have filled in the gaps). The point is that he includes the whole of this sentence under the heading 'this is what is written'. He seems to be saying that the whole of the Scripture (which we now know as the Old Testament), finds its focus and fulfilment *both* in the life and death and resurrection of Israel's Messiah *and* in the mission to all nations, which flows out from that event. Luke tells us that with these words Jesus 'opened their minds so they could understand the Scriptures', or, as we might put it, he was setting their hermeneutical orientation and agenda. The proper way for disciples of Jesus of Nazareth, crucified and risen, to read their Scriptures, is *messianically* and *missiologically*. Paul, though he was not present for the Old Testament hermeneutics lecture on the day of resurrection, clearly had his own way of reading his Scriptures radically transformed in exactly the same way with the same double focus. Testifying before Festus he declares, 'I am saying nothing beyond what the prophets and Moses said would happen – that the Messiah would suffer and, as the first to rise from the dead, would proclaim light *to his own people and to the Gentiles [nations]*' (Acts 26:22–3; my emphasis). It was this dual understanding of the Scriptures that had shaped Paul's CV as the apostle of the Messiah Jesus to the Gentiles.

On the whole, evangelicals have been good at the former (messianic reading of the Old Testament), but inadequate with the latter (missiological reading of it). We read the Old Testament messianically in the light of Jesus, in the sense of finding in it a messianic theology and eschatology we see as fulfilled in Jesus. In doing so we follow his own example, of course, and that of his first followers and the authors of the Gospels. But what we have so often failed to do is to go beyond the mere satisfaction of ticking off so-called messianic predictions that have 'been fulfilled'. And we have failed to go further because we have not grasped the missiological significance of the Messiah.

The Messiah was the promised one who would embody in his own person the identity and mission of Israel, as their representative, king, leader and saviour. Through the Messiah as his anointed agent, Yahweh the God of Israel would bring about all that he intended for Israel. But what was that mission of Israel? Nothing less than to be 'a

light to the nations', the means of bringing the redemptive blessing of
God to all the nations of the world, as originally promised in the title
deeds of the covenant with Abraham. For the God of Israel is also the
creator God of all the world. Through the Messiah, therefore, the God
of Israel would also bring about all that he intended for the nations.
The eschatological redemption and restoration of Israel would issue
in the ingathering of the nations. The full meaning of recognizing
Jesus as Messiah, then, lies in recognizing also his role in relation to
the mission of Israel for the sake of the nations. Hence, a messianic
reading of the Old Testament has to flow on to a missiological reading – which is precisely the connection that Jesus makes in Luke 24.

However, even if we accept that Jesus offers us a Messiah-
focused and mission-generating hermeneutic of the Scriptures, we
may still query the claim that somehow there is a missional
hermeneutic of the whole Bible such that 'mission is what it's all
about'. This uneasiness stems from the persistent, almost subcon-
scious paradigm that mission is fundamentally 'something we do'.
This is especially so if we fall into the evangelical reductionist habit
of using the word 'mission' or 'missions' as more or less synonymous with evangelism. Quite clearly the whole Bible is not just
'about evangelism', even though evangelism is certainly a fundamental part of biblical mission as entrusted to us. Evangelism *is*
something we do and it *is* validated by clear biblical imperatives.
The appropriateness of speaking of 'a missional basis of the Bible'
becomes apparent only when we shift our paradigm of mission from
our *human* agency to the ultimate purposes of *God* himself. For
clearly the Bible is, in some sense, 'all about God'. What, then, does
it mean to talk of the mission of God?

Whose Mission Is It Anyway?

God with a mission

Though the phrase *Missio Dei* has been misused in some theology virtually to exclude evangelism, it does express a major biblical truth.
The God revealed in the Scriptures is personal, purposeful and goal
orientated. The opening account of creation portrays God working

towards a goal, completing it with satisfaction and resting, content with the result. And from the great promise of God to Abraham in Genesis 12:1–3 we know this God to be totally, covenantally, eternally committed to the mission of blessing the nations through the agency of the people of Abraham. From that point on, the mission of God could be summed up in the words of the hymn, 'God is working his purpose out as year succeeds to year', and as generations come and go.

The Bible presents itself to us fundamentally as a narrative, a historical narrative at one level, but a grand, metanarrative at another. It begins with a God of purpose in creation; moves on to the conflict and problem generated by human rebellion against that purpose; spends most of its narrative journey in the story of God's redemptive purposes being worked out on the stage of human history; and finishes beyond the horizon of its own history with the eschatological hope of a new creation. This has often been presented as a four-point narrative: creation, fall, redemption and future hope. This whole worldview is predicated on teleological monotheism; that is, there is one God at work in the universe and in human history, and that God has a goal, a purpose, a mission that will ultimately be accomplished by the power of his Word and for the glory of his name. This is the mission of the biblical God.

To read the whole Bible in the light of this great overarching perspective of the mission of God is to read 'with the grain' of this whole collection of Scriptures that constitute our canon. This foundational point is a key assumption of 'a missiological hermeneutic' of the Bible. It is nothing more than to accept that the biblical worldview locates us in the midst of a narrative of the universe behind which stands the mission of the living God. All creation will render 'glory to the Father and to the Son and to the Holy Spirit, as it was in the beginning, is now, and ever shall be'.[1] That is a missional perspective.

Humanity with a mission

On the day of their creation, human beings were given their mission on the planet so purposefully prepared for their arrival – the mandate to fill the earth and subdue it and to rule over the rest of creation (Genesis 1:28). This delegated authority within the created order is moderated by the parallel commands in the complementary account, to 'till' and 'keep' the Garden (Genesis 2:15 NRSV). The care and keeping of creation is our human mission. We are on the planet with a purpose that flows from the creative purpose of God himself. Out of this understanding of our humanity (which is also teleological, like our doctrine of God) flows our ecological responsibility, our economic activity involving work, productivity, exchange and trade, and the whole cultural mandate. To be human is to have a purposeful role in God's creation. In relation to that creational mission, Christians need to be reminded that God holds us accountable to himself for our humanity as much as for our Christianity. There is, therefore, a legitimate place for ecological concern and action, for biblical earth-keeping, within our understanding of Christian mission responsibility – on the assumption that Christians too are humans made in the image of God (indeed being restored even more fully to that humanity in Christ), who have not been given some privileged exemption from the mission God entrusted to our species. This ecological dimension of our mission flows not only from creation, but also reflects an eschatological perspective: the biblical vision is of a new creation, of which Christ is the heir. Our care for the earth is an expression of our understanding of its future as well as its origin (similar to our concern for the human person).

Israel with a mission

Against the background of human sin and rebellion, described in the bleak narratives of Genesis 3–11 running from the disobedience of Adam and Eve to the building of the Tower of Babel, God initiates his redemptive mission of blessing the nations of humanity, beginning with the call of Abraham in Genesis 12. This is the essential missional purpose of God's election of Israel. Israel came into existence as a people with a mission entrusted from God for the sake of the rest of the nations. All that Israel was, or was supposed to be – all that Yahweh their God did in them, for them and through them – was ultimately linked to this wider purpose of God for the nations.

A missiological hermeneutic of the Old Testament, in its redemptive dimension, centres around this point. Israel's election was not a rejection of other nations but was explicitly for the sake of all nations. This universality of God's purpose that embraces the particularity of God's chosen means is a recurrent theme. Though not always explicitly present, it is never far from the surface of the way in which Scripture portrays Israel's intended self-understanding. We shall explore this missiological reading of the Old Testament more fully in the section 'Missiological Perspective on the Old Testament' below.

Jesus with a mission

Jesus did not just arrive. He had a very clear conviction that he was sent. But even before Jesus was old enough to have clear convictions about anything, his significance was recognized. Just as Luke ends his Gospel with the double significance of Jesus for Israel and for the world, so also right at the start he makes the same connection. It is there in the words of recognition spoken by Simeon as he cradled the infant Jesus, words appreciated by generations of Anglicans for their evening beauty in the *Nunc dimittis*, but rarely recognized for the missiological significance of their double messianic claim: 'Lord now let your servant depart in peace, according to your word. For my eyes have seen your salvation, which you have prepared in the sight of *all people*, to be a light for revelation to *the nations* and for glory to your people *Israel*' (Luke 2:29–32; my emphasis and translation).

It was at his baptism that Jesus received an affirmation of his true identity and mission. The voice of his Father at his baptism combined the identity of the Servant figure in Isaiah (echoing the phraseology of Isaiah 42:1), and that of the Davidic messianic king (echoing the affirmation of Psalm 2:7). Both of these dimensions of his identity and role were energized with a sense of mission. The mission of the Servant was both to restore Israel to Yahweh and also to be the agent of God's salvation reaching to the ends of the earth (Isaiah 49:6). The mission of the Davidic messianic king was both to rule over a redeemed Israel according to the agenda of many prophetic texts, and also to receive the nations and the ends of the earth as his heritage (Psalm 2:8)

Jesus' sense of mission – the aims, motivation and self-understanding behind his recorded words and actions – all have been a matter of intense scholarly discussion. What seems very clear is that Jesus built his own agenda on what he perceived to be the agenda of his Father. His will was to do his Father's will. God's mission determined his. In the obedience of Jesus, even to death, the mission of God reached its climax.

The church with a mission

As my quotation of Luke 24 above indicated, Jesus entrusted to the church a mission directly rooted in his own identity, passion and victory as the crucified and risen Messiah. Jesus immediately followed the text quoted with the words 'You are witnesses' – a mandate repeated in Acts 1:8, 'you will be my witnesses'. It is almost certain that Luke intends us to hear in this an echo of the same words spoken by Yahweh to Israel in Isaiah 43:10–12:

> 'You are my witnesses,' declares the LORD,
>   'and my servant whom I have chosen,
> So that you may know and believe me
>   and understand that I am he.
> Before me no god was formed,
>   nor will there be one after me.
> I, even I, am the LORD,
>   and apart from me there is no saviour.
> I have revealed and saved and proclaimed –
>   I, and not some foreign god among you.
> You are my witnesses,' declares the LORD, 'that I am God.'

Israel knew the identity of the true and living God; therefore they were entrusted with bearing witness to that in a world of nations and their gods. The disciples know the true identity of the crucified and risen Jesus; therefore they are entrusted with bearing witness to that to the ends of the earth. Mission flows from the identity of God and his Christ.

Paul goes further and identifies the mission of his own small band of church planters with the international mission of the Servant, quoting Isaiah 49:6 in Acts 13:47 and saying quite bluntly:

For this is what the Lord has commanded *us* [my emphasis]:

'I have made you a light for the Gentiles [nations],
   that you may bring salvation to the ends of the earth.'[2]

(This is a missiological hermeneutic of the Old Testament if ever there was one. As the NIV footnote shows, Paul has no problem applying the singular 'you' – which was spoken to the Servant – to the plural 'us'.) So again, the mission of the church flows from the mission of God and the fulfilment of his purposes and his Word. It is not so much, as someone has said, that God has a mission for his church in the world, as that God has a church for his mission in the world. Mission is not just something we do (though it certainly includes that). Mission, from the point of view of our human endeavour, means the committed participation of God's people in the purposes of God for the redemption of the whole creation. Mission, like salvation, belongs to our God and to the Lamb. We are those who are called to share in its accomplishment.

Putting these perspectives together, then, and summarizing the sections 'What Is the Bible All About?' and 'Whose Mission Is It Anyway?' above, a missiological hermeneutic means that we seek to read any part of the Bible

- in the light of God's purpose for his whole creation, including the redemption of humanity and the creation of the new heavens and new earth;
- in the light of God's purpose for human life in general on the planet, and of all the Bible teaches about human culture, relationships, ethics and behaviour;
- in the light of God's historical election of Israel, their identity and role in relation to the nations, and the demands he made on their worship, social ethics and total value system;
- in the light of the centrality of Jesus of Nazareth, his messianic identity and mission in relation to Israel and the nations, his cross and resurrection;

- in the light of God's calling of the church, the community of believing Jews and Gentiles who constitute the extended people of the Abrahamic covenant, to be the agent of God's blessing to the nations in the name of, and for the glory of, the Lord Jesus Christ.

A Missiological Perspective on the Old Testament

Evangelical Christians have traditionally had less of a problem reading the New Testament from a missional angle, which is hardly surprising given the dominance within the New Testament of the apostle Paul and his missionary travels and writings. So in the rest of this chapter I want to focus on how the above proposals can help us to develop a missiological reading of the Old Testament.

Certainly, *preaching* mission from the Old Testament usually rouses people's curiosity, mainly because it is unexpected. Many people, in my frequent experience, are surprised to hear a sermon on mission based on a text from the Old Testament. 'Mission' is widely viewed as a task originating from some words of Jesus on the mount of ascension. It seems to involve sending off somewhat peculiar but doubtless very worthy people to far-off parts of the earth to work for God in a bewildering variety of ways, and then to return from time to time to tell us about their adventures and ask for continued support. Since nothing of that sort seems to have happened in the Old Testament (not even Jonah came home on furlough to raise funds for a return trip to Nineveh), mission is deemed 'missing – presumed unborn' in that era.

A more sophisticated form of such a caricature is to be found in the way David Bosch relegates the Old Testament's contribution on mission to a subsection of a chapter entitled 'Reflections on the New Testament as a Missionary Document', in his magisterial survey *Transforming Mission*.[3] The Old Testament certainly provides essential theological preparation for the emerging mission of the New Testament church, but Bosch defines mission in terms of crossing barriers for the sake of the gospel (barriers of geography, culture, language, religion etc.). Since Israel received no mandate to *go to* the nations in that sense, there is, in Bosch's view, no mission in the Old Testament.

Apart from observing that in fact there are many 'barrier-crossing' episodes in the grand Old Testament story of Israel's journey with Yahweh worthy of missiological reflection, I would argue that Bosch has defined mission too narrowly. What follows is a brief survey of some of the key Old Testament themes which contribute to the broadening of the idea of mission that I have argued for above. This is, to be clear once again, not a search for bits of the Old Testament that might say something relevant to our narrowed concept of sending missionaries, but rather a sketch of some of the great trajectories of Israel's understanding of their God and his mission through them and for the world. We are not concerned about how the Old Testament gives incidental support to what we already do, but with the theology that undergirds the worldview Christian mission assumes.

I shall merely sketch below the missiological implications of four major pillars of Old Testament faith: monotheism, election, ethics and eschatology. A great deal more could be fruitfully explored in the same way.

The uniqueness and universality of Yahweh

According to the Old Testament texts, the faith of Israel made remarkable affirmations about Yahweh, affirmations that had a polemical edge in their own context and still stand as distinctive claims. Among them are the declaration that Yahweh alone is God and there is no other (e.g. Deuteronomy 4:35, 39). As sole deity, it is Yahweh, therefore, who owns and runs the world (Deuteronomy 10:14, 27; 1 Chronicles 29:11; Psalm 24:1; Jeremiah 27:1–12). This ultimately means the radical displacement of all other rival gods and that Yahweh is God over the whole earth and all nations (e.g. Psalm 96; Isaiah 43:9–13; 44:6–20; Jeremiah 10:1–16). The impact of these claims is felt in such widely varying contexts as the struggle against idolatry, the language of worship, and the response to other nations, both in their own contemporary international history, and in eschatological vision.

There is no doubt that the strength of the Old Testament affirmations about the uniqueness and universality of Yahweh as God underlie, and indeed provide some of the vocabulary for, the New Testament affirmations about the uniqueness and universality of Jesus (cf. 1 Corinthians 8:5–6, based on Deuteronomy 6:4; and Philippians 2:9–11, based on Isaiah 45:23). It is also noteworthy that these early Christian affirmations were equally polemical in their own historical context as those of ancient Israel, and in turn provided the primary rationale and motivation for Christian mission. We are dealing here with the missiological implications of biblical monotheism.

A fully biblical understanding of the universality and uniqueness of Yahweh and of Jesus Christ stands in the front line of a missiological response to the relativism at the heart of religious pluralism and some forms of postmodernist philosophy.

Yahweh's election of Israel for the purpose of blessing the nations

The Old Testament begins on the stage of universal history. After the accounts of creation we read the story of God's dealings with fallen humanity and the problem and challenge of the world of the nations (Genesis 1–11). After the stories of the Flood and of the Tower of Babel, could there be any future for the nations in relation to God? Or would judgement have to be God's final word?

The story of Abraham, beginning in Genesis 12, gives a clear answer. God's declared commitment is that he intends to bring blessing to the nations: 'all the families of the earth will be blessed through you' (Genesis 12:3, own translation). Repeated six times in Genesis alone, this key affirmation is the foundation of biblical mission, inasmuch as it presents the mission of God. The creator God has a purpose, a goal, and it is nothing less than blessing the nations of humanity. So fundamental is this divine agenda that Paul defines the Genesis declaration as 'the gospel in advance' (Galatians 3:8). And the concluding vision of the whole Bible signifies the fulfilment of the Abrahamic promise, as people from every nation, tribe, language and people are gathered among the redeemed in the new creation (Revelation 7:9). The gospel and mission both begin in Genesis, then, and both are located in the redemptive intention of the Creator to bless the nations. Mission is God's address to the problem of fractured humanity. And God's mission is universal in its ultimate goal and scope.

The same Genesis texts which affirm the universality of God's mission to bless the nations also, and with equal strength, affirm the particularity of God's election of Abraham and his descendants to be the vehicle of that mission. The election of Israel is assuredly one of the most fundamental pillars of the biblical worldview, and of Israel's historical sense of identity.[4] It is vital to insist that although the belief in their election could be (and was) distorted into a narrow doctrine of national superiority, that move was resisted in Israel's own literature (e.g. Deuteronomy 7:7ff.). The affirmation is that Yahweh, the God who had chosen Israel, was also the creator, owner and Lord of the whole world (cf. Exodus 19:4–6; Deuteronomy 10:14–15). That is, he was not just 'their God' – he was God of all (as Paul hammers home in Romans 4). Yahweh had chosen Israel in relation to his purpose for the world, not just for Israel. The election of Israel was not tantamount to a rejection of the nations, but explicitly for their ultimate benefit. If we might paraphrase John, in a way he would probably have accepted, 'God so loved the world that he chose Israel'.

Thus, rather than asking if Israel itself 'had a mission', in the sense of being 'sent' anywhere (anachronistically injecting our 'sending missionaries' paradigm again), we need to see the missional nature of Israel's existence in relation to the mission of God in the world. Israel's mission was to be something, not to go somewhere. This perspective is clearly focused in the person of the Servant of Yahweh, who both embodies the election of Israel (identical things are said about Israel and the Servant), and also is charged with the mission (like Israel's) of bringing the blessing of Yahweh's justice, salvation and glory to the ends of the earth.

The ethical dimension of Israel's 'visibility' among the nations

Naturally, then, there is an enormous amount of interest in the Old Testament around the way in which Israel related to the nations. It is far from being a simple relationship. On the one hand there is the ultimate vision of Israel being a blessing to the nations. On the other hand there is the calling for Israel to be separate from them, to resist their idolatry, to avoid their wickedness, to reject their gods and their ways. At the same time, Israel was a nation among other nations in the broad sweep of ancient Near Eastern macroculture, and so there is considerable missiological interest in the variety of ways in which the faith of Israel related positively and negatively to the cultures of other nations over the centuries. We could give much more missiological attention to the different responses of, for example, the patriarchal narratives to their surrounding culture; of the Deuteronomic materials to Canaanite culture; of the prophets to the relationship between Israel's experiment with royalty (king and temple) and Canaanite parallels; of the exilic and post-exilic communities to the world of Mesopotamian and Persian religion and culture; and these are just some of the possibilities.[5]

But the major point of interest here is, in its shortest expression, the missiological dimension of Israel's holiness. Israel was called to be distinctive from the surrounding world in ways that were not merely religious but also ethical. This is expressed as the very purpose of their election in relation to God's promise to bless the nations. In the context of, and in stark contrast to, the world of Sodom and Gomorrah, Yahweh says of Abraham, 'I have chosen him, so that he will direct his children and his household after him to keep the way of the LORD by doing what is right and just, so that the LORD will bring about for Abraham what he has promised him' (Genesis 18:19). This verse, in a remarkably tight syntax, binds together election, ethics and mission as three interlocking aspects of God's purpose. His choice of Abraham is for the sake of his promise (to bless the nations); but the accomplishment of that demands the ethical obedience of his community – the fulcrum in the middle of the verse.

Later, covenantal obedience is not only based on Israel's historical redemption out of Egypt, but also linked in Exodus 19:4–6 to their identity and role as a priestly and holy people in the midst of the nations. As Yahweh's priesthood, Israel would be the means by which

God would be known to the nations and the means of bringing them to God (performing a function analogous to the role of Israel's own priests between God and the rest of the people). As a holy people, they would be ethically (as well as ritually) distinctive from the practices of surrounding nations. The moral and practical dimensions of such holy distinctiveness are spelled out in Leviticus 18–19. Such visibility would be a matter of observation and comment among the nations, and that expectation in itself was a strong motivation for keeping the law (Deuteronomy 4:6–8). The question of Israel's ethical obedience or ethical failure was not, then, merely a matter between themselves and Yahweh, but was of major significance in relation to Yahweh's agenda for the nations (cf. Jeremiah 4:1–2).

This missiological perspective on Old Testament ethics seems to me a fruitful approach to the age-old hermeneutical debate over whether and how the moral teaching given to Israel in the Old Testament (especially the law), has any authority or relevance to Christians. If, as I believe, it was given in order to shape Israel to be what they were called to be – a light to the nations, a holy priesthood – then it has a paradigmatic relevance to those who, in Christ, have inherited the same role in relation to the nations. In the Old as well as the New Testament, the ethical demand on those who claim to be God's people is determined by the mission they have been entrusted with.

Eschatological vision: ingathering of nations

Israel saw the nations (including themselves) as being subject to the sovereign rule of God in history – whether in judgement or in mercy. This is a dimension of the Old Testament faith that we need to get our minds around, since it does not sit congenially with our tendency to a highly individualistic and pietistic form of spirituality (see Jeremiah 18:1–10; Jonah).

But Israel also thought of the nations as 'spectators' of all God's dealings with Israel – whether positively or negatively. That is, whether on the receiving end of God's deliverance or of the blows of his judgement, Israel lived on an open stage and the nations would draw their conclusions (Exodus 15:15; Deuteronomy 9:28; Ezekiel 36:16–23).

Eventually, however, and in a rather mysterious way, the nations could be portrayed as the beneficiaries of all that God had done in and for Israel, and even be invited to rejoice, applaud and praise Yahweh the God of Israel (1 Kings 8:41–3; Psalms 47; 67).

And, most remarkable of all, Israel came to entertain the eschatological vision that there would be those of the nations who would not merely be joined to Israel, but would come to be identified as Israel, with the same names, privileges and responsibilities before God (Psalm 47:9; Isaiah 19:19–25; 56:2–8; 66:19–21; Amos 9:11–12; Zechariah 2:10–11; Acts 15:16–18; Ephesians 2:11–3:6).

These texts are quite breathtaking in their universal scope. This is the dimension of Israel's prophetic heritage that most profoundly influenced the theological explanation and motivation of the Gentile mission in the New Testament. It certainly underlies James's interpretation of the Christ event and the success of the Gentile mission in Acts 15 (quoting Amos 9:12). And it likewise inspired Paul's efforts as a practitioner and theologian of mission (e.g. Romans 15:7–16). And, as we saw earlier, it provided the theological shape for the Gospels, all of which conclude with their various forms of the Great Commission – the sending of Jesus' disciples into the world of nations.

And finally, of course, we cannot omit the even wider vision that not only the nations, but the whole creation will be included in God's purposes of redemption. For this God of Israel, of the nations, and of the world, declares himself to be creating a new heaven and a new earth, with a picture of a redeemed humanity living in safety, harmony and environmental peace within a renewed creation. Again, this is a portrait enthusiastically endorsed in the New Testament, which sustains our hope today (Psalm 96:11–13; Isaiah 65:17–25; Romans 8:18–21; 2 Peter 3:13; Revelation 21:1–5).

Conclusion

Much more could be said, taking up other major themes of the Old Testament and reading them from the perspective of the missional purpose of God for his people and his world. From this angle also individual stories, events, persons and institutions come to have an added significance. At least I trust this sketch may have touched on some of what Jesus had in mind when he asserted that the mission of bringing the good news of repentance and forgiveness in his name to the nations is nothing less than what is written in the Scriptures that pointed to himself.

Further Reading

Blauw, J., *The Missionary Nature of the Church*, New York, McGraw-Hill, 1962.

Brueggemann, W., *Theology of the Old Testament: Testimony, Dispute, Advocacy*, Minneapolis, Fortress, 1997, pp. 492–527.

Burnett, D., *God's Mission, Healing the Nations*, rev. ed., Carlisle, Paternoster, 1996.

Hedlund, R., *The Mission of the Church in the World*, Grand Rapids, Baker, 1991.

Kaiser Jr, W. C., *Mission in the Old Testament: Israel as a Light to the Nations*, Grand Rapids, Baker, 2000.

Köstenberger, A. J., and O'Brien, P. T., *Salvation to the Ends of the Earth: A Biblical Theology of Mission*, Leicester, Apollos, 2001, pp. 25–53.

de Ridder, R., *Discipling the Nations*, Grand Rapids, Baker, 1971, pp. 14–87.

Rowley, H. H., *The Missionary Message of the Old Testament*, London, Carey, 1945.

Scobie, C. H. H., 'Israel and the Nations: An Essay in Biblical Theology', *Tyndale Bulletin* 43.2 (1992), pp. 283–305.

Wright, C. J. H., *Deuteronomy*, New International Biblical Commentary on the Old Testament, Peabody, Mass., Hendrikson, 1997, pp. 8–19.

Wright, C. J. H., *Knowing Jesus through the Old Testament*, London, Marshall Pickering, InterVarsity Press, 1992, pp. 136–80.

Wright, C. J. H., 'The Old Testament and Christian Mission', *Evangel* 14.2 (1996), pp. 37–43.

Notes

[1] Book of Common Prayer.

[2] Author's own translation.

[3] David Bosch, *Transforming Mission*, Maryknoll, Orbis, 1991. The relevant words are 'There is, in the Old Testament, no indication of the believers of the old covenant being sent by God to cross geographical, religious, and social frontiers in order to win others to faith in Yahweh ... Even so, the Old Testament is fundamental to the understanding of mission in the New', p. 17.

[4] This has been shown clearly, and in a way that underlines its importance for the whole mission of the biblical God through the people of God for the world, in the works of N. T. Wright, especially his *New Testament and the People of God*, London, SPCK, 1992, pp. 244–79; and *Jesus and the Victory of God*, London, SPCK, 1996.

[5] Walter Brueggemann is one of very few Old Testament scholars who have given serious and detailed attention to the nations as a theological reality in the Old Testament. See *Theology of the Old Testament: Testimony, Dispute, Advocacy*, Minneapolis, Fortress, 1997, pp. 492–527.

Chapter Thirteen

Cross-Reference Theology: The Cross in Conversation with Muslims

Ida Glaser

> See the ignorance of the Christian appealing for protection to the Lord who was suspended (on a cross).
>
> Jalal al-Din Rumi

Nothing is more central, to this book or to the Christian faith, than the cross of Christ. Yet nothing is more difficult to communicate to the world of other faiths. Paul found this in his own context, coining the classic phrases about the cross being 'foolishness to the Greeks and a stumbling-block to Jews'. The cross is still both for Muslims. For Muslims, Jesus did not die on the cross, did not need to die on the cross, and to suggest that he did so to pay for our sins is immoral. How then can we communicate what the cross means? What mission strategy can bridge the gulf of understanding? In this chapter Ida Glaser argues, with great sensitivity to historical and contemporary Islamic teaching about Jesus and the cross, that there can be no substitute for the patient telling and retelling of the

Gospel stories of the cross (and indeed the biblical story as a whole of which they are part). For the cross has no meaning in any abstract doctrinal framework apart from the story within which alone it makes sense. But such is the power of the cross that this patient, relational and cross-centred witness can never leave the witnesses themselves unchanged in the process.

Denial

Myself: What does the cross mean to you, as a Muslim?

Friend: It was the punishment they had in those days. But it didn't happen to Jesus. There was a swap. Probably the king who condemned him swapped bodies with him, and was the one who was crucified.

Myself: How do you think that differs from the way that Christians see the cross?

Friend: They see it as almost synonymous with Jesus Christ. It's the centre for them. All about their sins being forgiven and that sort of thing.

(Pause.)

Friend: Of course, Christianity and Islam teach very much the same thing. All the religions do. It's just common sense.

I was asked to write a chapter on how biblical theology and the cross develops in an Islamic context. To write about the Bible would have been easy. I, and others, have often reflected on how the contrast with a dictated text gives a new appreciation of the human dimension of the Bible. The contrast with a text that uses stories to illustrate laws and principles underlines the fact that, in the Bible, it is the story of God's involvement with human beings that matters. The contrast with an eternal Word that became Book makes us realize that the primary locus of revelation is not the Bible itself but Christ. The Islamic apologetic that insists on the corruption of the Bible sends us back to examine its human as well as divine origins, and to rethink the way we talk about inspiration and authority. I could have written a chapter like that quite comfortably.

But I decided instead to focus on the cross, and I have been anything but comfortable. I have realized anew that, after many years of trying to share Christ with Muslim people, I still struggle to find ways of bringing them to the cross. It remains, for them, the foolishness and the stumbling block (1 Corinthians 1:23) that it ever has been. It is easy to talk to Muslims about God, about creation and judgement and sin and godly living. It is even easy to tell them about Jesus' birth, life and teachings. But, when it comes to his death, even young children will say, 'He did not die.' This bare denial means that, as far as the Muslim is concerned, there is nothing to talk about. As with the Jews and Greeks of Paul's time, it is only God who can bring Muslims to the cross.

Perhaps the most interesting thing about the above (real) conversation is that my Muslim friend did not realize, until I pointed it out, an inconsistency that any Christian would have noticed. How could it be that Islam and Christianity are basically the same when Islam denies the event at the heart of the Christian faith? The question is: *what* is basically the same? What is 'religion' about? My friend's answer: it's about what God wants you to do. As one imam began a lecture, 'What is the purpose of a religion? To regulate the whole of life.'[1]

It was the *regulations* that, my friend thought, were, in principle, the same. I want to suggest that these similar principles are what we would know without any special revelation – the existence of God, our answerability to him, and enough about what is good to leave us without excuse at the judgement (Romans 1:18–20). Islam adds to this many of the biblical laws and stories, but they are in a different framework from their context in the Bible. It is this, rather than historical consciousness or even, I think, the evidence of the Qur'an, that underlies the denial of the crucifixion.

The Qur'an refers to the death of Jesus in several places. In only one is the death denied, the much quoted Surah 4:157:

(The Jews) said (in boast), 'We killed Jesus the son of Mary, the Messenger of Allah' – but they killed him not, nor crucified him, but so it was made to appear to them. And those who differ therein are full of doubts, with no (certain) knowledge, but only a conjecture to follow, for of a surety they killed him not.

In Surah 19:33, Jesus speaks of God's blessing on him on the days of his birth, death and resurrection. In 5:119–20 and 3:55 Jesus speaks of God 'taking him to himself' – a word that usually refers to death. The most common[2] current interpretation of this is that, as my friend suggested, someone[3] was made to look like Jesus and crucified, while Jesus himself ascended straight to heaven. His death is yet to come – at the end of times when he comes to bring Christians to Islam and to kill the Antichrist. It is after this that he will die and then the end of the world will come.

This is not the only interpretation that is possible for these passages. Chawkat Moucarry discusses the various interpretations that Muslims have offered for Surah 4:157, and adds his own suggestion that the verse denies the Jews' *boast* rather than the *fact* of Jesus' death.[4] Christians would agree that it was not really the Jews who were responsible – it was God's own initiative, and anyway the people who crucified Jesus were the Romans. Some Muslims find this an interesting idea, and some see the cross as a powerful symbol, but, in my experience, most persist in the belief with which they were brought up: Jesus did not die. One well-known Muslim polemicist entitles a booklet *Crucifixion or Cruci-fiction?* The story of our redemption is, he says, fiction.[5]

If the Qur'an has several places that refer most naturally to Jesus' death and only one verse that seems to deny it, and if other interpretations are possible, why does the emphasis on denial continue? It is not that Muslims have been unaware of the difficulties. Moucarry cites a classical commentator's exploration of six different objections to the idea that God should have deceived people by having someone crucified in Jesus' likeness.[6] It is not the text of the Qur'an that requires the circumvention of the cross, but the Islamic framework of thought in which Jesus *should not* have died on the cross, there is no *need* for Jesus to die on the cross, and the Christian understanding of the cross is *immoral*.[7]

Why should it not have happened? Because the ministry of God's Messenger should not finish in failure and disgrace. It would be dishonouring to God as well as the Messenger. Why is it immoral? Because each person should be punished for his own sin. It would not be fair of God to punish someone else on our behalf. The whole idea of God putting his Son to death like this is revolting. Why was there no need? Because, according to Islamic thinking, human beings are not fallen. They are only weak and ignorant, listening to Satan rather than to God. God is all-powerful, and can forgive us if he so chooses. What we need is guidance, and that is just what God has given us, through his prophets and books.

The Qur'anic Adam story has just this pattern: Adam and Eve are led astray by Satan, repent as soon as God reminds them of his command, and are simply forgiven. They are then sent down to earth, and told to be careful to follow God's guidance when it comes. A Muslim colleague summarized the differences between Islam and Christianity during a lecture on the Adam stories in the Bible and the Qur'an thus:[8]

Qur'an	Bible
Adam and wife tempted	Adam and wife tempted
'Fell'	'Fell'
Repentance	All have sinned
Forgiveness	Redemption needed
Promise of guidance	Saviour needed
Islam	Jesus Christ

Conversation

It is tempting for Christians to respond to all this by argument. The denial of the cross is a historical error, and we can seek to prove it so. We can present our arguments for Jesus being God's Son and for God's love and justice being met on the cross. Of course, history needs to be put straight, and reason is an important part of the discussion; but this does not take us to the heart of the problem.

The denial of Christ's death has been one of the common Muslim criticisms of Christianity since the time of Muhammad. It stands alongside criticisms of the divinity of Christ, the doctrine of the Trinity and the reliability of the Bible. All have their roots in the Qur'an

itself, and presumably therefore in Muhammad's interactions with
the Christians of his time. Regrettably, Christian responses have
often been centred around these same topics. But why regrettably,
when these things go to the heart of the Christian faith? Because, I
want to suggest, such discussions expose us to three dangers.

1. *The danger of starting from differences rather than similarities.* Any communication requires some common ground –
   at least a common language. Christians and Muslims can use
   the same words with different meanings, resulting in both
   sides convinced that they have won the argument, and no
   one the wiser about the other's faith.

2. *The corollary of neglecting to deal with deeper differences.*
   The danger of apologetics is that we can focus on the arguments, and not take into account the underlying differences
   that make sense or otherwise of incarnation and crucifixion.
   We can demonstrate the historical death of Christ on the
   cross to our entire satisfaction, but the Muslim is unlikely to
   accept it if it will not fit into his worldview.

3. *Focusing on these issues keeps us on Islamic ground, and
   can therefore make us lose sight of the distinctives of the
   gospel.*[9] (This third danger takes us nearer to the heart of the
   matter.) For example, the Islamic question about the divinity of Christ is how a human being can logically be divine,
   since God and humans are quite different. We believe that
   Jesus is God *and* man not because this makes logical sense,
   but because we have found that we can interpret the person
   of Jesus in no other way than by accepting the wonder that
   God has come to be with us. This is the Gospel distinctive.

The Islamic question about the Bible is whether we have the books
that God originally gave the prophets, or whether they have been
lost. We don't believe that God gave books in the Islamic sense of
word by word dictation. We believe that people wrote, under the
guidance of the Holy Spirit, so that Scripture can be fully inspired
and at the same time have a human form and history. This link

between the human and the divine is one key to our gospel in an Islamic context.

How, then, do we get to the root of the problem? Effective communication needs to start from common ideas, to take account of differences in worldview, and to lead to the gospel. It may be that, like Paul at Lystra where the worldview was very different to his (Acts 14:8–20), we can only take one step at a time. The cross came at the end of Jesus' earthly ministry, and his disciples, even with their Jewish education and Jesus' own teaching, did not understand it until after the resurrection. Communication of the cross needs to be done in context.

We look here at some ways of trying to communicate, and then go on to see how the cross can take us to the heart of the issues at stake between Muslims and Christians.

Beyond the orthodox

Muslims and their contexts are highly varied. Most of this chapter is written in the context of orthodox Sunni Islam, but the Muslims we meet may think in many different ways that suggest different ways of communicating the cross.

Some Muslims find the very idea of the cross offensive. They may refuse to meet in a room in which there is a cross, and some have even asked to be excused from wearing a school badge that incorporates a cross. Experience suggests that there are people who will not listen to any explanation, so vehement is their denial. In general, the cross is not the place to start in talking with such people. It may take many years of friendship and introduction to biblical ideas before they will be ready to recognize that Christian beliefs at least make sense on the basis of Christian assumptions.

Among twenty-first century British Muslims the situation may be different. Many have learnt about basic Christian beliefs at school, and may be curious to learn more. Some parents have heard the story of the cross and resurrection from their children, and may be ready for an explanation. The 'postmodern' climate enables young people to accept the possibility that someone else's faith is valid, even if it is in categorical opposition to their own. In such situations, a simple explanation, like the 'bridge' model, can make sense, provided that the ground has already been laid in teaching about sin, which separates us from God, and about God coming to us in Christ.

There are also practices within Islam that can act as a 'way in' to explaining the idea of atonement:

- *The Eid sacrifice.* At the height of the Pilgrimage to Mecca, Abraham's sacrifice of his son is commemorated by Muslims across the globe killing their own animal sacrifices. Orthodox teaching says that this is an obedient act of thanksgiving and remembrance, and in no way a sacrifice of atonement. However, some popular thinking has the idea of transferring sin on to the animal.

- *The aqiqa sacrifice.* On the seventh day after birth, many Muslims shave the baby's head and sacrifice a sheep or a goat. The animal is said to be offered in substitution 'blood for blood, flesh for flesh, bones for bones, skin for skin and hair for hair' for the child.[10]

- *Popular Shi'ism has ideas of redemptive suffering seen in the tragic figures of Fatima and Ali, Hassan and Husayn.*[11] In particular, the martyrdom of the latter gives rise to stories of his blood having healing efficacy, and weeping over his sufferings is a door to Paradise.

- *Honour and shame.* Muslim societies usually see shame as more important than guilt. There are occasions when the shedding of blood is seen as the only way of cleansing the shame and restoring family honour.[12] Some Christians have traced ideas of honour and shame in the Bible, and point to God's honouring Christ and dealing with our shame on the cross.[13]

Such ideas may help us to explain our understanding of the cross to particular Muslims, but in practice many will still see no need for it. They may have ideas of atonement, but they see it as available through their religious practices. They may even have ideas of mediation, but see Muhammad as the mediator approved by God. There remains the task of showing them why Jesus is needed.

Telling the story

The cross in abstract may make little sense: the story of Jesus captures interest and moves hearts. The suffering of the Messiah seems a *tragedy* taken by itself; but as the disciples on the road to Emmaus found, reading the Old Testament shows us that it is a *necessity*.

It has often been noted that the disciples after the crucifixion were very like present-day Muslims.[14] They believed strongly in one God. They hoped to see a visible kingdom for his people. They expected God to save his Messiah. They saw the crucifixion as a terrible tragedy. They knew nothing of the resurrection. They could only understand when Jesus took them right back through the Scriptures and the story of Israel; and when they realized that Christ was risen.

Many Christians working among Muslims have found it necessary to spend much time in telling the whole Bible story. We cannot expect Muslims to understand the atonement as a detached idea. I suspect that this is because it does not make sense as a detached idea: it only makes sense in the light of the God of Israel.

It also only makes sense because of who it is who died on the cross. Muslims are quite right when they suggest that one person being punished for another's sins is unjust. Ezekiel 18 recognizes this. It is different if a person *chooses* to pay someone else's penalty, and different again if someone chooses to bear an assault and not to fight back. Christians believe that both these things are happening on the cross. In Christ, God chooses to bear sin and its consequences rather than to punish us. In Christ, God also finds an acceptable sacrifice for our sins. Neither of these makes sense if God was not in Christ. If Jesus is, as Muslims believe, simply a prophet, the first is simply impossible. No human being can bear the consequences of sin against all other human beings, let alone against God. The second is unthinkable. How could one person be a sufficient sacrifice for everyone else's sins, even if this were just?

And how do we get to understand that God was in Christ? The New Testament does it by telling us the gospel stories. The epistles assume it – they never try to argue it. It is the gospel story that shows us who Jesus is. It is only at the end of that story, at the foot of the cross, that the centurion of old said, 'Surely he was the Son of God' (Matthew 27:54; Mark 15:39). Communication of the cross to Muslims, as to others, needs to be in the context of the whole story of Jesus.

Muslims who watch the *Jesus* video often accept the death of Christ it portrays. This is not surprising. It is unthinkable that the Christ portrayed in the Gospels should avoid the cross. It is also unthinkable that the Father portrayed in the Gospels would stop Jesus from taking his determined road. It was the Devil who tried to keep him from the cross – specifically at the temptations, and through Peter. In Gethsemane, the Father does not try to deflect his Son, but sends an angel to strengthen him for his trials.

Chawkat Moucarry's careful scholarly presentation of Christ in an Islamic context gives us an example of the centrality of the story.[15] He starts with an overview of Jesus in the Qur'an, and then explores Muslim interpretations of the denial of the crucifixion in some depth (see above). He focuses on the idea that the cross should not have happened: Muslims cannot see how Jesus could both be from God and be crucified. He then goes straight to Jesus' historical context by noting that the first-century Jews had the same problem. They concluded that, since he was crucified, he could not have been God's messenger. Muslims resolve the problem in the opposite way. Since he was God's messenger, they say, he could not have been crucified.

Moucarry moves from here to the gospel story, which, he suggests, offers a third possibility: that Jesus was both sent by God and crucified. 'Indeed,' he says, 'the Gospels teach us that it was precisely through Jesus' death on the cross that he fulfilled his mission as Messiah' (p. 141). He then tells the story of Jesus through Peter's encounters with him, showing how Peter moved from a denial of the possibility of Jesus' suffering to the focus on the cross in his epistles. It is only then that he goes on to the historical evidence for Jesus' death and resurrection, through the idea of the servant King and titles for Jesus in the Qur'an and the Bible, to the question of Jesus' relation to God.

Whether exploring Qur'anic interpretation in the academy or watching the *Jesus* video in the home, the cross is not an abstract idea but part of the history of God's life among his people.

Sentness and suffering

Kenneth Cragg has reflected on the cross in the context of Islam for many years. He has focused on the sin and suffering seen at the cross, on Christ's obedience and self-giving in going there, and on what it means that God sent Christ to hang there. His 1956 book *The Call of the Minaret*[16] explores these three levels, and observes that Muslims can accompany us in the first two, but not the last:

First, the cross is a human act: it has to do with ungodly opposition to the Servant of God. It is on the cross that we see the extent of human sin and rebellion, and the results of distorted religious understanding. Islam accepts the intent of the Jewish and Roman authorities to crucify Jesus. 'The cross,' argues Cragg, 'is the prototype of all. The cross bore a superscription in Hebrew, in Greek and in Latin. The human forces that made it what it was, as a human deed, are common to all humanity' (p. 270). We can, he suggests, point to the 'representative character of the cross' in showing us the human response to God. Such an analysis challenges the Muslim to move beyond ideas of human beings as weak and ignorant towards seeing our fallen and rebellious human nature.

Second, the cross is not only something that people did to Jesus: it is something that *Jesus* chose to do. His own message required him to suffer the consequences of people's hostility. He taught that we should not return evil for evil, but respond to hatred with love. Both to be loyal to his calling and to eschew violence in the face of expected opposition necessitated the cross. The cross, says Cragg, 'is what happens when a love like Christ's encounters a world like Jerusalem' (p. 270). Muslims accept Christ's willingness to obey God to the point of death. We want to tell them that God permitted him this obedience: a death in forgiveness rather than hatred. This is a death that accepts and deals with the evil that causes it.

Third, the cross is an act of *God*. This is where we part company with most Muslims. That people wanted to crucify Jesus, and that he was willing to be crucified, they agree. That God could also have wanted it seems senseless to them. It only makes sense if this is not only God choosing this death for his prophet, but that 'God was in

Christ, reconciling the world to himself' (2 Corinthians 5:19). It is not that the sacrifice of someone else 'somehow placates a propitiating God from without', but that Christ himself 'expresses the divine love already active towards sinful humanity' (p. 272). We can only make sense of the cross in the context of the incarnation.

Cragg has developed such themes into an explanation of the incarnation and the cross starting from Qur'anic ideas. Chapters 2–4 of his *Christ and the Faiths* (SPCK, 1986), lay the foundations. He starts from the idea of the greatness of God, as expressed in Mary's Magnificat and the *Allahu akbar* cry of Islam. He focuses on Mary's 'His mercy is on them that fear him' (Luke 1:50) and the parallel Muslim ideas of *rahmah* (mercy) and *taqwa* (piety or godly fear) in the context of an unbelieving world. In this way, he lays a firm foundation of common ground between Muslim and Christian, while signalling differences in the way that we interpret these ideas.

He goes on to reflect on the shared idea that God speaks through prophets. Must these prophets not have some 'capacity for revelation', he asks? Muslims say that the Qur'anic words are given with no participation by the prophet: it is only after their receipt that he transmits and interprets them. Cragg argues that he must have a capacity to receive. 'God and his Messenger' frequently go together in the Qur'an. That is, the human recipient of revelation matters. Human and divine cannot be quite so incompatible as some Muslims suggest.

He then reflects on the Bible's telling of the messages of Christ and of Jeremiah, and argues that the message cannot be separated from the messenger. Neither can the rejection of the message be separated from the rejection of the messenger. We find that Jeremiah's sorrow at this rejection can scarcely be distinguished from God's sorrow (e.g. Jeremiah 12:5–11).

All this implies, suggests Cragg, that God as Sender is not only associated with the message that is sent, but also with the messenger. And this 'association' is in the context of the sufferings of the messenger. He recognizes that this has taken him into ideas that are anathema to Islam – 'association' of anything with God (*shirk*) being the unforgivable sin. Cragg's exploration of the idea of 'sentness' has taken him towards the idea that God became so associated with his Messenger that God not only sent, but also personally came and suffered. It has taken him to the cross.

What do we see on the cross?

What do such attempts at communication with Muslims do to our theology of the cross? They not only drive us towards different expressions of our faith, but also lead us to appreciate different aspects of it and develop new insights into it. I have found that the Islamic emphasis on revelation has led me to see the cross in terms of revelation as well as atonement. This is not, of course, an either/or. The revelation is in the atonement. What is revealed is not a doctrine or an idea of atonement, but God in Christ reconciling the world to himself.

Muslims see the Qur'an as the prime locus of revelation, as the eternal Word of God come to us in a Book. Biblically, Christ is the eternal Word of God, come to us as one of us. If God was in Christ, and if the cross is the focus and climax of his ministry, what do we see when we look at him there? Because the cross is both the heart of Christianity and missing from Islam, we see some of our crucial differences there.

We see ourselves

Muslims may deny the 'fall' but, on the cross, we see the full extent and effects of sin. *This* is what human beings will do when confronted with the absolute goodness of God himself. *This* is what God has to do to deal with human wickedness. It is not Christ's sin but ours that we see exposed on the cross; and this focus on what we see takes us to another concept that is particularly relevant in many Islamic contexts – shame. Shame is about our sin being seen by ourselves and by others.

Muslims agree about the wickedness that wanted to kill Jesus. The main point of Surah 4:157 in its context is not denying Christ's death but putting the Jews to shame for their persistent rejection of God's message. This is right. The New Testament also puts them to shame for their treatment of Christ, but for an opposite reason. The Qur'an says, 'You killed him not.' The apostles frequently tell their Jewish audience, 'You killed him' (Acts 2:23, 36; 3:13–15; 4:10; 5:30). This comes to a climax in Stephen's sermon in Acts 7, with its relentless exposure of the goodness of God and the rejection of his prophet that culminates in the rejection of Christ.

That sermon was addressed to Jews, but the New Testament addresses humanity more widely, and makes it very clear that we are all implicated in Christ's death. The cross shows us as nothing else does that we are fallen, and that religious or moral guidance is never enough. Here is the best of messengers bringing the best of guidance. Not only do the religious people send him to the cross; his most faithful disciples deny and forsake him. I can see the wickedness of the world and of myself in the light of the cross.

We see *God*

'God was . . . in Christ' (2 Corinthians 5:19). For the Muslim, this is an impossibility, because the human and the divine are two totally different realities. For the Christian, accepting the compatibility between divine and human implied by the belief that God made humans 'in the image of God' is a wonder. God who *can* come to be with us *does* come to be with us, and to become one of us. And, when he comes, he becomes totally involved in our lives, to the extent of entering our pains and our death.

This is God who is holy and just and righteous and loving; but the comparison with Islam brings out other aspects of him.

This is God who does not overlook sin. Muslims believe that God can forgive by sovereign mercy: since he is not affected by human actions, he can simply wipe away the penalty for sin. In Christian terms, this is not really forgiveness, since it does not deal with the pain and the offence that sin causes. In the cross, we see how sin affects God. We see a God who is not aloof from the world, but is deeply wounded by it.

This is God who allows evil its full extent. When sin corrupted God's good creation, he limited its effects for the sake of his creation

(Genesis 3:22–4; 4:13–16; 6:3; 11:6–9). He could have put an end to the wickedness at the cross by destroying its perpetrators,[17] or by rescuing the victim; but he did not. On the cross, we see God allowing evil to have its full effect – not on us, but on himself.

This is God who is not ashamed of his shameful creatures. According to custom, as in most Muslim cultures, the prodigal son's father should never have welcomed him back, and should never have gone to seek the elder brother. Both sons were shaming him by their actions, and the only way he could have kept face would have been to cast them off completely. But the father's love overcomes his shame – he honours them both by going out to them. On the cross we see our completely honourable Messiah exposed to shame for us.

This is God triumphant. In Islamic thinking, God's honour and triumph are reasons for denying the cross. It is dishonouring to God's prophet, and therefore to God, we are told. 'We honour Jesus more than you do' is a common criticism. In Christian thinking, it is not Christ whose dishonour we see on the cross, but our own. We see Christ's honour in his obedience to the Father. We see his triumph in fighting sin and Satan to the very end.

And, of course, we see God honouring Christ and triumphing over all his enemies in the resurrection. In denying the crucifixion, Muslims seldom think about the Christian teaching about the resurrection. We, who see that 'God was in Christ', see that it is a greater triumph to go through death to resurrection than to escape death. This is not only a triumph over the people who wanted to kill him, but over sin and Satan for all time.

We see ourselves anew

'God was reconciling the world to himself in Christ' (2 Corinthians 5:19). On the cross, we do not just see God – we see him doing something. He conquers sin and Satan, not just to show himself Lord, but to rescue us. How can that be?

For Muslims, the idea that someone should die for our sins seems unfair. But there is another way of looking at this. Paul also says, 'if anyone is in Christ, he is a new creation' (2 Corinthians 5:17

NRSV). Most Muslims come from cultures that function collectively, in ways that are incomprehensible to many Western individualist Christians. They know that if you are a member of a family you are implicated in all that happens to that family. In particular, one person can shame the whole family; and the honour of a family is shared by every member of it. Paul is telling us that if we are members of Christ we are implicated in all that happens to him.

He can even say that those who are in Christ have died with him (Romans 6:3ff.; 2 Corinthians 5:14). We can see ourselves, in Christ, on the cross. We see our sin that put him there, but we also see the shame and the penalty for our sin nailed there. And, if we are implicated in Christ's death, we are also implicated in his resurrection. We have brought shame on him, but he has borne it. Now, we can share in his honour and triumph.

Cross-reference Theology

> If we mean to live in this world, it has to be said that cross-reference theology is the only one that there is.[18]

Theology is always done in a context, whether recognized or not. The job of Christian theologians is to understand and express afresh the 'old, old story' for the current generation. We look to the Scriptures and their context, but also to the church and to the world. If our theology is to help rather than hinder our mission, it must be done in 'cross-reference' to the world to which we are called.

It is my belief that such cross-reference theology will always refer to the cross. Compared to all other worldviews, it is above all the cross that makes Christianity distinctive. It continues to be the foolishness and the stumbling block that it ever was, because it simply does not fit into any scheme other than that of the biblical salvation story. Theological reflection in the context of any other system is likely to take us again and again to the cross at the heart of our faith.

Christians called to minister among Muslims frequently testify to this. People consulted during the writing of this chapter told me:

- The cross has become so much more precious to me.
- I have grown in appreciation of the Creator God who is almighty, yet humbled himself on our behalf.
- I keep seeing the significance of grace, and that's what the cross is all about, isn't it?
- I began to think more of God's love being sacrificial, embracing suffering. This leads me to marvel at his grace and to love him more.

This is no new phenomenon. Samuel Zwemer, one of the best-known missionaries in the Arabian peninsula, wrote a whole book on *The Glory of the Cross* towards the end of his life.[19] He writes with a rare passion, and here is its origin: 'The following chapters are the result of meditation on the passion of our Lord and his Death on the cross in the midst of men who deny the historicity of the crucifixion and the necessity of the atonement.'[20]

Islam's very denial of the cross can make us realize afresh its significance. I trust that this short chapter has helped readers to do just that.

But this is not only a theological significance. We cannot appreciate the cross in our thinking without it impacting our living. And this is, perhaps, the most important aspect of cross-reference theology. Muhammad chose the temporal victory of the *hijra*: Jesus chose the very different victory of the cross. Which will we choose? Interaction with Muslims brings this challenge into sharp relief. Constance Padwick wrote in 1938, 'It is no easy achievement to meet the *hauteur* of Islam without answering *hauteur* but with penitent love.' And she quotes Temple Gairdner of Cairo (1837–1928):

> We are claiming the right to have it said to us, 'Ye are they which have continued with me in my temptations' ... (Christ) too knew what it was to fall back on the Spirit, to realize and to confess that only by what seemed like weakness must all that strength be met, *only* by the foolishness of the Message, *only* by the scandal of the cross.[21]

Our days are no different. There are still social and political tensions between Muslims and Christians worldwide. There are still millions of Muslims who struggle with oppression and sin every day. The calls to mission, to peacemaking, to being salt and light in the world are no less urgent. Responding to the calls is no less costly.

The cross is not only part of the Bible story and the gospel story: if we are to communicate with Muslims, it must also be part of *our* story. We must allow *our* sin – communal and national as well as personal – to be exposed and dealt with at the cross. We must follow the obedience and meekness that led Christ to it. We must show in our lives the God who is involved in human affairs; who does not overlook sin; who accepts the effects of sin, but does it with forgiveness; who is not ashamed to be associated with sinful people; and who triumphs through death.

Roland Muller's research on what makes an effective missionary among Muslims yields a startling result. What the subjects of his research had in common, apart from love for Jesus, for the Bible and for Muslims, was that they had all suffered deeply, either in their personal lives or as the result of their ministry.

> Suddenly, I realized that Muslims weren't attracted to evangelists, they were attracted to God ... They may not know it, and might not express it in those words, but when they see God in his beauty, lived out in the lives of his people, they are attracted to him. In order for Jesus to truly shine through a life, the hard exterior has to be broken and removed.[22]

In Gethsemane, Jesus begged his Father, 'If it is possible, may this cup be taken from me' (Matthew 26:39). If there had been any other way, we can be sure that the Father would have spared the Son. There was no other way for him if we were to be saved. There is no other way for us if our Muslim friends are to see him.[23]

Notes

[1] This was a talk given to a group of Christian theological students in Oxford.

[2] Another interpretation, popularized by the Ahmadiyya, is that Jesus was put on the cross, but that he did not die there.

He swooned, and later revived and went to preach in Kashmir, where his grave can still be seen.

3 The most popular candidate is Judas, although some, like my friend, think it was Pilate.

4 *Faith to Faith: Christianity and Islam in Dialogue*, Leicester, Inter-Varsity Press, 2001, ch. 10.

5 Ahmed Deedat, *jamaat.net/crux/crucifixion.html,* accessed 22 January 2003.

6 Moucarry, *Faith to Faith*, pp. 134–37.

7 See Kenneth Cragg's analysis in *Jesus and the Muslim*, repr., Oxford, Oneworld, 1999, ch. 6.

8 Dr Jabal Buaben of the Centre for the Study of Islam and Christian–Muslim Relations, Selly Oak, Birmingham. The main Qur'anic stories can be found in Surahs 2:30–39 and 7:11–25.

9 I am indebted to Dr David Thomas for giving me the seed of this idea.

10 See A. A. Thanvi, *Bahishti Zewar*, trans. F. Ud-din, Taj, 1990, p. 284. Two animals are offered for a boy, one for a girl.

11 See M. Ayoub, *Redemptive Suffering in Islam*, Hague, Mouton, 1978.

12 This idea is behind the so-called 'honour killings' of women whose chastity has been broken in some Muslim communities.

13 E.g. B. Musk, *Touching the Soul of Islam*, Marc, 1995, ch. 4; and E. W. Huffard, 'Culturally Relevant Themes about Christ', in *Muslims and Christians on the Emmaus Road*, ed. J. D. Woodberry, Monrovia, Calif., Marc, 1989, pp. 161–74.

14 See e.g. the introduction to Woodberry, *Muslims and Christians*, pp. ix–xv.

15 Moucarry, *Faith to Faith*, part 3.

16 Oxford University Press. Page references are to 2nd ed., Collins, 1986. Interpreting the cross is dealt with in sections IX and X of ch. 10. See also Cragg's *Jesus and the Muslim*, George Allen and Unwin, 1985.

17 Qura'nic prophets are often rescued by God's judgement on their opponents. See e.g. Surah 7:59–93.

18 K. Cragg, *The Christ and the Faiths: Theology in Cross-reference*, SPCK, 1986, p. 13.

19 First published by Oliphants in 1954.

20 Ibid., p. 5.

21 'North African Reverie', in *International Review of Mission*, vol. 27, no. 107 (1938), pp. 341–54.

22 *Tools for Muslim Evangelism*, Essence, 2000, p. 24.

23 Although I have written this chapter, many of the ideas in it have come out of discussions with friends and colleagues as I have researched it.

Chapter Fourteen

Christian Mission Today: The Power and Weakness of the Cross

David Zac Niringiye

The cross of Christ, Paul affirmed, was the power of God demonstrated in weakness. Yet often the message of the cross has been preached by those in positions of power – political, colonial or economic. Those, however, who have taken the mission of the cross in true weakness, poverty and suffering (and especially those who have been martyred for their witness), are those who have most to teach us about its transforming and life-giving power. In three moving stories of African Christian leaders, David Zac Niringiye takes us to the Church of Uganda, one of the largest and liveliest parts of the worldwide Anglican communion, though probably less familiar to most readers of this book. Through their testimony in different generations, we are challenged about the true nature of conversion, about our obsession with safety when mission must mean taking risks, and about where the true source of our identity and security lies.

Christian mission is our response to God's mission in Christ; it is about following Jesus. Every context presents opportunities and challenges to Christians as they seek to live and serve as witnesses to God's kingdom that is 'present and yet to come'. Theological convictions lead to different views of mission, but it is also true that the context has an impact on the understanding of God's mission. The present world context of socio-economic inequalities, poverty, famine and wars dictates that we reflect on the meaning and manifestation of God's mission in the context of human pain and suffering. This is especially so given the mass of suffering humanity contrasted with a minority that seem to be removed from such pain. The *World Development Report 2000/2001: Attacking Poverty* paints part of the picture thus:

> At the start of a new century, poverty remains a global problem of huge proportions. Of the world's 6 billion people, 2.8 billion live on less than $2 a day and 1.2 billion on less than $1 a day. Eight out of every 100 infants do not live to see their fifth birthday. Nine of every 100 boys and 14 of every 100 girls who reach school age do not attend school. Poverty is also evident in poor people's lack of political power and voice and in their extreme vulnerability to ill health, economic dislocation, personal violence and natural disasters. And the scourge of HIV/AIDS, the frequency and brutality of civil conflicts, and rising disparities between rich countries and the developing world have increased the sense of deprivation and injustice for many.[1]

Moreover, the Christian church is numerically strongest among the poor. This brings to the fore fundamental questions about the content and meaning of the Christian mission and faith and its universality in the context of such socio-economic and political disparities.

However, what these statistics do not show is the vulnerability of the churches and people in the North and West where most of the socio-economic wealth and power lie, in the hands of a largely godless society. It is possible therefore to be oblivious to the 'poverty of the heart' and the dehumanization that results from material idolatry. The church is also vulnerable because it is a minority in a largely post-Christian society.

These issues invite honest reflection as to the meaning of being evangelical and Anglican at two levels. First, what should be our response to the fact that most of the membership of the global Anglican communion are socially disadvantaged and politically dispossessed? Second, the evangelical community in the West is a minority of a minority, suffering not an economic crisis, but a crisis of confidence in the gospel. How do we make sense of our evangelical Anglican identity in this global context?

As evangelicals, we shall quickly want to say that it is in the gospel, the *evangel*, that we find the meaning of God's mission in our world and hence the nature of Christian mission and faith. However, although the gospel is adequate whatever the human condition, we are often blind to the fact that our understanding of it is inadequate and flawed, and our mission praxis is often a reflection of our particular historical-cultural conditioning.

My contention is that it is by turning to the understanding and experience of the gospel of the people who live in those conditions of deprivation and dispossession – the vulnerable and weak – that we shall broaden our horizons in appreciating the nature of God's mission today and the power of the gospel. This will give us fresh confidence to face the opportunities and challenges of witnessing for Christ. For, as Paul pointed out to the Ephesians, it is only 'together with all the saints' that we are able 'to grasp how wide and long and high and deep is the love of Christ, and to know this love that surpasses knowledge' (Ephesians 3:18–19).

The saints I have selected are three African church leaders from the Church of Uganda, from different generations faced with different opportunities and challenges. The Church of Uganda is one of the largest evangelical sections in the Anglican communion; a people who have known weakness and adversity in a very turbulent and often violent history, part of the World Bank poverty statistics. They are Apolo Kivebulaya, famed Ugandan pioneer missionary to the Congo; Erica Sabiti, the first African Archbishop of the Province of the Church of Uganda, Rwanda and Boga-Zaire, as it was then called – the Anglican province covering present-day Uganda, Rwanda, Burundi and the Democratic Republic of Congo; and lastly, Janani

Luwum, successor to Erica Sabiti, and murdered by the infamous Idi Amin regime.

These saints point us to an appreciation of the fact that Christian mission is about carrying the cross and following Jesus. Their stories give us a fresh understanding of 'Christ crucified', as the 'the power of God' and 'the wisdom of God' (1 Corinthians 1:18,21). They reveal that the motif of the cross is not only about atonement but is the substance and core of Christian life, mission and ministry – for the foolishness of the cross is the wisdom of God! They share the apostle Paul's passion to 'know Christ and the power of his resurrection', recognizing that it also entailed 'the sharing in his sufferings, becoming like him in his death' (Philippians 3:10).

Apolo Kivebulaya

Kivebulaya was one of the early converts to Christianity in Buganda as a result of the work of God through missionaries of the Church Missionary Society (CMS). The first CMS missionaries arrived in Buganda at the King's Court in 1877. Although Kivebulaya accepted the faith as an adult in the 1880s, his faith was rekindled during a revival in 1893 that was propelled by the work of George Pilkington.

At the time, Pilkington was engaged in translating the Bible into Luganda along with his Ugandan colleague Henry Wright Duta. However, the strain of hard work with little rest, coupled with anxiety and discouragement over what Pilkington, like other missionaries, considered to be a lack of depth among the Baganda (*Buganda* is the region; *Baganda* the people; *Luganda* the language), had begun to take its toll on him. He retreated to the island of Kome in Lake Victoria for a holiday. While at Kome he had a 'revival' experience, which he shared with his fellow missionaries on his return to Mengo mission station, in Buganda. He suggested holding a series of special services to enrich the spiritual life of the young church, and the idea was welcomed enthusiastically.

People flocked to the services and for many church members this was a time of spiritual awakening, and of a new commitment to

Christian service. As a result many of those who committed themselves volunteered as catechists and missionaries to unreached lands in Buganda and beyond. Every month 'missionary meetings' were organized by the church council at which some evangelists reported on their work and called for fresh recruits. It is reported that within one year of the beginning of the revival 260 new evangelists were at work, occupying 85 stations of which 20 were beyond the borders of Buganda. Among them was Apolo Kivebulaya.

He resolved to abandon the path towards becoming a chief that his involvement in the politico-religious wars in Buganda (late 1880s and early 1890s) assured him, to serve as an evangelist. He was deployed by the nascent Mengo Church Council to serve in Toro Kingdom, at the foot of the Mountains of the Moon, the Ruwenzoris. It was while he was traversing the Ruwenzori range, preaching the gospel and planting churches, that he gazed westwards and saw smoke emerging out of the jungles of the Ituri Forest in the Congo. As he stared he said to himself, 'There, from where smoke is emerging are people for whom Christ died. I must go and tell them about him.' So when the CMS missionaries sought for evangelists to go and open a mission in Mboga in eastern Congo, Kivebulaya was the first to volunteer.

Ibrahim Katalibara tells the story of Apolo's first journey to Mboga:

> After Apolo crossed the Semliki he stayed at the hut of Mwemi, who asked him what he was going to do at Mboga. 'I am a *nyakatagara* (diviner),' said Apolo. 'Good,' said Mwemi, 'for I am *nyakatagara* to the Mukama Tabaro.' Apolo answered him, 'I also prophesy and I will prophesy for you in the morning.' 'That's good,' said Mwemi, and cooked food for him – a true sign of fellowship.
>
> When the day broke, Apolo said, 'I want to get off early, but I'll show you my divine before I go.' He opened the Gospel of St John and read, 'For God so loved the world that He gave His only begotten Son, that whosoever believeth in Him should not perish, but have everlasting life,' and explained to him Jesus, that 'Who so believeth shall be saved'.[2]

Nyakatagara Kivebulaya went and lived among the people of Mboga, learnt their language and told them of the One who was crucified for them. The Church of the Province of Congo today owes its beginnings to the pioneering life and work of this barefoot evangelist, Apolo Kivebulaya.

Kivebulaya's account challenges us. It was Kivebulaya's encounter with the crucified-risen Christ by the power of the Holy Spirit that compelled him to enter the world of those whom he recognized as still living in estrangement, so that they too might encounter Christ as well and appropriate their redemption. His resolve to live, serve and die, if need be, among the people of eastern Congo echoes Paul's words about the compulsion of the love of God in the cross of Christ: 'For Christ's love compels us, because we are convinced that one died for all, and therefore all died. And he died for all, that those who live should no longer live for themselves but for him who died for them and was raised again' (2 Corinthians 5:14–15).

People for whom Christ died

From the standpoint of the cross, his perspective to those outside Christ was also transformed. They were no longer to be defined by their living conditions or level of civilization, but rather as 'people for whom Christ died'.

The challenge today is not to judge people by their skin, class, ideology, religious affiliation, sexual orientation, economic status – developed or underdeveloped – or level of civilization. But like Kivebulaya, we need to see people from the perspective of the cross – people for whom Christ died. Therefore, like our Master, who by incarnation entered into 'our world' to affirm our creatureliness, we choose to enter their world, affirming their humanity and communicating to them the message of redemption. This entering into has an edge. On the one hand, it enables us to understand the manifestation of human degradation and alienation; and on the other it gives credibility to the message of the Christ crucified, and to us his messengers.

Understanding is a prerequisite for mission because mission begins with the affirmation of God's creation. The gospel story begins with the creation account. Understanding is not to be construed as condescension, or as comprehension through compromise or as a process of abstraction, but rather as empathy, a subjective incarnation responsive choice of entering into, identifying with those who do not yet know that they have such a choice. Empathy is the recognition and affirmation of the self, the human in them; indeed recognition of us with them – the solidarity of being human.

This is what endeared Diana, Princess of Wales, to so many in the UK and beyond. She became an ambassador for the marginalized and disenfranchised, although she was herself privileged. Notwithstanding her beauty and charm, which made her the icon of the media, it was her vulnerability and capacity to empathize with the 'lepers' of our world that endeared her to so many. She was not afraid to be associated with their 'leprosy' because she was well acquainted with her own. She could identify with the rejected because she knew the sting of it in her life. Their pain was her pain; their rejection hers. No wonder she worked tirelessly for their recognition and liberation because, in a sense, their liberation was hers as well. No wonder she was greatly loved in spite of the royal blunders that beleaguered her life: we saw ourselves in her.

Empathy inspires us to live and work for liberation, and enables us to communicate in intelligible idiom the possibility of fullness of life. Intelligibility is necessary for both the communicator and the receptor; hence the mandatory responsive choice of incarnation if mission is to be authentic, credible and efficacious. Mission in these terms ceases to be perceived as a *project* but rather as a *sharing of the life* given by grace through faith in the crucified One.

Erica Sabiti

Erica Sabiti succeeded Leslie Brown in January 1966 as the first African archbishop of the Province of the Church of Uganda, Rwanda, Burundi and Boga-Zaire. Brown, consecrated six years earlier and enthroned by the Archbishop of Canterbury in 1961, was the first archbishop. He had also been bishop of Namirembe diocese, literally the 'established church' of the Kingdom of Buganda. When Brown announced his intentions to relinquish the see to an African, the leadership and church in Buganda not only wanted the maintenance of the status quo but also expected it – their own Muganda as bishop of Namirembe and Archbishop of the Province. (*Muganda* is an individual of the Baganda.) To the Baganda, a non-Muganda succeeding Brown would be tantamount to failure by the church to recognize the founding role of the Baganda in the growth and spreading of the church beyond Buganda. It was also feared that Namirembe would lose its pre-eminence in the church in the emerging Uganda, be relegated to the status of just one diocese among others, and that its cathedral would lose its identity as the premier worship centre for Buganda.

Moreover, for the people of Buganda, such a marginalization mirrored the contest that had hitherto dominated the political arena in the emerging nation state. Uganda, a colonial creation out of several kingdoms and outlying districts, had been independent for just over three years. It was a time when the tensions arising from ethnic and regional loyalties, spurred by a colonial legacy, were at their height, especially between the Kingdom of Buganda and the central federal government. In the ensuing rearrangement of political space, the people of Buganda were increasingly feeling marginalized and dispossessed. How was Sabiti, considered by the powerful Buganda elite as 'the wrong choice', to deal with such an explosive situation at his accession of the archiepiscopal see?

In his charge at his enthronement in St Paul's Cathedral, Namirembe, 25 January 1966, Sabiti pointed to the cross of Christ as the answer not only to the divisions in the church but to all social and political evils in the land. It is devotion to the cross of Christ, he pleaded and argued, that forms the people of God into one community, God's family. He stated:

> All our unhappy divisions, political, denominational, tribal and racial, disappear at the foot of the cross, where we meet together as sinners before our Saviour. When we allow the Lord Jesus to rule our lives, then we grow together as a family, we

are one in Him, we are called by God to serve all His children, of all tribes and races, in order to bring them to Christ and become living stones within his Church.[3]

Sabiti was a *Mulokole* (saved one), an evangelical, who had grown to learn through the revival movement that Christian life and service is about devotion to the cross of Christ. He was one of the few clergy who were part of the East African Revival movement, a movement of renewal and reform, originating from among the indigenous lay people of the church in Uganda, and members of the Ruanda Mission, a small mission formed out of the Church Missionary Society (CMS) in the late 1920s.[4] At the core of revival ethos were two motifs: the cross of Christ – a central motif of the gospel; and the clan community – a defining element of traditional-cultural society. And for the adherents to the revival, the *Balokole* (plural of *Mulokole*), it is the integration of the two motifs that defined Christian life, mission and service.

According to the revival, as for any evangelical movement, the defining story of the gospel is the Christ-event; that is, the historical birth, life, death, resurrection and ascension of Jesus of Nazareth, and the coming of the Holy Spirit at Pentecost. The hinge of the Christ-event is Jesus' death on the cross, the defining moment of his salvation mission. Therefore, authentic Christian faith, in revival terms, is a function of the relationship of an individual in community with the cross of Christ.

Patricia St John expressed revival ethos well:

> To let God's light shine on our sin can only cause us to flee to the cross and the ground at the foot of the cross is level. There is only one common denominator there: our need of Jesus because our sin and pride, and all the barriers, classes and arti-ficialities men [*sic*] have erected melt away. There is only one class at the cross: humble, forgiven sinners, rejoicing because Jesus has forgiven them and this forms a bond between them that cannot be broken.[5]

Thus for Sabiti, encounter with the Christ of the cross diminishes the significance of all other marks of our individuality and identity, because

Christ crucified restores to us true identity, which is being in relation with God and neighbour. Those marks of identity when surrendered at the cross are transformed into resources for service. It is devotion to Christ crucified that creates true *koinōnia* among those who are in Christ, an essential element to Christian mission in a world torn apart by humankind's greed and self-centredness.

Five years later Sabiti was to reiterate the same message of the transforming power of the cross of Christ for Christian mission and service. In his archiepiscopal charge to the Provincial Assembly of the Church in December 1970, he summarized the story of the church thus: 'service to the suffering; unity of the people; the knowledge of God'.[6] Expanding on these themes, Archbishop Sabiti explained:

> If we look at our history, it is clear that our Church has made gifts of the highest value to the life of the people of Uganda, Rwanda and Burundi ... The first gift we have given is practical service to the poor, the weak and the sick. Poverty, ignorance and disease have for centuries broken the will and taken our people. In response to these needs we have built a school system that reaches into every community of our land, we have built hospitals, introduced cash crops, helped farmers and worked to improve community services ...[7]

Reflecting on the theme of the unity of the people, he asserted:

> If we look at our history, we see that we have been and must remain men of unity. Our history is one that shows a continuing struggle to break down the walls that divide men; a struggle to transcend the divisions of tribe, clan, language, culture and race, which have for too many years held us back and even weakened us and too frequently prevented us from doing what God has given us to do.[8]

On the knowledge of God, Sabiti amplified:

> If we look at our history, we also find that our Church is an Evangelical Church. I do not mean Evangelical as a Church party, but Evangelical in the only true sense of that word. We have stood for the fact that the most important issue in life is the

relation we have with God ... We have sought in many practical ways to improve the life of the people of Uganda. But from the beginning we have known that the greatest gift we have to offer is Christ himself.[9]

According to Sabiti the church's historical mission was in obedience to Christ crucified and this meant service to the world; its identity, unity in a context of sociocultural diversity; and its *raison d'être*, the evangelical gospel leading to a faith relation with God.

Recovering community

Sabiti's plea to the church in Uganda three decades ago is relevant to the church today and to anywhere in our world, not least in the evangelical community in the UK. The Christ of the cross confronts us not only with our alienation from God but also from neighbour and creation. But he also starts us on a journey of restoration. This restoration is engendered through a continuous process of conversion, which occurs as we continually repent of our self-centredness that characterizes our estrangement, and open ourselves to the fullness of God. This fullness is itself not possible without true fellowship with our neighbour, as we are grasped by the Spirit of the risen Christ, who continually points to our alienation and hostility that was nailed to the cross. Devotion to the Christ of the cross ought to demolish the barriers of race, colour, gender and any other criteria of identity in community. The power of the cross transforms the 'I am' to 'we are'. It is the rediscovery of genuine community among those devoted to Christ.

Western civilization and culture has extolled the sense of individual autonomy, individual freedom and choice, and has located the essence of being human in the 'self' excluding the 'other'. This philosophy of life is pervasive and has even entered into some of the distinctive marks of being evangelical. It is reflected, for example, in the emphasis on crisis-based individual conversion and 'personal' salvation. I was struck by the extent of this pervasive individualism while at a missions conference as it was reflected in the worship. The lyrics of most of the popular choruses that we sang together were addressed in the first person singular: '*I* love you Lord', '*I* worship you', 'You died for *me*' and so on. We hardly sang as *we*. Our witness to the cross of Christ dictates that we recover 'community' in being Christian.

Janani Luwum

Janani Luwum, then Bishop of Northern Uganda, was elected in May 1974 to replace Archbishop Erica Sabiti, who was retiring that year. This was at a time when Idi Amin, the brutal military dictator, had entrenched his position as president of Uganda.

Luwum's accession to the archiepiscopal see was bound to lead to confrontation with the Amin regime. First, he was an Acholi, from the northern part of the country, the home country to deposed President Obote and heartland of his support, and by extension, of Idi Amin's opposition. Second, he was a *Mulokole*, courageous and bold. As Kevin Ward has observed, Luwum was a deeply spiritual man and 'intellectually the most competent person', godly, fearless and with a pastoral heart.[10] Third, he presided over the Church whose 'established position' was Amin's envy. The Protestant Church had hitherto enjoyed the benefits of being the quasi-established religion of Uganda, since its victory over the Roman Catholics in 1892. From the time of Amin's violent overthrow of the Republican government, which he considered to be pro the Anglican Church, his project was to 'establish' Islam.

As Bishop of Northern Uganda, Luwum must have intervened on several occasions on behalf of many who had 'disappeared' at the hands of the military machine of the regime. He had mourned with many whose loved ones had been killed. Now as archbishop he continued to exercise his pastoral duty at a national level, advocating for those who dared not face the regime's reckless officers. On several occasions he confronted Amin, protesting his regime's brutality and demanding that the government live up to its mandate to protect the lives and property of the citizens, rather than unleashing its military machine on a defenceless population. This did not go down well with Amin who was committed to eliminating any form of real, imagined or potential challenge to his regime. So Luwum, now considered to be an enemy and a political saboteur, would inevitably face Amin's terror apparatus.

It is difficult to ascertain the extent of Luwum's support and involvement in efforts to remove Amin from power. At the time there were several efforts to get rid of the regime by military means, of which Luwum was certainly aware. However, given his forthrightness in attacking the regime for its carnage, and his personal association with some of those found to have been planning to remove Amin from power, it was only logical that he should be accused of being a collaborator with 'enemy forces'. The Idi Amin regime was serviced by a sophisticated and powerful intelligence network.

In early January 1977, Luwum was accused, together with Bishop Yona Okoth of Bukedi diocese in eastern Uganda, of collaborating with three other men in a clandestine plan to overthrow Idi Amin and his government. The fateful day was Wednesday 16 February. Idi Amin summoned all the religious leaders to a meeting at the International Conference Centre, Kampala. Present were all the bishops of both the Roman Catholic Church and the Church of Uganda, leaders of the Islamic faith, diplomats, senior military officers, and the whole Cabinet. To this gathering Amin displayed an array of guns. At the end of the gathering Luwum was arrested together with two government ministers and subsequently killed.

It is instructive to note that on the day before that fateful day, Luwum's wife, Mary, pleaded with him to get out of Uganda, but Janani refused on the basis that he was not guilty. And on the day of his death, Mary pleaded again, telling him that if he went to the meeting at the International Conference Centre, he would not return. Luwum replied, 'If I die, my blood will save Uganda.'[11] About two hours before his death, as Luwum and all the bishops listened to the charges against him, Luwum turned to Bishop Festo Kivengere and whispered, 'They are going to kill me. I am not afraid.'[12] He was neither afraid nor ashamed of being identified as an enemy of a regime that was killing its own people, and which had therefore lost its legitimacy to govern. He was willing to pay the ultimate price of his pastoral service and mission. He was not afraid of death but rather embraced it as a consequence of serving Christ crucified. Although he faced his accusers as though guilty, he knew he was fulfilling his calling as a minister of the Christ crucified and was therefore *not afraid* to face the consequences. It is said that when the last orders were given to Luwum to see the president, he turned and smiled to his brother bishops and said, 'I can see the hand of the Lord in this.'[13]

He died a criminal's death. The death was brutal. An eyewitness account of the damage on his body is graphic:

1. There was a hole in his throat below his Adam's apple through to the back of his neck.
2. There were deep wounds on both armpits. It appeared as though his chest had been shot in the armpit, and the chest was bandaged.
3. There was a hole on his left lower stomach going through his back. It could be a wound inflicted by something like a sword.
4. His back had been broken by cutting it with a sharp instrument.
5. Lastly, his loins had been cut off, and around the lower area was all bandaged. There was no other wound apart from a few bruises on the left leg.[14]

Suffering with the flock

We know that Luwum was not the first to suffer such bestiality at the hands of Amin's butcher machine. He was to be numbered among the thousands who 'disappeared'. Those who were picked by the military machine and killed were said to have 'disappeared' and never accorded a decent burial. In seeking effectively to serve those under his care, Luwum suffered what they suffered. He died like them, and indeed with them, and thereby authenticated his mission and that of the church by sharing in 'the suffering of his flock'. He suffered their pain and died their death. This is what Professor Mahmood Mamdani, a recognized social political analyst of Uganda's political history, a non-Christian, has acknowledged: that Luwum was murdered 'not because he was a devout Christian, but because he was an ardent nationalist'.[15]

However, the significance of Luwum's death is not just in how he died but, more importantly, that he saw his death as part of his service and mission. The premonition that his 'blood would save Uganda' attaches vicarious significance to it.[16] This vicarious factor in his death was a result of choice. It gave it a special quality and value, and distinguished his death from other such deaths. Luwum could, like many, have fled the country, but rather he chose to face the consequences of his stand with the oppressed and hunted. It is Luwum's sense and consciousness of mission expressed in his vision to 'save Uganda' that accords his death the character of Christian mission.

Christian service and action, motivated by commitment to the Christ crucified, will lead to suffering with the oppressed at the hands of the oppressor, but it works for their liberation from oppression as part of the process of sharing the life that Christ gives. But it also seeks the *liberation of the oppressor* from the tyranny of his estrangement from God and neighbour. The title of Festo Kivengere's book *I Love Idi Amin* echoes this double edge of Christian mission. Idi Amin, from whose tyranny Ugandans needed liberation, was not excluded from God's mission. Festo saw Amin not just as a brutal dictator but also as one for whom Christ had died. Kivengere could therefore write later, 'We love President Idi Amin. We owe him a debt of love, for he is one of those for whom Christ shed His precious blood. As long as he is still alive, he is still redeemable. Pray for him, that in the end he may see a new way of life, rather than a way of death.'[17]

Mission as Conversion

Christian mission progresses by conversion. A fresh encounter of the incarnate-crucified-risen Christ, which we experience as we enter into the world of the 'other', opens our eyes to the shared humanity in those who are dehumanized by Satan, self, and society. Recognizing a shared human identity entails conversion, a turning towards God, towards their humanity and our own. True conversion is a three-dimensional process. It is incongruent with the act of God in Christ for our redemption to separate these dimensions and to boast of having experienced any one or two without the other. The tragedy is that we often speak of conversion as a two-dimensional process involving the self and God. We must also be converted to the humanity of others, especially to those whose material circumstances denigrate them.

However, as we attempt to enter the world of the oppressed, distressed and disempowered, we are confronted by our own fear: the fear of losing our comfort and security, fear of becoming like them, the fear of pain and death. Fear hinders conversion. The only way towards conversion is by turning our back to fear, by turning to the cross of Christ. We must repent of fear. For fear not only manifests insecurity; it is also a mark of our unwillingness to be vulnerable by empathizing with those to whom God sends us. At the core of it, fear manifests our alienation from their humanity and our reluctance to surrender our idols of safety, for the greater value of human freedom that the Christ of the cross offers.

Christian mission is therefore Christ's invitation to us to deny ourselves, take up the cross and follow Jesus (Mark 8:34). Kivebulaya, Sabiti and Luwum encourage us to follow their example and to shun the easy and safe way. Safety poses a major hindrance to Christian mission. The issue of safety is reaching idolatrous proportions as a result of modern technology and progress in medical science. Evangelical Christian mission agencies are even developing policies that are dominated by safety as a priority value.

I recall corresponding with a mission organization based in the West, some time in the early 1990s. They wanted to send a short-term missionary to help in the work among university and college students in Nigeria. This organization had an enviable track record of missionary involvement in several parts of the world. The process of selection of the candidate had matured and a date set when the young man would relocate to Nigeria. However, the news coming out of Nigeria at the time was not good. The political situation was unstable, and civil unrest had been reported in various parts of the country. Then came a fax from that mission, wondering whether we should proceed with the plans, given the unstable political situation. The question that the representative asked me was 'Is it safe?'

I reflected over the contents of the fax and particularly the question 'Is it safe?' I certainly could not guarantee safety in Nigeria of all countries, with a historic post-independence track record of political turmoil and violence. But I also wondered whether the question of safety was primary in deciding the next step. I wrote to the mission and entreated them that although it might not be safe and that I could not guarantee it, I was confident it was the right thing to do.

The desire for safety is expressed in processes and mechanisms that eliminate risk. Yet risk is the essence of faith. Modern-day preoccupation for safety and security is the antithesis to incarnational suffering-service. Preoccupation with safety alienates, but our search for the good of humankind will lead us to reflecting on reconciliation and fellowship in Christ.

There is need for a fresh discovery and encounter with the crucified One and a continual surrender of fear. Our devotion to him will enable us continually to repent and surrender the question 'Is it *safe*?' We shall learn to ask, 'Is it *right*?' Like Jesus, in the moment of reckoning in the garden of Gethsemane, we must resolve to step out of our comfort zones and share his life with those among whom it may not be safe to, among those whose life and condition has become 'safe' due to their ignorance of the One who died for them.

Christian Mission: Power for and among the Powerless

Kivebulaya, Sabiti and Luwum fit Paul's categorization, when he wrote to the Corinthians:

> For consider your call, brethren; not many of you were wise according to worldly standards, not many were powerful, not many were of noble birth; but God chose what is foolish in the world to shame the wise, God chose what is weak in the world to shame the strong, God chose what is low and despised in the world, even things that are not, to bring to nothing things that are, so that no human being might boast in the presence of God. (1 Corinthians 1:26–9 RSV)

They, like the Corinthians, were not only weak in the eyes of the world but like Paul chose weakness, having discovered that 'He is the source of your life in Christ Jesus, whom God made our wisdom, our righteousness and sanctification and redemption' (1 Corinthians 1:30 RSV). God's decisive action to restore meaning and fullness to life was in the incarnation of Christ that climaxed in his death. Hence the cross models for us the way of Christian mission in a world characterized by pain and suffering – life through death, power through weakness, wisdom through folly. Indeed, the cross of Christ commends itself to us as the paradigm for life and Christian mission today.

The crisis of confidence in the gospel in the West is not about the ineffectiveness of the gospel. It may be traced to the desire by the church to have recognition in the public arena. And yet the power of the gospel lies in the transformation of the 'low and despised in the world, even things that are not, to bring to nothing things that are, so that no human being might boast in the presence of God' (1 Corinthians 1:28–9 RSV).

The Christ of the cross confronts us, our conception of Christian mission and our exercise of the task of missions at all levels. At the motivational level, the compulsion and urgency for missions arises from the encounter of the self-giving love manifest in Christ's volitional surrender to death on the cross. Second, at the methodological level, paternalism and power will give way to vulnerability and partnership, not just for pragmatic expediency, but as the only way engendered by repentance and conversion, the only response to an encounter with the weakness and power of the Christ of the cross. The triumphalist posture resulting from the overvaluation of the significance of numbers and material resources characteristic of much evangelical assessment of mission today needs to give way to suffering-service.

Let us heed the caution of Samuel Escobar, the Latin American missiologist: 'This new century will be characterized not by mission to the poor but mission *by* the poor. This new movement in mission can only be prevented by the power of rich Christians.'[18]

Notes

1. The World Bank, *World Development Report 2000/2001: Attacking Poverty,* New York, Oxford University Press, 2001.

2. This is old in Anne Luck, *African Saint: The Story of Apolo Kivebulaya,* London, SCM, 1963, p. 70.

3. Erica Sabiti, 'Charge to the Church of Uganda, Rwanda and Burundi,' Provincial Assembley of the Church of Uganda, December 1970.

4. The Ruanda Mission was founded in protest to what was perceived by its founders to be liberal and modernist theological influence in the CMS. (Note: 'Rwanda' is the modern form of 'Ruanda'.) Three principles were affirmed in their constitution: (1) The Ruanda Council and the missionaries of the Ruanda General Medical Mission [RGMM] stand for the complete inspiration of the whole Bible as being, and not only containing, the Word of God. (2) Their determination is to proclaim full and free salvation through simple faith in Christ's atoning death upon the cross. (3) They are satisfied that they have received from the CMS full guarantees to safeguard the future of the RGMM on Bible, Protestant and Keswick lines (Stanley Smith, *Road to Revival*, Oxford, SCM, p. 42).

5. *Breath of Life*, London, Norfolk Press, 1971, p. 161.

6. 'The Proceedings of the Second Meeting of the Second Provincial Assembly held at Bishop Tucker College, Mukono, December 9, 10 and 11, 1970; Appendix B: The Archbishop's Charge to the Church of Uganda, Rwanda and Burundi, December 1970'. Provincial Assembly Papers, COU Archives, p. 4.

7. Ibid.

8. Ibid.

9. Ibid.

10 Kevin Ward, 'The Church Amidst Conflict', in Margaret Ford, *Janani: The Making of a Martyr*, London, Marshall, Morgan and Scott, 1978, p. 83.

11 Ford, *Janani*, p. 86.

12 Ibid.

13 Ibid., p. 87.

14 Henry Okullu, *Church and Politics in East Africa*, Kenya, Uzima, 1980, pp. 6–7.

15 M. Mamdani, *Imperialism and Fascism in Uganda*, Nairobi, Heinemann, 1983, p. 56.

16 Obviously this term is used in the relative sense of one who dies for others, not in the unique sense of the vicarious *atoning* death of Jesus.

17 Festo Kivengere, *I Love Idi Amin*, London, Lakeland, 1978, p. 63.

18 Samuel Escobar, Seminar at the Overseas Ministries Study Centre, New Haven, Conn., December 1999.

Chapter Fifteen

Encouraging Mission-Mindedness: The Quest for an Ethos of Mission Spirituality in the Church

Tim Dakin

If mission is of the essence of the church, and part of evangelical defining identity, why do so many churches, even evangelical ones, lack a vibrant and intentional mission spirituality? Tim Dakin explores what mission spirituality should involve and how it is inhibited by some of our inherited Christendom ecclesiologies. He then moves on in the second part of this chapter to illustrate his thesis, positively and critically, from the early history of the CMS and its relation to the clerical structures of the church. But what kind of church do we need to be? Dakin critiques 'blueprint' ecclesiologies and finds hope in some more radical forms of emerging church dynamics. In his final section he draws on the resources of 1 Peter, written to churches that knew themselves to be 'aliens and strangers' in the midst of an often hostile culture, as we in the West increasingly do. He explores the ethical, evangelistic and eschatological challenges of what it means to be God's holy people in mission.[1]

Introduction

David Bebbington tells us that evangelicalism is characterized by four key attributes: conversionism, activism, biblicalism and crucicentrism (cross-centredness).[2] We might call this the 'quadrilateral' of evangelical spirituality. Bebbington's four characteristics are echoed in the aim of this book, which is to encourage Christians in their calling to be Bible-based, cross-centred and mission-minded (mission-minded incorporates both conversionism and activism). It is the third aspect that I want to focus on here as a major factor in our evangelical ecclesiology. My basic point is that our understanding of the church follows from putting mission first. Thus the call to be mission-minded is about *the intentionality and the implications of evangelical mission spirituality.* Moreover, I aim to show how the ecclesiology of evangelical mission spirituality relates to a wider debate about the nature of the church. In this wider debate, the intention of the evangelical mission spirituality is to encourage missional communities as agents of transformation. A church that is mission-minded has this ethos. First Peter shows how this ethos is Bible-based and cross-centred and how leadership is about encouraging us to stand fast in this faith.

Mission Spirituality

Intentional mission

I remember, as a child, hearing stories about missionaries like Gladys Aylward and Amy Carmichael. I recall being told about their amazing commitment, despite terrible setbacks and difficult circumstances. Aylward and Carmichael came from very different social backgrounds, but what united them was a dedication to evangelistic mission. In this they are an example for us today: they remind us what it means to be mission-minded – to live out the gospel intentionally so that others may come to know Christ and to be willing to do this wherever God calls, even in another culture.

Of course it is easy to romanticize about the heroism and determination of missionary pioneers. But what is most encouraging about their example is that their calling cannot be extrapolated from an existing state of affairs: to be intentional about world mission was, and is, to be 'outside the box'. In the face of the changes in contemporary culture and the forces of globalization we need the encouragement of other people's example to reach forward into new ways of intentional witness.

It is easier to ask difficult questions than to give convincing answers. For some, contemporary changes and challenges are mesmerizing: we are like rabbits in the headlights, or like the centipede in this poem that is thrown into a paralysis of self-doubt on meeting a toad:

> A centipede was happy 'til
> One day a toad in fun,
> said, 'Pray, which leg goes after which?'
> This strained his mind to such a pitch
> He lay distracted in a ditch
> Considering how to run.[3]

Becoming intentional

> Do not be conformed to this world but be transformed by the renewing of your minds.
>
> Romans 12:2 NRSV

I suggest that we can read Romans 12:2 as a call to be mission-minded, that is, to be open to ongoing transformation through a renewal resulting from mission engagement. Paul's use of the word *mind (nous),* does not restrict this transformation to a renewal of our theology and worldview; rather here mind also implies 'disposition', 'practical reason' and 'resolve'. Bringing these together, Paul is inviting us into a renewal of *intentionality.* To be deliberately intentional for mission is to be mission-minded, to cultivate a mission spirituality. Paul encourages us by the mercies of God to be mission-minded people, people who are not conformists. This is an invitation to discover the reality of transforming mission in the church's relations with God, the world and itself.

In a pair of chapters which outline the development of the Western missionary movement,[4] Andrew Walls argues that there are three necessary conditions on which the missionary enterprise has depended throughout its history: 'The first necessity was a body of people with the degree of commitment needed to live on someone else's terms', 'the second need was for a form of organization that could mobilize committed people', and 'the third factor necessary to overseas missions was sustained access to overseas locations, with the capacity to maintain communications over long periods' (p. 221).

I would say that the first of the three necessary factors is the most fundamental: a mission spirituality embodied in a community of people committed to mission service. I would also argue that the implications of putting mission spirituality first, and of integrating this into our theological understanding of the church (our ecclesiology), would lead to a revision of the Anglican tradition. The implications would be very far-reaching.

'Spiritual agents alone are suitable for spiritual work.'[5] This axiom was foundational to the formation of CMS missionaries in training. The axiom highlights both the origins of world mission in spirituality and also the ongoing importance of spirituality as the resource for mission. Yet it is often the development and impact of the 'the ways and means' of doing mission (organization and techniques) that become the focus for mission thinking and practice, rather than the most fundamental condition for mission which is the renewal of the church through an intentional spirituality of mission. Formation for mission begins with mission spirituality, mission-mindedness.

In the development of the Western missionary movement it was only when the prevailing horizon of Christendom and the given forms of Christian life were reworked that world mission emerged. Mission spirituality is the revival and ongoing renewal of the church's mission, but this needs to be integrated into the theological understanding of the church and not seen as a specialism. It is this opportunity of integrating mission spirituality into ecclesiology that the contemporary climate offers.

Spirituality and mission

> From a Christian perspective, spirituality is not just concerned
> with prayer or even narrowly religious activities. It concerns
> the whole of human life, viewed in terms of a conscious rela-
> tionship with God, in Jesus Christ, through the indwelling of
> the Holy Spirit and within a community of believers.[6]

Philip Sheldrake's definition helpfully sets the broad parameters of
Christian spirituality. Writing about how for one leading Anglican evangelical, John Stott, mission and spirituality come together, James Gordon
says, 'Mission and spirituality overlap in life under the cross: "mission
sooner or later leads us into passion ... every form of mission leads to
some form of cross. The very shape of mission is cruciform".'[7]

Yet, if we take mission as a focus for spirituality, such a focus
will also result in a process of broadening spirituality as the results
of mission are included. Sydney Evans recognizes this in an article
on 'Anglican Spirituality' where he says (very datedly), first that
there is a need to assess 'the effect on Anglican spirituality of the
spread of the Anglican version of Christianity first to the colonies
and then to the wider ambience of dominions and empire'. And secondly that 'The growth of indigenous churches of the Anglican Communion in the Third World brings into the Anglican experience fresh
interpretations of Christian response in art, music, dance, patterns of
community and spontaneity less fettered by history.'[8] In any assessment of these changes for Anglican spirituality it is important to
acknowledge that the cultural diversity referred to here is a result of,
and at the heart of, *mission.* Thus interculturalism is not a goal in
itself: Christian fellowship is only through Christ and for the sake of
knowing a greater Lord: as Max Warren said, 'it takes a whole world
to know Jesus Christ'.[9] Christ is our focus, and yet he is known in a
diversity of contexts through the Spirit.[10] A mission spirituality must
include an 'intensity' and an 'extensity' in its commitment to Jesus.[11]

I believe that we need to hold together both the focused passion
and the breadth of mission spirituality. And this further requires an
understanding of the work of the Holy Spirit as the *mission encour-
ager.* This is not just at the theological level, but at the level of lived

experience where the questions of mission strike right at the heart of who we are and what we believe – the gut level. For at the level of daily experience we face many theological questions, which are raised precisely because we are passionately engaged in practical commitment to world mission (as indeed it was in the New Testament church). We are vulnerable in both realms – theological and practical, and in both realms we need the help of the Holy Spirit.

Transition to Mission

The search for mission after Christendom

If we ask how the above approach helps us develop an Anglican ecclesiology grounded in a mission spirituality, we need first to consider how mission did emerge within Anglicanism. We cannot explore what kind of church embodies a mission spirituality without first passing through the narrow gate of the historical emergence of mission in the Western Christian context.

As already noted, Andrew Walls suggests that there are three necessary conditions for the emergence of mission, but what is it about the nature of Western Christianity that makes these factors *necessary* for mission movements to emerge? Basically, Walls suggests that Western Christianity, because it was fundamentally tribal and territorial, needed to break out of its own identity to do mission: 'Western Christianity is a tribal religion; and tribal religion is fundamentally more about acknowledged symbols, and custom and recognized practice, than about faith' (p. 220). Tribal religion takes a territorial form, as Walls says:

> The political development of Europe ensured that the Western experience of Christianity would be in territorial terms. On one side lay Christendom, Christian territory, the assembly of Christian princes and their peoples, subject to the law of Christ, territory in which idolatry, blasphemy, and heresy could have no place; on the other side lay heathendom, the world outside.

One form Christian mission takes in this context is the crusade, 'the attempt to extend the territory within which the Law of Christ would be observed'. Crusade-type mission ultimately failed and other forms emerged. In fact, one such form of mission, which was foreign to the European experience, is *mission after Christendom*. This kind of mission implies 'a readiness to enter someone else's world instead of imposing the standards of one's own. It required learning another's language, seeking a niche within another's society, perhaps even accepting a situation of dependence' (p. 220). The three conditions of the Western mission enterprise were necessary because fundamentally, European Christianity did not change (and perhaps is only just beginning to change), despite the fact that the missionary movement pointed to, and enabled, the establishing of a non-Christendom, extra-European, Christianity.

Both Roman Catholic and Protestant mission required the same three conditions because both endorsed a Christendom mentality, even after the Reformation,[12] and 'left the foundational assumptions of European Christianity essentially untouched' (p. 220). The particular form the mission movement took in Anglicanism displays the fundamental tension which the three conditions imply – the tension between a Christendom mentality and the new mission dynamic. It is a tension that still needs to be addressed in contemporary mission spirituality. Walls clarifies the challenge faced by those with a vision for world mission also committed to the Anglican church: 'Western Christianity, being essentially territorial in conception, has always operated on a territorial understanding of Christian ministry. That understanding was also monarchical: the ordained pastor in his parish' (p. 222). This inherent clericalism was a major challenge to the missionary movement.

Church Mission Society and mission after Christendom

This challenge needed a prophetic-practical response. The history of the CMS illustrates one such response and highlights the changes that needed to take place in understanding the sort of mission cooperation into which the Spirit was directing the church. The CMS arose out of the evangelical revival (as nurtured by the influence of German Pietism in England). This movement is the first of Walls's three necessary factors for it produced those committed to a new form of world mission, a mission after Christendom. But the tension between this vision and the ecclesial context became clear in establishing the second necessary condition, the mission organization.

The CMS leadership was committed *both* to the vision of evangelistic mission *and* to the Anglican Church order. It therefore naturally sought for evangelical, ordained missionaries, but none offered themselves.[13] The question was whether the clerical norm for ministry could be broken by deploying non-ordained catechists as missionaries. The tension was exacerbated by the lack of support from senior bishops and in the end an alternative to sending catechists was found.[14] Thus the CMS maintained the clerical norm by deploying ordained Lutheran colleagues willing to accept Anglican strictures and yet having a vision for a mission after Christendom.[15] In this way the CMS negotiated a synergy between world mission and an established national church, but the clerical norm was questioned and was soon challenged.

This uneasy initial development was eased by the subsequent support of bishops and by those who were episcopally ordained offering themselves for missionary service. However, the fundamental paradigm of the clerical norm would now be challenged by practical developments rather than by the implications of world mission being systematically applied in the CMS and the Church of England. Walls identifies three factors that eroded the clerical norm: (1) 'the rise of medical missions'; (2) the still more transformative influence of 'the steadily increasing indispensability of the woman missionary';[16] and (3) the lay expansion of CMS and its development into a voluntary lay society. Walls notes that 'around 1812, the CMS began to develop local auxillaries' (p. 234).

The clerical norm was thus challenged, not in a planned or systematic way, but more by accident and pragmatic evolution. The rise of medical mission meant that the medical superintendent, rather than the ordained missionary, was the senior figure in mission hospitals. And with new openings for outreach to women and the growing significance of education in mission, the sheer weight of numbers of women missionaries eroded the clerical norm. For example, between 1895 and 1904 the CMS sent 425 women and 391 men.

Lastly, the significance of lay involvement and support for world mission, through a wider membership, led to applications from a wider circle beyond that of the clergy and their networks. Not the least of these new human resources were the young (graduate) volunteers who began to offer for mission service and who were to become the leaders in a second wave of development of the mission movement in Anglicanism in the 1880s.

With these kinds of developments we see a challenge that goes to the heart of the Christendom culture, that is, the clerical norm. It would therefore be right to ask if the new mission organization really was a radical expression of mission spirituality, or was it just the means by which a Christianity, which still had a Christendom perspective, was able to carry on as it always had while sponsoring world mission? Any answer to this is complex. But a way of exploring this is to suggest that the clerical norm should be seen as one way of holding together a whole framework of Christian community. We may therefore suggest that the wider order, the nexus, of Christian community is what is being questioned by the emergence of lay mission rather than the need for an ordained ministry.

The voluntary association, as a lay society, is not an ideal nor a blueprint for the church's mission: it emerged in the practical call to mission but it has significant implications for church in the era of 'mission after Christendom'. The most significant thing it did was to point towards the ethos of a mission spirituality and how this is worked out in the church being a mission community. However, we do need to note that this work remains incomplete. As Brian Stanley says, 'The paradox of much evangelical Christianity was that it sought to use the model of the believers' church to shore up the creaking structures of Christendom in Europe and even reconstruct them overseas.'[17]

Communities of mission service

The commitment of the CMS to Anglican order was born out of a vision for the renewal of the church. It was therefore as believing Christians that the ordained leaders of the CMS sought to release renewal into the church for the sake of releasing resources for world mission. What was not thought through were the implications of a lay voluntary mission association for the clerical norm as the means by which the Christian community had been ordered and maintained. The lay voluntary association, as in previous generations, refocused Christian community around a practical prophetic vision for world mission in which structures were secondary to the creation of mission community.

In another essay Walls says, 'There never was a *theology* of voluntary societies.'[18] However:

> Untheological development as it may have been, the voluntary society had immense theological implications. It arose because none of the classical patterns of Church government, whether Episcopal, Presbyterian, congregational, or connexional, had the machinery (in their late eighteenth century form anyway) to do the tasks for which missionary societies came into being. By its very success, the voluntary society subverted all the classical forms of Church government, while fitting comfortably into none of them (p. 247).

I would call this prophetic-practical ecclesiology. Voluntary societies enabled a renewal within the structures of the church. Thus, although the voluntary society is one means by which the Western church became missional, its status as a necessary factor should not hide the fact that it also released a rediscovery of Christian community. The challenge to the clergy norm was the invitation to move from a church where community is focused in structure (i.e. in which 'blueprint ecclesiologies' are influential), to church as *communitas* where community is sustained by a shared vision for mission.

> Structure and community in fact need each other. Ideally, moments of community can serve to cleanse and renew structure, and it should be the goal of structure itself to serve and help to realize community effectively ... The Church needs such communities, not to live its life for it, but to show it should be living that life and to encourage it so to live. Orders, missionary fellowships or whatever it may be, can foster the renewal of local congregations and encourage cross-cultural mission.[19]

Mission spirituality both gives rise to, and is born of, such *communitas,* and it is this that, I believe, needs to be placed at the heart of an Anglican ecclesiology, in its mission, faith and order.

Beyond Blueprint Church

Challenging blueprint ecclesiology

Nicholas Healy, in a creative and complex book,[20] argues that much modern ecclesiology has been deficient because it has adopted a blueprint method, which has resulted in arrogance and idealism. This blueprint ecclesiology has five elements:

> One is the attempt to encapsulate in a single word or phrase the most essential characteristic of the church; another is to construe the church as having a bipartite structure. These two elements are often combined, third, into a systematic and theoretical form of normative ecclesiology. A fourth element is a tendency to reflect upon church in abstraction from its concrete identity. And one consequence of this is, fifth, a tendency to present idealized accounts of the church. (p. 26)

Healy goes on to argue, first, that the blueprint approach to ecclesiology obscures the rich complexity and variety of how an understanding of the church is built up from an interpretation of Scripture, historical development, the construal of God's presence, and the present church context. Second, that the whole methodology results in ecclesiology not doing its proper job: it becomes both idealized and restricted. Instead, ecclesiology should be about the practical task of helping 'the concrete church in performing its tasks of witness and pastoral care' (p. 38) and also the broad-ranging prophetic task of addressing its context. Thus Healy will neither give up the big story, the metanarrative, of the Christian tradition, nor allow this story to float away from its embodiment in the life of even the sinful church.

The alternative approach is for the practical-prophetic tasks of ecclesiology to be done acknowledging both the church's embodied practice as well as the ultimate horizon of the Christian theological imagination, 'in keeping with an orientation to Jesus Christ as ultimate truth' (p. 40). But these tasks are not to be compromised by merely merging our theological horizon with our cultural contexts. This can lead, for example in the West, to the assimilation of dominant humanistic beliefs in the outworking of ecclesial practice.

I suggest that mission spirituality is an expression of this combination of both the theological imagination and the practical response to Jesus as Lord in a given context. Such spirituality will not allow us to short-circuit our view of the church by either idealizing it or avoiding its embodiment in particular contexts. Healy suggests that we idealize the church because we do not take as constituent both the concrete reality of church life and the sinful nature of that reality and thus, in thinking of the church as having two parts, the spiritual and embodied parts or the divine and human, we fail to fulfil a truly mission spirituality. We also fail to do full justice to the wider context of the church's life if we fail to recognize the necessity of interreligious apologetics.[21] Both these patterns of failure emerge in our tendency to develop blueprints of the church.

So what sort of ecclesiology adopts a theological horizon, engages with the breadth of cultural contexts and the wealth of the tradition, while acknowledging, but not succumbing to blueprint ecclesiology? It is an ecclesiology of the *quest for truth lived out in the drama of God's mission.*

Church and the drama of mission

At the big story level, Healy focuses on the choice between an ecclesiology based on an *epic* or a *dramatic* theology. Here he is drawing on Hans Urs von Balthasar: 'The relations between God, world and church are best conceived, he believes, as something like a play. The play can be described in terms of one or other of two types of Christian horizons and theological styles, the epic and the dramatic' (p. 53). This may sound innocuous, but it has significant implications. Healy associates the modern, blueprint model approach with *epic* theology, which 'steps out of the drama to take an external spectator's perspective ... the epic horizon can be seen especially in church documents, catechisms, and those large scale systematic theologies in which Christian life is laid out as a whole as if nothing further needs to be done or known'. In contrast to this tidy approach, in which the final state of the church is thought to be essentially present, *dramatic* theology 'takes the perspective of a participant in the drama ... it displays the conflictual nature of Christian existence ... the ongoing dramatic struggle that constitutes discipleship' (p. 53). Here our discipleship is to express our gratitude in responding to God as his collaborators: 'God calls each one of us to respond to our own unique mission' (p. 63), and the church is called to help us to do that in relationship with Christ (who is himself the mission) and under the director of the drama of mission: the Spirit-director.

Healy sees dramatic ecclesiology helping the church do two things: 'to witness to its Lord in the world and to help the individual Christian in her task of discipleship' (p. 74). He believes that the church, in these two tasks, has not been helped either by pluralist ecclesiology or by inclusivist ecclesiology. The pluralist option, which sees the church as just one community of faith pointing, along with others, to the same assumed common reality of God, does not take diversity seriously. The inclusivist option, which sees the church as representing the anonymous Christianity of all, does not acknowledge that faith traditions make non-negotiable claims about truth and salvation.

Three dimensions of the mission ethos of ecclesiology

Let me draw out three fundamental, grammatical dimensions to the ethos of an ecclesiology that has a mission spirituality. First, we only know truth within the drama, not outside it, so we do not possess the totality of truth prior to the eschaton. The Scriptures already give us God's truth, but in the 'not yet' of faith we still 'know in part, but then we shall know fully'. Rather we receive truth in a relationship of trust in the faithfulness of the Director: 'We receive the truth in the gift of the self-presence of God by the Spirit, by which we are led in Christ to the Father' (p. 104). This is why Healy rejects pluralistic relativism. I would call this the *eschatological* dimension.

Second, the church's mission is *that tradition of inquiry after truth* in which the question is what response should be made to the *unsurpassable claims of Jesus as Lord.* This being so, the church must participate in *debate as part of its mission,* including the necessity of interreligious apologetics. This might be termed the *evangelistic* dimension of mission spirituality.

Third, the church's mission is *a 'bricolage' of engagement* leading to diverse contextual patterns of the church as a concrete community. This diversity will be both internal (formational) and external (evangelistic). For Healy this implies a *penitential history* approached theologically (while using the tools of history, sociology and ethnography), to reveal the Spirit's movements in the actual mission of the church (not an idealist normative model). This dimension is the *ethical* dimension of the church's community life.

Church as communion in mission

In *Transforming Communities,* Stephen Croft plots a careful course between the various 'models' of church that incorporate an emphasis on church as community or communion. [22] He suggests that the emerging approach for the Anglican church must go beyond a given structure, while recognizing the value of inherited structures. We need a trellis but also need to accept it is not the vine. 'The trellis which the Church of England and many other churches have employed as the basic framework for church life is that of the single parish and the stipendiary minister' (p. 70). The minister has been the linchpin in the inherited structure as the one who fosters community. It is this framework which the emergence of the mission agencies questions, and it is a framework being questioned in new ways today. 'In essence the framework for developing the church outlined here is about refocusing a sense of Christian identity and of Christian mission through the intentional development of missionary community and therefore of social capital' (p. 172).

Croft outlines four aspects of the relational ethos of the church – the church's relationship with God, herself, the world and to time. How each aspect is addressed implies a certain approach to the church's mission context. In Croft's opinion, in Britain 'as our society as a whole becomes more secular, the Church as whole will need to invest significantly more time in establishing Christian identity through small gatherings as well as public ones so that the Christian witness to life in its totality can remain both supported and distinctive' (p. 92). For Croft our calling is to be like God in his community of mission (p. 118); to be greater than the local parish and diocese (p. 131); to be concerned with formation and evangelism (p. 138); and to reflect the values of a pilgrim church (p. 151). Croft recognizes that these four aspects are part of the backdrop, of relationships and community, which enable a more focused attention on developing transforming communities.

Mission Spirituality in Church

First Peter and the church's ethos of mission spirituality

First Peter is a letter that offers a profound practical-prophetic ecclesiology for Christians who need encouraging to be mission-minded. At the end of 1 Peter, the apostle says, 'I have written this short letter to encourage you and to testify that this is the true grace of God. Stand fast in it' (5:12 NRSV). Here we see the intentionality of leadership, encapsulating the advice given in the previous 11 verses to fellow leaders. It seems to me that if we include the ordained ministry as part our understanding of the church, we should focus on the intentions of leaders and not on structures. We need leaders who intend, by their *fellowship,* to encourage others to stand fast in the faith. This kind of leadership turns inherited models of hierarchy into functional (missional) relationships for encouraging a mission-mindedness at the heart of the church's community ethos. Leaders should be those who encourage mission, not oppose it (as happened in history). In so doing they may affect the future more than they can ever anticipate.[23]

> 'elect exiles . . . according to the foreknowledge of God the Father, in the sanctification of the Spirit, for obedience to Jesus Christ and for sprinkling with his blood' (1 Peter 1:1–2).

I believe that the mission spirituality of 1 Peter encourages the relational ethos of a missional church. Who we are is what matters. 'Theological identity, not geographical location, is the author's concern ... The meaning of belonging to Christian community is the major focus of what the letter has to say.' This ecclesiological teaching is set in a trinitarian framework of divine actions that generate the elect community of believers: 'God's choice, the Spirit's sanctifying acts, and Christ's giving of his blood.'[24]

In 1 Peter both the trinitarian mission and the Word of God are taken as given. The epistle opens with a trinitarian greeting to the Christians in 'exile' and the first chapter concludes with the importance of the enlivening Word of God. This double reality – Trinity and Word – provides the general orientation for the church's ethos of mission spirituality. The Spirit is the one who creates this 'force field' (1:10–11) in which we are held in place within our particular context as resident aliens.[25]

Within this framework of the theology (missiology) of the first part of 1 Peter, we can draw out three aspects of the ethos of a mission spirituality: the *ethical* implications of holy community, the disturbing reality of *evangelistic* identity, and the mystery of *eschatological* belief.

The ethical character of holy community

Images of the Christian community, for example 'chosen race', 'royal priesthood', 'holy nation' (2:9) abound in 1 Peter, but we get a feel for the ethos of this community only if we first set these images in the context of the call to be holy. This call is based on the character of God: 'be holy, for I am holy' (1:16). So the apostle urges his readers to a mission intentionality: 'prepare your minds for action; discipline yourselves; set all your hope' (1:13). This intention means not conforming to the world but being transformed into the holiness of God. This intentional missionary holiness needs to be combined with the command to 'love one another deeply from the heart' (1:22). It is this combination of holiness and love that tells us what it means to 'let yourselves be built into a spiritual house' (2:5). The same combination determines the ethos of the 'spiritual house' at the heart of 1 Peter. This 'spiritual house' has Christ as its cornerstone and is a building made up of living stones, that is, those who have been born again and purified by God's Word.

It is the combination of community and holiness, rooted in the character of God, that is most stretching in 1 Peter because it is inescapably linked with suffering – Christ's and ours. The first chapter acknowledges the suffering of various trials (1:6) and recognizes that there is a hiddenness about faith (1:8), and chapter 2 has a stark presentation of Christ's suffering (2:18–25). The eucharistic prayer of the Kenyan liturgy sums up this calling of being identified with Christ in the phrase 'We are because He is.'

This living out of the ethical demands of Christian mission is best accomplished by communities of commitment and witness:

> It is my contention that the malaise of the church in the main-stream denominations is due at least in part to a neglect of that aspect of church life which can be expressed in these small communities: depth of friendship and relationship; disciple-ship within structures of mutual accountability; worship and prayer which arise from and are closely related to shared lives; and a common sense of purpose enabling one another to share in the mission of God . . . In previous generations that sense of belonging might have been facilitated by a full-time minister. It now needs to be generated by the intentional formation of a community.[26]

I believe that we are now in the era of generating the ethos of holy community. It includes a mission spirituality that gives people the confidence to build on the past and move into the future. We face a major challenge from Islam, which understands the requirement for holiness in no uncertain terms. The five pillars of Islam are the spiritual structures of the Dar el Islam – the House of Submission. We find scattered in 1 Peter 1–2 five values of Christian community that characterize the ethos of the Spiritual House of the Living Stone: word (obeying the truth; 1:22); love (1:22); worship (2:5); witness (proclaiming the praises; 2:9); and work ('living such good lives'; 2:11). This is the 'House of Holiness'.

The evangelistic character of Christian community

The purpose of Christian community is not just inward looking but includes the church's relation to the world. First Peter describes Christians as *resident aliens*. The word used (1:17; 2:11) is *paroikos,* designating those who are permanently resident but are not citizens. In 2:11 it is combined with *exiles* (also used in 1:1), which has a similar meaning. When we lived in Kenya, our family had to have resident-alien passes, which now also include a photo. One can be easily identified as a non-citizen. When we returned to the UK, where we are citizens, we found that the sense of being a resident alien continued; we underestimated the demands of relocation and establishing a new way of life.

It is interesting that *paroikos* is the word from which we derive parish! The English understanding of parish has come to mean quite the opposite of the life of a resident alien as exemplified in 1 Peter. In our culture, to be parochial is to be so rooted and settled in the local situation that we do not look beyond it. The question we face today in Western mission is whether our parochial Christendom model of faith will do, whether it is the 'local' as in parish or the 'local' as Christendom. I doubt if the parish system of the Church of England is the best way for the church to be in mission today. I think we need to rediscover what it means to be a 'parish' in the old, 1 Peter, sense – that is, to be *paroikos – resident alien*. 'We believe that the designation of the church as a colony and Christians as resident aliens are not too strong for the modern [American] church – indeed, we believe it is the nature of the church, at any time and in any situation, to be a colony.'[27]

The church continued to use the term *paroikos* to describe itself in the early centuries. It regarded itself as an alien colony: 2 Clement 5:1 uses *paroikia* in the same way as 1 Peter – a community of resident aliens. Irenaeus calls churches *paroikiai*. This plural then became the term used for individual congregations. *Ekklesia* is the singular used for the whole church, of which *paroikiai* are constituent churches. 'Strictly, then, the parishes are societies of resident aliens on earth whose true citizenship is in heaven'.[28] The new, emerging ways of being church in mission need to be based on the old ways of being a distinctive and authentic spiritual house, that is, of helping people live their Christian lives in the world. Miroslav Volf forcefully challenges the understanding that finds the identity of the church primarily in its gathered form: 'Properly understood, the church is not a gathering but a community that gathers, and the church's work is therefore done both when the community is gathered and when it is dispersed in the world.'[29] This moves us beyond a pietistic and private faith towards authentically engaged Christian citizenship.

In the British context, many have come to believe in the inevitable decline of the church as part of a secularization thesis. I think this is fundamentally flawed. Our culture is not straightforwardly secular. It is certainly no longer dominated by institutional Christianity, but there is an interest in spirituality. I believe one response is to develop an evangelistic perspective based on the call to holy community. Fundamental to this is what Volf calls the 'soft difference' of being resident aliens as a missional stance.[30] Volf distinguishes between hard and soft difference. Hard difference is rooted in fear and lack of identity; soft difference includes an ability to be gently different from others on the basis of a clear identity. 'For people who live the soft difference, mission fundamentally takes the form of witness and invitation. They seek to win others over without pressure or manipulation, sometimes even "without a word" (1 Peter 3:1)' (p. 16). I think that the major challenge we have is to be authentic Christians, to be the spiritual house *(oikos pneumatikos)* that is most truly itself in mission, basing its evangelism on the call to holiness, not techniques.

Do we see exile as a victim image or as a positive way of constructing reality? Kenneth Leech suggests that both Ephesians and 1 Peter are needed for understanding a spirituality of exile. Ephesians affirms a 'no longer stranger' in relation to God and one another. First Peter sees Christians as still resident aliens in dispersion.[31] Michael Nazir-Ali also suggests that one of the *Shapes of the Church to Come*[32] is that of exile: 'the church needs to prepare itself for an experience of exile, when it does not, automatically, have a seat at the table and when the dominant assumptions of the culture are indifferent or hostile to the gospel values the church seeks to promote'. This leaves

us in the kind of vulnerable position in which refugees find themselves. Jesus was a refugee in both Egypt and in Nazareth. His parents must have gone through a double process of resettlement. Jesus
passes on to others in their mission learning the vulnerability that this
would have taught the family. When the seventy are sent out, their
vulnerability is part of their mission: 'The vulnerability of the seventy consists of two things: first the opposition and indifference they
will face; and secondly their small numbers in the face of a large task.
They go then not in their own strength, but in reliance upon God. This
reliance is the first aspect of the mission they – and we – undertake.'[33]

The eschatological nature of ecclesiological belief

Questions about suffering and evil present a huge challenge.
Inevitably the answer must always be more than a resolution to a
particular issue and always more than an intellectual understanding
of why there is evil. Whether we are Christians or not, we face the
same foundational question of 'Why?' As Christians, the question
is part of our understanding of God, and I suggest it is one of those
'before the foundation of the world' issues that shapes the nature of
our belief more than any other issue.

In 2002 we have all been faced afresh with this question with reference to 11 September 2001. My personal and professional experience included a visit to Rwanda and Burundi where I visited the
genocide sites where thousands of Christians were murdered by other
Christians in churches. This was not only a question of unbelievable
inhumanity, but a colossal challenge to my faith: How could Christians
do this? What sort of Christianity was brought to these countries that
allowed this? And what sort of God is this that allows all this anyway?

The personal dimension was exacerbated by the knowledge that
the CMS was taking on a new level of responsibility for one of those
mission organizations (Mid-Africa Ministry), which had actually
brought the gospel to Rwanda and had planted the churches that had
nurtured some of those Christians who had been caught up in the
genocide. I was to be the person heading up this new integrated mission and I needed answers. I found the foundations of my faith

shaken anew. The most stark question was 'Could I believe in a God who would allow such a world to be created, in which the gospel could appear to be so useless with the result that terrible things could be done in the most Christian country in the world (Rwanda was 97 per cent Christian)?'

First Peter tells us that Christ was chosen, as the Lamb to be slain, 'before the foundations of the world'. Our religious belief cannot be framed in terms merely of contrast with this world: we don't cope with suffering now merely because heaven will be better. We need something deeper. We need to know that the God who made heaven and earth has shared in the cost and risk of creation; more than that, we need to know that he is still involved and that he can make a practical difference.

John Stott concludes a recent article on 11 September with these words from P. T. Forsyth: 'The Cross of Christ . . . is God's only self-justification in such a world as ours.' Stott adds, 'By the Cross[34] of Christ, God justifies us, but he also justifies himself.'[35] *God's mission, which included the cross, is foundational.* The cross is the place where God's practical commitment is enacted. The response of faith is to recognize that it was *God* who was acting in Christ on the cross. The God revealed in Christ is not just showing solidarity with human suffering and sin. He is also taking responsibility for the possibility of restoring things anew and he is reaching out to those who are lost, even in the deepest of places (1 Peter 3:19). This is a Holy Saturday perspective that links together what God has done before the foundations of the world with those things yet to be revealed. On the basis of the Jesus we do know, we come to believe in the one who was both chosen before the foundation of the world and also the one who is yet to be revealed. The outworking of this *before and after* of Jesus is the mission to reach out to others with this faith.

Conclusion

Both Walls and Healy make it clear that ecclesiology needs to come to the fore in our understanding of God's mission. But both have indicated that we need to acknowledge the wider perspective of mission spirituality, either because it was out of movements of mission spirituality that mission practice emerged in the church, or because ecclesiology needs to be set in a wider prophetic-practical context. This wider perspective provides the alternative background to that of Christendom and is needed in both the Western world within which Christendom emerged, and in the ecclesiological traditions that came out of Christendom and were exported and planted in other parts of the world. The need for the church to express a mission spirituality is both the *prophetic* challenge not to set up blueprints for church, and the *practical* challenge of creating community.

Notes

1   This chapter is an extended version of an article published in the January 2003 *CMS Newsletter,* p. 554.

2   *Evangelicalism in Modern Britain*, London, Unwin Hyman, 1989, p. 3.

3   A. Carmichael, *Edges of His Ways*, Christian Literature Crusade, London, 1955.

4   'The Protestant Missionary Awakening in its European Context' and 'The Missionary Movement: A Lay Fiefdom', in A. Walls, *The Cross-Cultural Process in Christian History*, Edinburgh, T. and T. Clark, 2002, chs 11, 12.

5   L. Nemer, *Anglican and Roman Catholic Missions*, St Austin, Syler Verlag, 1981, p. 95.

6   From Philip Sheldrake's preface to William Countryman, *The Poetic Imagination: An Anglican Spiritual Tradition*, London, Darton, Longman and Todd, 1999, p. 10.

7   *Evangelical Spirituality*, London, SPCK, 1991, p. 302, quoting J. R. W. Stott, *The Cross of Christ*, Leicester, Inter-Varsity Press, 1986.

8   *A Dictionary of Spirituality*, London, SCM, 1983, pp. 15–16.

9   See Andrew Walls's reflections on the intercultural nature of the church and the 'full stature of Christ' in his chapter 'The Ephesian Moment', in idem, *Cross-Cultural Process*, ch. 4.

[10] An example of new comparative Christology is Volker Kuster, *The Many Faces of Jesus Christ*, London, SCM, 2001.

[11] These terms are used in relation to mission by Daniel Hardy, e.g. *Finding the Church*, London, SCM, 2001, ch. 8.

[12] In fact, Walls suggests that the Protestant Reformation killed the goose that laid the golden eggs by undermining the significance and effectiveness of the religious orders which had been the organizational means for world mission.

[13] For example, the evangelical circle around Charles Simeon, one of the leaders who established the CMS, produced no missionary. 'From its beginning it was a voluntary society, but in its early years it was essentially a clerical society, a network of Evangelical clergy who kept up a correspondence based on their knowledge of their of own parishes and congregations.' Quoted from 'The Mission Movement a Lay Fiefdom' in Andrew Walls, *The Cross-Cultural Process in Christian History,* New York, Orbis Books, 2002, p. 23.

[14] See M. Hennel, *John Venn and the Clapham Sect*, London, Lutterworth, 1958, appendix C, pp. 282–3.

[15] See Paul Jenkins, 'The Church Missionary Society and the Basel Mission: An Early Experiment in Inter-European Cooperation', in *The Church Mission Society and World Christianity, 1799–1999*, eds K. Ward and B. Stanley, Grand Rapids, Eerdmans, 2000.

[16] See the essays in Ward and Stanley, *Church Mission Society*, by Jocelyn Murray, 'The Role of Women in the Church Missionary Society, 1799–1977'; and Guli Francis-Dehqani, 'CMS Women Missionaries in Persia: Perceptions of Muslim Women and Islam, 1884–1934'.

[17] 'Christian Missions and the Enlightenment: A Re-evaluation', in *Christian Missions and the Enlightenment*, ed. Brian Stanley, Grand Rapids, Eerdmans, 2001, p. 15.

[18] He goes on, 'The voluntary society is one of God's theological jokes, whereby he makes tender mockery of his people when they take themselves too seriously. The men of

highest theological and ecclesiastical principle were often the enemies of the mission movement.' Quoted from 'Missionary Societies', in *The Missionary Movement in Christian History*, Edinburgh, T. and T. Clark, p. 246.

[19] Simon Barrington-Ward, *CMS Newsletter*, 'Missionary Movements: A New Phase', published in *Love Will Out a Theology of Mission for Today's World: CMS Newsletters 1975–1985*, Basingstoke, Marshall Pickering, 1988, pp. 185, 189.

[20] Nicholas M. Healy, *Church, World and the Christian Life: Practical-Prophetic Ecclesiology*, Cambridge, Cambridge University Press, 2000.

[21] This is an important move because it begins to develop a foundation for how to assess the *outcomes* of world mission, that is, the emergence of churches in contexts where there is no European Christendom background and where other religions have provided the background cultural perspective. Healy is not only easing us out of European modernism, but is also easing us into a world church context.

[22] *Transforming Communities: Re-Imaging the Church for the Twenty-First Century*, London, Darton, Longman and Todd, 2002. In Chapter 4 Croft reviews and critiques five models of emerging church: (1) chain of cinemas (lots of up-front ministry); (2) local franchise (adopts a successful formula); (3) unit of production (makes disciples); (4) growing/healthy churches (quality control emphasized); (5) mirror of society (need centred). He is careful to note the positive aspects of each of these.

[23] Here is Walls's critique of the lack of support from Christian leaders for the emerging Western missionary movement:

> Few in ecclesiastical leadership had the remotest idea that the so often struggling movement was to be instrumental in the transformation of the demographic composition of the Christian church. A movement that arose in the heart of Christendom helped Christianity to survive the death of Christendom. A project that was soaked in the Enlighten-

ment helped to produce a Christianity whose strength now lies in its independence of the Enlightenment. An expression of Christianity that arose from interaction with deep currents in European culture has helped to foster a Christianity that will depend on its critical interaction with the ancient cultures of Africa and Asia (*The Missionary Movement in Christian History*, Edinburgh, T. and T. Clark, p. 235).

24 M. E. Boring, *1 Peter*, Nashville, Abingdon, 1999, p. 53. See also E. Clowney, *The Message of 1 Peter*, Leicester, Inter-Varsity Press, 1994, appendix A, pp. 227ff.

25 To develop a doctrine of the Holy Spirit is notoriously difficult and yet vitally important for mission spirituality. John McIntyre, for example, in acknowledging the centrality of the church's evangelism, shows how the doctrine of the Holy Spirit differs from that of Christology in being much more diffuse, and yet he sees the hard work of engaging with pneumatology as of great importance for the church's mission. See his book, *The Shape of Pneumatology*, Edinburgh, T. and T. Clark, ch. 1.

26 Croft, *Transforming Communities*, pp. 72, 80.

27 S. Hauerwas and W. Willimon, *Resident Aliens: Life in the Christian Colony*, Nashville, Abingdon, 1989, p. 12.

28 G. Kittel, G. Friedrich and G. Bromiley, eds, *Theological Dictionary of the New Testament*, Grand Rapids, Eerdmans, 1985, p. 245.

29 'The Nature of the Church', *Evangelical Review of Theology* (2002), p. 75.

30 M. Volf, 'Soft Difference: Theological Reflections on the Relation between Church and Culture in 1 Peter', *Ex Auditu* 10 (1994), pp. 10–16.

31 Kenneth Leech, *Through Our Long Exile*, London, Darton, Longman and Todd, 2001, p. 8.

32 Eastbourne, Kingsway, 2001, p. 200.

33 John Holmes, *Vulnerable Mission*, Cambridge, Grove Books, 2001, p. 14.

[34] P. T. Forsyth, *Justification of God*, London, Duckworth, 1916, p. 32.

[35] John Stott, 'Responding to Evil', *e.g.*, 7 December 2001, London Institute for Contemporary Christianity, London.

Chapter Sixteen

Seeing God through African Eyes: An English Parish Shares the Life and Mission of the Church in Kenya

Phil Baskerville

How can people in an ordinary British parish church benefit from what God is doing in other parts of the Anglican communion where there is life and growth? How can they even overcome the ignorance of the realities of worldwide Anglicanism that is sadly endemic in many parishes? One answer is to go and see for yourself. Phil Baskerville tells the story of how, in different parishes, he has been involved in taking groups of parishioners on a kind of extended field trip to Kenya, and how it became a mind- and heart-changing experience not only for those who went but also for the whole church. The secret of success, according to Phil, lies in thorough preparation and orientation, clear objectives, plenty of opportunity for reflection, and a strong sense of ownership and involvement by the whole church (not just by those who made the trip). Here is a model of how to engage a church's collective heart in mission that is truly relational and experiential and helps to dissolve the myth that mission is only about 'sending missionaries'.

Introduction

Mission is at the very heart of the gospel! Good news can only really be 'good news' when it is shared with others. And yet, one of the effects of living in the midst of an increasingly individualistic society as we do in Britain, is to create an increasingly inward-looking church. For many in our churches, the concept of reaching out to others with 'good news' is not on the agenda. It is hard enough just keeping our feet on the map, never mind looking out beyond ourselves ... and if it is hard enough to generate some kind of concern for 'local mission', it is often impossible to encourage interest in world mission and our part in the worldwide church.

- Think of the struggles undertaken by the mission committee (if there is one) to keep mission interest alive in the parish.
- Think of the difficulties in trying to encourage people to attend 'mission meetings'; even when link mission partners are present, the attendance is sometimes poor.
- Think of the problem of trying to help people move beyond just giving money to various societies or mission partners that the church may support, into an active growing partnership in the gospel.

Yet one of the great strengths of the church in many other parts of the Anglican communion is their focus on mission, and their effectiveness in telling others about Jesus. The church in South America and Asia and Africa is experiencing a time of tremendous growth, and as Anglicans in Britain we need to learn humility so that we are able to listen to and learn from our brothers and sisters overseas.

But, 'It's difficult to become excited and enthusiastic about world mission, and to feel really part of the worldwide church if you have never been to it!' These sentiments I heard expressed on one occasion reflect the feelings of many in our churches. So this chapter recounts an attempt by a fairly ordinary parish (whatever that may mean) to try to address that challenge of engaging with the world-wide church by taking a team of people out to Kenya, to be able to listen to, and learn from, Christians in Africa simply living out their faith.

This venture is the third time I have been involved in this kind of project (twice with my previous parish of St Bartholomew, Roby) and I am writing most of these reflections in Dubai airport on our return journey to England!

The invitation to be part of the team carried with it the challenge to 'see God through African eyes' as we spend time with Christian brothers and sisters in Kenya. It would be an opportunity to experience some of the joys and frustrations of life in a developing country, and to be able to learn from the growing church overseas – its challenges, struggles and successes. It would also be an opportunity to broaden and deepen our understanding of mission partnership. And finally it would be an opportunity to learn more about God, to deepen our relationship with him and to understand better his call to serve him in our individual lives as well as in the corporate life of our church.

Preparation and Training

The opportunity to be part of the team was presented to the whole church family about a year before the visit took place, with a concern that the members of the team would reflect the diversity of our church family – mixed in terms of age, financial ability (this is not just for the wealthy members of the church), and spiritual maturity. The group would therefore not be perceived as representative of just one segment within the church. The reason for this was partly so that on return, the diversity of the individual members would better enable the lessons learnt to reach the *whole* church family.

So, within the group of 10, there were PCC (parochial church council) members, treasurer, church warden, youth and children's workers, lay reader and clergy representation, as well as those new to the Christian faith, or 'seeking' to know more about Jesus. Two members had completed the Alpha course the previous year. Although the group represented our church diversity well, this was more a case of fulfilled hopes than a deliberate policy – the membership of the team was open to all.

One of the most important aspects of the venture was in the training and preparation of the team, enabling the group to acquire tools with which to be able to look and listen more effectively when overseas.

For long-term mission partners, cross-cultural training and preparation is regarded as essential, and often much time is spent on this. But for many short visits, or even for mission partners working overseas for shorter periods, this training is often lacking – and yet it is a vital part of understanding the culture of our hosts, and also our own culture and its effects upon us.

It is often only when we step outside our own culture and come face to face with a different culture that we become more conscious of how strong a hold the culture in which we have been raised has upon us. We need to be aware of our own culture-flavoured perspective of life and faith – of how much our own worldview is a product of our cultural upbringing. When we begin to appreciate this, then we are better able to learn from another culture. When we fail to do this properly, real learning can be restricted.

The training we arranged involved some basic language learning, as well as the opportunity to engage in, and think through, some of the cultural issues that will arise. It included use of video, discussion, role play, Bible study, eating a Kenyan meal together as well as welcoming visitors from overseas and allowing them to share their stories and experiences (see Appendix A on page 316 for more details). The language sheets were themed around different aspects of the visit – vocabulary of visiting, of travelling, of church life and so on.

The content of the training is important, but also regularly meeting together enables relationships to grow within the team, and a degree of trust to develop in preparation for sharing lessons learned while overseas. Even though teams can be diverse in terms of both age and spiritual maturity, meeting regularly encourages a sense of growing together.

The Visit

The programme we organized was largely dependent on pre-existing links: a children's home we support, a Kenyan clergyman who had already visited our parish, and link mission partners. The individual elements will vary from parish to parish, but in our case included those pre-existing links as well as opportunities to 'dig deeper' and to make new links. One weekend involved each individual in the team staying in a local home – eating and sleeping with the family for two nights, sharing in the life of the home, attending the local church.

Faced with the challenge of a growing church in Africa, we also had the opportunity to meet local bishops, clergy and lay leaders – to hear of their vision and hopes and struggles. We were able to see how the church is trying to respond to the challenge of teaching this growing church – its training of leaders, both ordained and lay. One of the challenges facing a rapidly growing church is the strategy for training leaders. The average parish in Kitale and Eldoret dioceses has 15 churches with usually just one trained, ordained leader. Therefore lay training is vital. We spent some time in these dioceses, where we visited the directors of TEE (Theological Education by Extension) – a programme designed to train lay leadership for the church and to develop understanding of Scripture, as well as teaching practical ministry.

We also spent a morning at a local theological college, where students are being prepared for the ordained ministry. Strategically, part of their course involves training them as TEE leaders so that on entering parish ministry they are able to train their own lay leadership.

Another important element of the visit was regular (daily) opportunity to meet together as a team for reflection, worship and prayer.

We would talk about the experiences of each day – the people we had met, conversations we had engaged in, active and 'passive' ministry. Much of the visit involved simply watching and listening to our hosts as we shared in their daily lives, their joys and struggles; but there were also occasions where we were involved in up-front leading and speaking, and prayer – often daunting, but also exciting and humbling. Throughout the visit, we attempted not to make the itinerary so busy that there was no space for quiet reflection (see Appendix B on page 317 for more details).

Small Team or Whole Church?

One of the potential difficulties that can arise in taking a small team overseas is trying to share the experience with those left behind. How can the whole church be a part of the venture, and so be able to learn from the experience – not just as individuals, but corporately? We have tried to address these questions at the three different stages – *before, during* and *after* the visit:

1. *Before the visit* there were regular discussions, reports and updates with both the mission committee and the PCC, all of which helped to develop a shared vision and ownership of the venture. Magazine articles can help keep the wider church family informed and up to date. We invited our children and youth groups to 'design a logo' for the team, with the invitation to speak to the groups involved. The logo was later used on prayer cards, T-shirts and mugs!

   Each preparation meeting was also open to those who would not be going out with the team, and the final meeting was an open afternoon for the whole church family – which included a presentation (with slides and video) of the different stages of the itinerary; a cross-cultural game; a live-link phone call with one of our Kenyan hosts, ending with eating Kenyan food together. Finally, the evening before we left we had a commissioning service for the team, led by a local bishop (see Appendix C on pages 318-320).

2. *During the visit* we had prepared prayer cards with details of the itinerary and a map of Kenya, so that the church family could follow our progress, and pray with us each day.

We had some 'Team for Kenya' mugs made – not as a fund-raiser, but rather to encourage prayer – 'When you reach for your morning cup of tea or coffee, pray for us'! (On our return, one church member said how this simple idea had revolutionized his prayer life!)

Each Sunday (and also during our midweek prayer meeting), we set up a phone link – a live 10 minute report by phone relayed through the sound system during our main 10.30am services and accompanied by pictures sent by email (from a digital camera), so our church family could see and hear what was happening. Technological developments mean that there are so many opportunities here to keep in touch – the use of video cameras could be another possibility.

3. *After the visit* itself there will be various opportunities to address meetings and hold presentations. The evening service after our return will be a 'Kenya Special' – an opportunity to hear in more detail some of the first impressions and initial responses to the events and experiences of the visit. There are also invitations to share with other churches – either in midweek meetings or in leading the Sunday service.

Some of these opportunities will be immediate, but others will be long term and will, I hope, lead to further opportunities to develop this partnership in the gospel.

In my former parish the taking of a team overseas in 1991 and again in 1994 was a catalyst for a number of developments – the opportunity to welcome brothers and sisters from overseas who came to stay in the parish, as well as encouraging a number of people from the parish to work overseas (short and long term). As a result, mission became genuinely two-way!

Challenges

This kind of venture presents a number of challenges – most obviously to the local church involved, but also to the wider church, and to our mission societies.

The main challenge to the local church will be to incorporate the experiences and lessons learnt by a group of individuals into the corporate life of the church – such that these experiences will have a bearing upon the mission of the church, local and international. Talking to the incumbent of my former parish (Rev Geoff Pearson) – now 11 years and 8 years since those earlier team visits – his reflections are helpful.

For the individual members of these two teams (15 in all), their experience has had a very deep effect upon their faith and ministry – two couples became full-time mission partners; two are now (lay) readers; one is ordained and one married to a clergyman and involved in full-time ministry; one has been involved in work in India through the Guide movement; three have been involved in support of mission partners and one became a Christian through his visit! Each person's life has changed significantly through the experience.

For the church family as a whole the effects have been interesting, although it is more difficult to attribute change directly and solely to the team ventures. Certainly the church is much more a 'sending' and 'receiving' church than it was before the two visits, as mentioned earlier. In summer 2002 three church members went out to Tanzania to visit and work with link mission partners (who themselves had been leaders of the second team in 1994). Giving to the 'core' mission societies supported and to individual mission partners has increased. Reflection and lessons learnt have affected the preaching and teaching ministry. Practical examples and illustrations from overseas are now familiar and understood by the church family. One example is that of a deeper appreciation of the power of the cross to bring healing and wholeness even in the midst of deep suffering; an experience from the overseas church that can bring hope to our own situations. We witnessed the God who walks alongside us in our suffering and who offers resurrection.

Overall, the effect has been not to fling wide the gates to world mission, but to keep them open! It has allowed the steady trickle of mission links to enrich the ongoing life of the church.

Much depends on the starting point of the church. Where there is deep parochialism this kind of venture can powerfully broaden horizons. For churches where there is a long history of mission partnership this kind of hands-on preparation and sharing can deepen understanding. From this experience we eagerly await what God may have in store for us as a church.

I also feel, however, that challenges may well be presented to the wider church. It could be argued that this kind of activity will work well in parishes where there are former mission partners, or overseas partners living. But what of parishes where there is no such involvement? Perhaps here is a role for the wider church family – a sharing of people resources to help in the preparation and planning.

Perhaps here is a further role for our mission societies and mission partners; and perhaps encouraging this type of partnership should form part of the training programme and preparation for overseas work. Helping to develop creative and imaginative mission partnerships has also been a part of the thinking of mission societies; here is another role, which could prove exciting.

A Final Note

As mentioned at the beginning of the chapter, this venture, which I have found exciting and commend to you, is just one attempt by an ordinary parish (or rather two parishes) to engage with the worldwide church; thus deepening our partnership in the gospel. We are not unique – I am sure many other parishes could write of their own partnership experiences and of the lessons they have learnt. Using whatever method, the challenge for us all is to walk alongside brothers and sisters overseas and to learn from their example of life and faith – a wonderfully enriching experience that can bring blessing not only to our local churches, but also to the worldwide church. Through such experiences we can begin to discover the real meaning of being gospel partners.

Appendix A: Training Programme

Session 1:	Tues 29 Jan.	Introductory session
Session 2:	Tues 26 Feb.	Cultural awareness: 'Values and virtues'
		Language sheet (1)
Session 3:	Wed 27 Mar.	Cultural sensitivity / Bible study (Romans 12)
		Language sheet (2)
Session 4:	Mon 15 Apr.	Crossing cultures: video
		Language sheet (3)
Session 5:	Tues 14 May	Crossing cultures
		'At home with language'
		Language sheet (4)
Session 6:	Tues 11 June	Kenyan meal / Hospitality issues
		Language sheet (5)
Session 7:	Tues 2 July	Visit of Revd Hubert Weyao
		'Kenyan Christianity' 1
		Language sheet (6)
Session 8:	Tues 6 Aug.	'Kenyan Christianity' 2 / Kenyan visitors: sharing their faith
Session 9:	Tues 3 Sep.	Language summary
		Final updates
		Prayer
Session 10:	Sat 7 Sep.	Church Family Day at Barnston Church Hall

For more information regarding trips to Kenya, email
Phil Baskerville at *phil@kabare.freeserve.co.uk*.

Appendix B: Itinerary of the Visit

September 2002

Date	Programme	Accommodation
Mon. 9	travel to Birmingham; fly to Dubai	Flight
Tues. 10	arrive in Nairobi; on to ACK St Julian's Centre	Limuru
Wed. 11	orientation/acclimatization at St Julian's	Limuru
Thu. 12	leave St Julian's; travel to Testimony	Eldoret
Fri. 13	Testimony Faith Home: time in school (CU)	Eldoret
Sat. 14	visit diocesan office (TEE); meet Bishop Kogo	Eldoret
Sun. 15	TFH involved in service; phone home church	Eldoret
Mon. 16	leave TFH; visit parish of Revd Hubert Weyao	Kitale
Tues. 17	visit Kitale diocesan office (TEE dept.)	Kitale
Wed. 18	meeting with Bishop Kewasis; travel to Rondo	Rondo
Thu. 19	quiet day: rest and reflection	Rondo
Fri. 20	leave Rondo; travel to Kapsabet / local homes	Kapsabet
Sat. 21	stay in local homes	Kapsabet
Sun. 22	attend local churches; phone home church	Kapsabet
Mon. 23	day at St Paul's Theological College	Kapsabet
Tues. 24	travel to Lake Baringo; rest and reflection	Baringo
Wed. 25	rest and reflection	Baringo
Thu. 26	rest and reflection	Baringo
Fri. 27	leave Baringo; travel to St Julian's	Limuru
Sat. 28	time with Nairobi Primary School parents	Limuru
Sun. 29	local church (phone home); travel to airport	Flight
Mon. 30	arrive in Birmingham	Home

Appendix C: Commissioning Service, St Michael and All Angels, Pensby

Prayers for use at the commissioning of the Kenya Team

Evening Service 8 September 2002

Introduction

Song: 'Men of faith'

The minister says:

> Blessed are you, God and Father of our Lord Jesus Christ!
> By your great mercy we have been born anew
> to a living hope through the resurrection of your Son from
> the dead,
> and to an inheritance which is imperishable, undefiled,
> and unfading.
> Once we were no people, but now we are your people,
> declaring your wonderful deeds in Christ,
> who called us out of darkness into his marvellous light.

All **Let my prayer rise before you as incense,
the lifting up of my hands as the evening sacrifice.**

1   O Lord, I call to you; come to me quickly;
hear my voice when I cry to you.
Set a watch before my mouth, O Lord,
and guard the door of my lips;

All **Let my prayer rise before you as incense,
the lifting up of my hands as the evening sacrifice.**

2   Let not my heart incline to any evil thing;
let me not be occupied in wickedness with evildoers.
But my eyes are turned to you, Lord God;
in you I take refuge; do not leave me defenceless.

All **Let my prayer rise before you as incense,
the lifting up of my hands as the evening sacrifice.**

Interviews with members of the Kenya Team

Song: 'Let Everything That Has Breath Praise the Lord'

The Word of God
> Bible reading: *Revelation 7:9–17 (read by a member of the Kenya Team)*

ADDRESS: BISHOP GEOFF TURNER

Song: I lift my eyes to the quiet hills

The commissioning

The bishop says:

God our Father, Lord of all the world, through your Son you have called us into the fellowship of your universal Church: hear our prayer for your faithful people that in their vocation and ministry each may be an instrument of your love, and give to your servants whom we will send out in your Name the needful gifts of grace through our Lord and Saviour Jesus Christ, who is alive and reigns with you, in the unity of the Holy Spirit, one God, now and for ever.

Amen

The bishop addresses the members of the team:

You will go to places you have not seen before, and to people you have not met before. Your hosts will welcome you as representatives of your families, and of this community, and of this church and parish.

Will you receive with gratitude the hospitality which is given to you, in whatever form it takes?

I will, with the help of God.

Will you fulfil all the duties of a guest in that country, even when your duties seem strange or burdensome?

I will, with the help of God.

Will you gladly accept opportunities to express our faith in Jesus, and to pass on the love and greetings of those who sent you, whether you are speaking to one person or to many?

I will, with the help of God.

Will you go with an open heart and an open mind, so that when you return you may be ambassadors for the people who welcomed you?

I will, with the help of God.

The bishop says:
> In the Lord's Name we send you out to see a new country and
> to greet new people
> to listen and to learn to experience human friendship and the
> love of Christ
> and to return to us with a blessing for us all.

The Lord bless you and watch over you, the Lord make his face shine upon you and be gracious to you, the Lord look kindly on you and give you peace; and the blessing of God almighty, the Father, the Son, and the Holy Spirit, be among you and remain with you always.
Amen.

Song: 'Jesus Christ, I think upon your sacrifice'

Intercessions (led by members of the Kenya Team)

Hymn [HTC] 446: 'We trust in you'

Blessing

Chapter Seventeen

Anglicans in Social Transformation: Hope on a Brazilian Rubbish Tip

Simea Meldrum de Souza

In this chapter, Simea Meldrum de Souza takes us to another part of the world, Brazil, and to what for most of us would be another world altogether but for Simea is her home and her parish, the civic rubbish tip in Olinda, the community who live there and the church that now thrives there. Simea tells the story of the community: its struggles and betrayals, the slow but life-giving effect of patient, incarnational Christian ministry, and the eventual transformation achieved by the combination of gospel witness and sociopolitical advocacy and action. The concluding chapter of this section powerfully shows how the truth of the Bible, the redemption of the cross, and the practice of costly mission are integral to one another in real life – especially life lived close to the threat of death, decay and desolation. That is where the church most dramatically witnesses to the power of God's love and the triumph of God's grace.

Our Personal Story

Brazil is one of the largest countries in the world in terms of both wealth concentration and social contrast. Since the revolution in 1964 a militant feeling for human rights has invaded the seminary and influenced the new clergy and bishops of the Episcopal Anglican Church of Brazil, with the result that the church has invested its efforts in liberation theology for almost 30 years. Consequently, many traditional Anglicans now redefine the mission of the church from a liberation point of view, with evangelism and church growth condemned as proselytizing. Human rights, such as culture and land ownership, should be respected, and many leaders of the church are social activists.

When the diocese of Rio de Janeiro, under the leadership of Bishop E. K. Sherrill, inaugurated the missionary district of northeastern Brazil, the bishop sent Paulo and Marcia Garcia to plant an evangelical and missionary district. From its beginning, the project had a clear vision of growth and expansion throughout the northeast. The strategy was to reach the upper-middle classes, in an area where the vast majority of people represent the poorest Brazilians. This was so that the church in this region would become rapidly independent of outside financial support and maintain its own continual growth. The old British chaplaincy church in Recife, Holy Trinity parish, with four thousand members and several church plants, is now our cathedral. It is a church that thrives through its outreach movements (marriage and youth encounter weekends, cursillos [retreats] etc.). However, there is a rapid turnover among the membership and, because of its luxurious air-conditioned church building and its elegant congregation, it is difficult for simpler people – the vast majority of the population – to participate in church activities. Consequently the Anglican Episcopal Church in northeastern Brazil became known as an elitist church.

In 1980, Bishop Edmund Sherrill sent us, Revd Simea and Ian Meldrum, as a husband-and-wife couple to the city of Olinda to plant an Anglican church, once again among the upper-middle classes. However, the Lord had other ideas.

The population of Olinda is less sophisticated than that of the capital city of that region, Recife, and many of the suburbs are transformed *favelas* (slum areas). This is a different situation from that of Holy Trinity church, which has no *favelas* near it. Olinda, considered a dormitory to Recife, has a population of around 450,000 as compared with the two and a half million in Recife. The smaller city has had a complex and violent political history, due to party ambitions, which have resulted in projects that have had little continuity and been of short duration as the government has changed every four years. The city has eventually become economically unviable as only 20 per cent of the population have maintained their tax contributions up to date. As a result, education, health, sanitation and other services have been neglected and have fallen into disrepair. Although a tourist city (the original city is still very beautiful) with the proud title of 'A World Patronage from UNESCO', today the city produces 150 tons of rubbish every day, but has no adequate collection and disposal system. Among the many problems in Olinda are

- drug abuse and associated violence
- school absenteeism
- premature sex and teenage pregnancy
- child labour

The city has 64 known slum areas and 70 per cent of the population live in social conditions considered below the poverty level. With slums near our home, street children and beggars, hungry children always at the door, and, above all, with a whole community of more than a thousand families *living off the city rubbish tip* this situation brought a new context to the mission of the Anglican Church in the north-east of the country. The church began to show a new face and proclaim a different message to the poor, the excluded ones.

Motivated by an evangelistic programme based on environmental education, the youth of Emmanuel parish, where I was the assistant minister responsible for the youth programme at the time, began a social solidarity action in a community of approximately 50 families who lived and survived on the rubbish that was tipped in an open area of the city. On 16 October 1993 we made our first contact with this community. From that date we returned at monthly intervals taking 50 basic food parcels to be distributed among the families, with the intention of giving some immediate relief from hunger and the total abandonment that those families suffered from the local authorities – no social help came from local government.

At the beginning of 1994, when we were making home visits, a family told us how hunger had forced them to consume human flesh – surgical waste, dumped illegally by a local hospital. I brought this fact to the attention of the church during a Sunday sermon. Unknown to me at the time, some employees from a national TV network were present in the congregation. You can imagine what happened next! Overnight it became a national and then an international scandal. Olinda became famous for what one report called 'the misery that leads to the practice of cannibalism'. Following visits from journalists from several different parts of the world, a local scandal turned into what seemed like a Hollywood production. The government, which had previously said that they had no plans or financial resources to help those families, were now being pressured by the international press to take action.

The local health minister became ill; the state secretary for health had to explain why the hospitals were being allowed to dump their waste illegally on open ground instead of incinerating it as the law required. But nothing positive was done to help the families involved and the misery continued.

Meanwhile the community of families grew, due to an ever-increasing unemployment rate and the large number of young people reaching adulthood with no professional qualifications. Now there were 120 families living on the tip and eating the rubbish. The majority would sort through the rubbish, looking for plastic, glass, metals and paper to sell on to middlemen. A family with at least four children was able to average around R$30,00 a week (US$9 or about £6 sterling), which was obviously not enough to feed themselves without also eating whatever waste food they could also find. And of course they would look for any food scraps. This latter led to yet another scandal when a local supermarket dumped a quantity of sweetcorn meal which they had mixed with rat poison as part of their pest control, and then, without thinking of the consequences, threw the contaminated food in the waste bins. These were then transported to the tip – with obvious consequences.

In the middle of all these social problems, the gospel has to be understood in its entirety, principally as the 'good news' for all, and it has to touch the roots of problems like these.

The Mission of the Church Is to Reveal the Lordship of Christ

The living Christ is exalted as Lord of the universe. He has power over nature, as his miracles showed, but the same power is at work today in human lives. The work of restoration realized by Christ does not limit itself to a new life given to the individual, but touches the restoration of the universe, and that includes the social and economic order. Thus the pastoral and prophetic mission of the church goes beyond individual and spiritual questions. If Christ is Lord of all human existence, it is the task of the church to pay attention to social and political issues as well.

- The rubbish collector needs to be part of the economic development plan for the city, because he or she is (1) a person, and (2) an agent who is an important educator of others concerning the expense of urban sanitation and the preservation of the environment.
- The child, and the teenager who is out of school because he needs to work in order to survive, is not being prepared to enter a competitive market labour force. His destiny is unemployment, vice and violence.
- The politicians are becoming accustomed to not having any supervision or inspection by the population in general, which leads to a political system of corruption, oppression, exploitation and, finally, to military intervention.

The presence of the church in situations of extreme misery is difficult because the exercise of *mercy* and *compassion* must not generate *paternalism* or *dependence*. Those families on the rubbish tip had many vices and, manipulated by politicians for years – exchanging votes for benefits – had developed a culture of dependency, and conformity to an oppressive system. The good news of the gospel must bring something new to the lives of the poor, liberty to the prisoners, vision to the blind and liberation to the oppressed.

Thus the presence of the church in day-to-day life, facing the challenges of survival, has developed an image of God who is present, who participates, who cries with them, who seeks to learn with them about the struggles and injustices. Many times we feel impotent when we can only sit with them, live alongside them, and demonstrate that at least we are feeling their pain – 50 basic food parcels were shamefully insufficient for this expanding community. God loves poor sinners, who need a sign of his presence and of his love and provision for them.

In the first meetings with those families I met Dona Jo, a lady just over 50 years old and popular in the community as a well-known spiritualist leader. She lived with an eight-year-old son in a cardboard home. Her past was sad, but even though she was deeply involved in black magic she had an evangelical hymn book and liked to sing with me some of the beautiful old hymns. She always had her ritual clothes on, but her eyes showed a deep thirst. The neighbours were impressed that I was willing to enter that dark house of ill repute and sing Christian hymns with Dona Jo. But I was able to see the power of God at work transforming a precious life. However, she was still afraid to break her ties with the evil rituals: she was a known leader and her life would be at risk. As the years passed our friendship grew, she feeling more and more the love that God was showing her, and I becoming certain that one day she would have an encounter with Jesus. One night, Dona Jo came to me in tears saying, 'Pastor Simea, I have already lost four sons through gunshots and three of them were involved in drug trafficking; and when you arrived here, you found me living among the rubbish. I have lost everything in my life and this religion of mine has taken everything. I no longer have the strength to live; please give me a word.' How I had prayed and waited for that moment! She was ready to receive Jesus. And it was at that moment that Dona Jo began to know the power of love in her life.

Later, she had a strong experience as she was cured of cancer, and this gave her more confidence that nothing could separate her from the love of Christ. Today, Dona Jo is a strong witness for Jesus in the surrounding community. Before, a *Mãe de Santo* (Saint's Mother) and now a servant of the Holy One. What a sign of the love of God.

The Mission of the Church and the Restoration of Society

The restoration begun by Christ occurs initially in the church. It is in the church that the original order of society, established by God, must be restored. In the church the differences exhibited between the social classes, economic and racial distinctions, together with the preconceptions that give rise to them, disappear as Christ is Lord of all and transforms us into one unique people (Galatians 3:28; Ephesians 2:14). In the church we seek the harmonious coexistence between the church and other institutions such as the state, civil society and the family. The bosses continue to be bosses, but learn to exercise their authority without oppression, and the workers learn to be subordinate without recrimination and any sense of inferiority. In the church Jesus Christ established between Christians, just distribution of goods is destined for all. Thus the diaconal, servant activity of the church, both within herself and outside in society at large, demonstrates that the gospel brings relief to the needs of the poor and oppressed, with resources coming from the rich and equipped.

Such a role may be easier when Christians are involved in civic leadership, because we can speak through biblical principles that can be applied to social, political and economic questions. However, this is not the case in Olinda. Despite being a historic city with Roman Catholic origins, the city leaders had never applied biblical principles to their political and administrative attributes. Instead, the church initiated this when it began to assume public services that people should have received from town council or public administration – services such as crèches, child shelters for street children, professional training for the more needy and unskilled, help given to those who seek out material from the rubbish for reuse, and so on.

As well as the misery among the 120 families eking out an existence on the rubbish tip, there was also a growing resentment towards other responsible groups outside the church. We put pressure on the government to act and begged for proper treatment of the rubbish, transforming the open tip into a landfill tip. Various technicians and government departments began the work. However, what was to be done with families who needed the tip for survival? What participation would they have in the process of transforming the environment where they earned their daily bread, such as it was? In meeting with the technicians, the church was invited to help in the process of taking the families off the tip. But was this right? How would they survive?

The church began to pray and, providentially, during that time our diocese was playing host to a meeting of MISSIO, a Lambeth Committee. As part of their programme, MISSIO were to visit some of our churches and new missions. So they came to see our work on the tip. We talked about our struggles and asked that they help us with a letter to the government, speaking of their visit and requesting that more attention be paid to the plight of the families who were about to lose everything, and of the need to look more closely at the question of human rights in such a situation. All the visitors signed the letter, specifying the countries and provinces they represented within the Anglican communion. Some months later we received a reply from the government: the 120 families were to be taken off the tip and relocated on a nearby area of land donated by the government, together with the necessary building materials to construct basic brick and mortar houses.

We celebrated with much joy! The church was advocating these families' human rights, and also had participated in helping to build the houses, which had running water, electricity and paved roads. Thus Union Village, as they chose to call it, was born. The restoration of that community signalled to the world the importance of human dignity, the value of life, and the kind of society in which the church firmly believed and was struggling to achieve.

It was a further surprise to us when some of the leaders of the community then came to us and requested a place of worship, an Anglican parish church for their new community. Once again we were able to raise the funding from local clothing sales and later, with help from World Vision, to buy the necessary land and erect a simple building. Thus the Living Waters Anglican parish was begun. Able to accommodate a hundred people, we began to hold regular services and Sunday school. Later, we added a dental clinic and ran professional training courses. Now instead of 12- and 13-year-olds becoming pregnant, a youth group began of young people wanting to make a difference and wanting to seek God's direction for their relationships. Children, teenagers and young people are all having their lives and futures restored.

Gabriel is married to Maisa, parents to Rafael, Rafaela and Gabriel – all refuse sorters. Gabriel aged 47, suffers from alcoholism and his family is being destroyed. He was mixed up, literally and metaphorically, in the detritus of life, had lost his self-respect, and his relationship with his wife and children was of the worst possible kind. One day Rafael, 16 years old, was invited to the young people's meeting and joined the guitar classes. Soon he came to know Jesus as his Saviour, and the history of his family began to change. Two years later, even his aunts are church members, and his father is one of the leaders of the recyclers association of Olinda. Rafaela dances in the worship dance group and at the age of 15 is an example to other teens. Gabriel is now an assistant Sunday school teacher.

It is important to remember that transformation of society is never complete, due to the fact that the effects of sin are never eliminated from our present world. It is at best a partial restoration. We cannot establish complete justice in the present world, but by our social action we can announce and point towards the will of God. And for some, the church brings real and lasting change – the enthronement of Christ in their lives and the recognition of the presence of the power of God. If the church manages to transform some of the distortions within the social order (injustices, oppression, corruption), the people involved are blessed by the gospel of the cross of Christ. This is the gospel that forgives, restores, redeems, and leads to worship and commitment to the kingdom of God – the kingdom that will never be perfect in this world, but will be so at the end of time, and towards which marches all human history and the universe in which we live. Then

Christ will return in glory, and the prince of this world will be banished. A new heaven and a new earth will be established, where justice will reign in all its fullness (Isaiah 65:17; 66:22; 2 Peter 3:13; Revelation 21:1). Thus the church announces with anticipation the kingdom of justice to be introduced by Jesus Christ at his coming. But in the meantime that kingdom functions within and through a provisional society governed by the laws of Christ; namely, the church.

The Mission of the Church Is to Be Socially Responsible

What are the responsibilities of the church in this provisional restoration of society? We can look at them in three fundamental aspects; the church has a ministry that is *educational, political* and *social*.

The church's educational ministry

The church must teach its members about work and rest. Only God sustains human beings – from him come the forces and conditions that enable us to work and, thus, obtain our daily bread. Work was created by God to give pleasure and fulfilment to humanity: we cannot be fulfilled if we have no work, because the human being was created with this vocation, as written in Genesis 1 and 2. Sin removed the pleasure from work, together with the grace that accompanied our labour in the beginning. With the fall, societal distortions were introduced in relation to work, income generation, socioeconomic contrasts, and the use and abuse of natural resources. But in Christ, humanity can find a new respect for nature, natural resources and our neighbour. In Exodus 20:8–11 we learn that it is necessary that those who work have a day of rest, the Sabbath day, and now the Christian Sunday. Physical rest is linked to the spiritual. Without Jesus Christ there is no real rest on Sunday. It is necessary that we cease from our work, as God rested from his (Hebrews 4:3).

The pulpits of our churches play a fundamental role in relation to the teaching aspect of our task. The church can raise the enthusiasm of the worker, assuring him that even the most humble will be lifted up and honoured by God. In Christ, workers find the joy and satisfaction that should accompany daily work. The sorters of recyclable material are a suffering and rejected people. As a result of this rejection, they have developed a culture similar to the animals with whom they coexist among the rubbish. The competition among them for survival, and the relationships that do not guarantee love and continuity, are the main causes of this. They do not know if they will cling on to life for another day. The children look upon death as something normal, as the drug traffickers murder with hardly a qualm those who get into debt – even for small sums of around R\$5,00 (£1). The teenagers do not know what it is to respect, to love, to have dreams, to look forward to marriage. The love of a father and mother is unknown to most. And it is within this environment that the gospel encounters its great challenge: to recreate human life, for children, young people, adults and the elderly.

The refuse tip association was in the hands of politicians and technicians who were interested only in projects that would generate more income for themselves and their NGOs (non-governmental organizations). Simple things such as a hydraulic press could make a huge difference, but for the technicians this was not a priority. So, the church, receiving help from the Secretary General of the Anglican communion, was able to provide a press that has brought a new commercial freedom to some of the sorters. The association grew to over a hundred members as the sorters began to see the results of their work. They began to learn how to negotiate with the big firms and began to see that God can open doors and raise the needy from the ash heap (Psalm 113:7).

Yet again the local government changed and all the support that the NGO had been giving in training and technical support stopped. As before, the sorters ran to the church for help. We began planning meetings and praying. In that situation, only Jesus could open the doors, because all the important information was with the NGO and technicians from the local council. We began to look for new partners and discovered that there was to be a national meeting of rubbish sorters and street dwellers. Nothing like this had happened before! We were able to support seven of our sorters to travel to the Brazilian capital, Brazilia. In total, five thousand rubbish sorters from all over Brazil gathered. The talks, the statements by the sorters, and from important technicians in the area of recycling, all this new information began to open the eyes of our little group of simple men and women. We returned greatly enthused to reopen the association. We did so with a deep sense of gratitude, as we could see the powerful hand of God once again prising apart closed doors.

Against the will of the local government and the NGO, the association was reopened. Strength and courage came through the joy and communion acquired during our prayer and Bible study meetings. But the association was still inexperienced in standing up to aggressive market forces in recyclable materials. Even large shops were discovering that tins, paper and plastics can generate considerable sums; the big firms were looking towards the rubbish tip, wanting a closed contract with the town council. What would happen to the over four hundred sorters and their families? One day my cell phone rang. It was a technician from a co-operative in Belo Horizonte, a large Brazilian city further south in Brazil: 'Pastor I have good news for you. The European Union is interested in "adopting" your sorters in Olinda.' I jumped for joy! How the Lord is faithful! He had told us in our meetings that he would raise up a powerful help for us that would overcome all the obstacles. Thus as he had healed and done signs and wonders, he would do them again here too, right in the middle of the Olinda rubbish tip.

The pulpit can also teach and reprimand those engaged in social sin. We can denounce the charging of excessive interest rates on the part of moneylenders; denounce the excesses in the misuse of consumer products, the invasion of values, the love of money; denounce failures in relation to the suffering of the poor. We can censure those who are lazy and parasitical. God created human beings and ordained them to cultivate the land, and with this gesture condemned the lazy and the indolent. Nothing is more opposed to the very order of nature than to lead a life of 'drink, eat and sleep' without looking to preserve, cultivate, produce and multiply in all aspects of life (Psalm 128:3; 2 Thessalonians 3:10–12). And what can we say in relation to unemployment among the young and poor caused by the greed of the rich? The church has a huge responsibility to denounce this sin, teaching that to take away a man's right to work is a sin of the most serious kind. Work is a gift from God, and to take it away is to take the life of someone. The poor worker depends upon his day-to-day work to scrape together enough for his next meal, contrary to the rich, who own palatial properties, have huge bank balances, pensions and so on. Thus to promote unemployment is an attempt on the life of the poor, and consequently a sin against the commandment 'You shall not kill' (Exodus 20:13 RSV).

So, we can conclude that the church has an enormous social responsibility in its teaching ministry in relation to the biblical principles about work, rest, the concentration on income, the use of material possessions and natural resources, and the fight against poverty.

The church's political ministry

How can the church relate to the state? When we read Romans 13:1–7, a passage where the apostle Paul mentions the civil authorities and our duties towards them, we can conclude that the church and the state are two institutions that proceed from God. The church and the state are two instruments of God for the establishment of his kingdom on earth. The church is the forerunner of the coming kingdom, and the state in its turn should maintain the actual, provisional order of human society. So, between the two institutions should exist durable links, and not simple, occasional relations. According to Romans 13 the state should maintain social order in society (cf. 1 Timothy 2:1–2). The church has the responsibility to intercede for the state so that there may be tranquillity, with dignity and mercy. And from Jeremiah 29:7 we can deduce that it doesn't matter what form of government the country adopts, even under the most hostile authorities: the people of God have the role of working for the good of the country so that the nation may prosper and be blessed.

When we perceived that there were political and economic interests behind the action of the local council and the NGOs that were helping ARO (The Association of Recyclers of Olinda), and that these interests were preventing the association from expanding throughout Olinda and becoming self-supporting, we had the conviction that God was at work in a miraculous way. This was clear when he raised up international agencies to bring new resources. And suddenly also the presence of foreign students, young volunteers, gave visibility to our work before the politicians. The fact that this small community had awakened international interest made the politicians aware that their stance was now visible and so all would see their non-cooperation. Thus, the church had played its role as a prophetic presence, a royal priesthood and a political agent as well.

Some technicians accredited to the European Union came to visit us in Olinda. The church was the articulator, organized the meetings, located and invited the political and social authorities as well as the sorter representatives. As the community now realized that only God could have brought them to such a place, they were ready to give him the praise and exalt his holy name. The first meeting was a battle. Some of the politicians broke their promise to be present, but the mayor called them all to a second meeting where an official agreement was signed to begin planning the joint project. The refuse sorters of Olinda will be strengthened in their association as it becomes the centre for the recycling industry in Olinda. This project is still in the planning stage, but the sorters and the government have seen the power of God at work and the lordship of Christ has shone forth. We are preparing a thanksgiving service and continue to pray that the name of Jesus will be exalted.

The church should also, when necessary, warn the authorities when they forget the divine sense of their office. When state authorities are engaged in the abuse of power, the committing of injustices against the poor, weak and oppressed, then the church must speak out prophetically. If the church stops watching over the state, it becomes an accomplice in social injustice, and thus fails to fulfil its political mission.

And finally, the church should, as part of its task, defend the poor and weak against the powerful exploiters and oppressors. There is no intrinsic sin in being rich and assuming powerful positions, but the church should be clear in its preference for the excluded and the victims of social injustice. The church often does not position itself in this way because it welcomes the oppressors and powerful within its congregations and accepts their offers of bribes. The absence of a group of poor people within any congregation should be an alert signal. The rich who exploit human misery in times of calamity, those who take sides within a social situation in order to gain wealth and protect themselves, show attitudes that should be carefully critiqued under the light of the Word by the church, and especially in view of the prophetic ministry of those who denounced the cruel oppression in Israel. We can portray the social responsibility of the church as part of its mission that should be carried forward by a church that is politically free, dependent on the Word of God, and relevant to the society in which it lives (James 2:15–16; 1 Thessalonians 4:11–12; 1 Timothy 5:8; Isaiah 10:1–2).

The church's social ministry

According to the Bible, the church has an important task alongside the poor, the orphans and the widows. The authority for her social ministry is in the biblical teachings, beginning in Genesis and ending in the book of Revelation. 'Out of the most severe trial, their overflowing joy and their extreme poverty welled up in rich generosity' (2 Corinthians 8:2).

As always, the richest are the least generous. It was thus when Jesus walked the earth, and it continues to be so. The Christians in Corinth needed to hear of the case of the Christians in Macedonia. Paul showed that the Macedonian believers were much more generous towards the poor than were their Corinthian counterparts. I ask myself if generosity relates only to money, because many times we see people who have no way to support or help others, be it with money or in any other way, *helping anyway.* Opening one's hand with the little one has is pure generosity, precious in God's sight. (Remember the simple offering of five loaves and two fish?) Sometimes, emotionally hurt people help others in a worse state. It is a simple question of the desire to give. Our challenge is to find what we *can* give, whether we will miss it or not, and get out of our heads the idea that we have nothing to give.

Finally, we are nearing our objective of being able to make known the year of grace of our Lord Jesus Christ in Olinda. The

social action with the refuse sorters is a preparation for the coming
of our Lord and Saviour for these people who were always marginalized by the established church. They have no resources to enable
churches to grow, no real income. They have not collaborated for the
development of society, because until now they have had no place in
the system. They do not have an appropriate culture to pass to the
historic culture of the church, but they do have their own culture. Yet
these are those whom Jesus sent to confuse the wise and powerful.
Jesus is revealing that they have the knowledge to survive in the
midst of struggles and trials. They know what it means to suffer and
'to bring into existence that which did not have the means to exist'
(cf. 1 Corinthians 1:28).

And so, with ordinary people – like Gabriel and Maisa, Fernando
and Maria, Adilson and Linda, Patricia, Rafaela, Gleidson, Flavio,
Erivaldo, Dona Jo with all her joy in the Holy Spirit – a community
of love, courage and vision is being formed to make a difference in
Olinda, as part of God's strategy for the evangelization of northeastern Brazil. What explosive power there is when the gospel, the
cross and the Word, all combine. This is what the Lord has promised in his Word, and today we are beginning to see it happen:

> Thus says the LORD: In this place of which you say, 'It is a
> waste without man or beast,' in the cities of Judah and the
> streets of Jerusalem that are desolate, without man or inhabitant
> or beast, there shall be heard again the voice of mirth and the
> voice of gladness, the voice of the bridegroom and the voice of
> the bride, the voices of those who sing, as they bring thank
> offerings to the house of the LORD:
>
>> 'Give thanks to the LORD of hosts,
>>   for the LORD is good,
>>   for his steadfast love endures
>>   for ever!' (Jeremiah 33:10, 11 RSV)

And that desperate place most feared in Olinda, where on average
three young people die violently every week, yet where Jesus walks,
is again making history, as we hear the voices of children, young
people, men and women, praising the Saviour, the Lord of Lords.